Life Stori

D0143369

# LIFE STORIES

## The Creation of Coherence

*Charlotte Linde*

*New York    Oxford*
OXFORD UNIVERSITY PRESS
1993

## Oxford University Press

Oxford   New York   Toronto
Delhi   Bombay   Calcutta   Madras   Karachi
Kuala Lumpur   Singapore   Hong Kong   Tokyo
Nairobi   Dar es Salaam   Cape Town
Melbourne   Auckland   Madrid

and associated companies in
Berlin   Ibadan

## Copyright © 1993 by Charlotte Linde

Published by Oxford University Press, Inc.
200 Madison Avenue, New York, New York 10016

Oxford is a registered trademark of Oxford University Press, Inc.

All rights reserved. No part of this publication may be reproduced,
stored in a retrieval system, or transmitted, in any form or by any means,
electronic, mechanical, photocopying, recording or otherwise,
without the prior permission of Oxford University Press.

Library of Congress Cataloging-in-Publication Data
Linde, C. (Charlotte)
Life stories : the creation of coherence / Charlotte Linde.
p. cm.   Includes bibliographical references and index.
ISBN 0-19-507372-X (cloth).  —  ISBN 0-19-507373-8 (pbk.)
1. Discourse analysis, Narrative.   2. Cohesion (Linguistics)
I. Title.
P302.7.L56   1993
401'.41 — dc20   92-25763

1 3 5 7 9 8 6 4 2

Printed in the United States of America
on acid-free paper

*This book is for my parents.*

# ACKNOWLEDGMENTS

This work has been many long years in the making, and my debts to friends and colleagues are correspondingly great. I am grateful to Eleanor Rosch and Dan Slobin for introducing me to autobiography as an area of investigation. My interest in discourse analysis and my understanding of its place in linguistic theory are due to William Labov. I am indebted to Joseph Goguen for pointing out to me that an 80-page article that keeps growing probably wants to be a book, and to George Lakoff and John Robert Ross for encouraging me to include that book in their edited series—which did not, unfortunately, last as long as the writing process. I am grateful to Dorothy Holland and Naomi Quinn for their encouragement and invaluable editorial assistance with an earlier version of Chapter 6 which appeared in Holland and Quinn (1987). I am indebted to my colleagues Penelope Eckert, Brigitte Jordan, Jean Lave, and Geoffrey Nunberg for help in the process of actually finishing the manuscript. I have also been greatly aided by discussions with A. L. Becker, Penelope Eckert, Veronika Ehrich, Gelya Frank, Nathan Hale, Robin Kornman, Elizabeth Krainer, Willem Levelt, Michael Moerman, James Peacock, Livia Polanyi, Larry Selinker, Sandra Silberstein, and James Weiner. My thanks to Brent Powers, for every kind of help and encouragement.

I would like to thank Cambridge University Press for permission to reproduce portions of the transcription notation from Atkinson and Heritage (1984).

My primary debt is to the people who told me something of their lives and whose stories are treated here dispassionately as objects for analysis.

# CONTENTS

A NOTE ON TRANSCRIPTION CONVENTIONS, xi

1. The Creation of Coherence in Life Stories: An Overview, 3
2. What Is a Life Story? 20
3. Methods and Data for Studying the Life Story, 51
4. Narrative and the Iconicity of the Self, 98
5. Coherence Principles: Causality and Continuity, 127
6. Coherence Systems, 163
7. Common Sense and Its History, 192
8. Conclusion, 219

REFERENCES, 225
INDEX, 235

# A NOTE ON TRANSCRIPTION
# CONVENTIONS

This work cites narratives taken from a number of studies that use differing transcription conventions. While some version of the Sacks–Schegloff–Jefferson system used in conversation analysis is now widely used by authors working in a variety of theoretical paradigms, neither this system nor any other serves as a universally accepted standard. This is because selecting a system of transcription conventions is not a value-neutral choice between equivalent representation systems. Rather, the choice is at least partly dictated by one's theory, one's analytical interests, and one's relation to one's audience (Ochs 1979).

The transcription systems used for discourse data generally represent some form of modified standard orthography. Such modifications are made to represent certain characteristics of speech delivery, including pauses, stress, lengthening of words, unusually high or low volume, register changes such as colloquial pronunciations, and laughter during speaking. Certain modifications of the punctuation system are also used to represent aspects of the conversational interaction, such as two speakers speaking at once or a second speaker beginning immediately after the previous turn without pause. The transcription may also record nonlinguistic features of the interaction, such as a participant's entering or leaving the interaction, attention to or manipulation of objects, and eye gaze. The degree to which such indications are made differs depending on the specific focus of a given analysis.

In transcriptions of my own data, I have used a simplified subset of the Sacks–Schegloff–Jefferson system that is as close to standard orthography as my analysis will allow. My reason for doing so is that it takes time to learn to use elaborately notated transcription systems, and a work intended for an interdisciplinary audience cannot assume that all its readers already possess this familiarity. In addition, I have noticed that readers confronted with extensive unfamiliar transcription conventions tend to skip the examples, which is the worst possible outcome of a choice of transcription system. I have chosen to leave examples from Sacks's and Goodwin's work in their original form, however, since an accurate retranscription would necessitate returning to the original tapes, and an inaccurate retranscription would be worse than an overelaborate one.

For readers unfamiliar with this transcription system, the remainder of this note explains the transcription conventions used in the various examples of this book. The specification of the transcription conventions used in conversation analysis is based on the version given by Atkinson and Heritage (1984).

## Simultaneous Utterances

Utterances starting simultaneously are linked with single or double left-hand brackets:

TOM:   I used to smoke a lot when I was young
   [[
BOB:   I used to smoke Camels

## Overlapping Utterances

When overlapping utterances do not start simultaneously, the point at which an ongoing utterance is joined by another is marked with a single left-hand bracket at the point where the overlap begins:

TOM:  I used to smoke a lot
          [
BOB:              He thinks he's real tough

When overlapping utterances do not start simultaneously, the point at which an ongoing utterance is joined by another is marked with a single left-hand bracket, linking an ongoing with an overlapping utterance at the point where overlap begins:

TOM:  I used to smoke a lot more than this
          [   ]
BOB:          I see

In my transcripts, a short overlapping utterance is indicated within the embedding utterance, enclosed by slashes:

P:  All it did was bend the rear fender //P: Yeah// of the bike

## Contiguous Utterances

When there is no interval between adjacent utterances—that is, when the second utterance is latched immediately to the first (without overlapping it)—the utterances are linked together with equal signs:

TOM: I used to smoke a lot =

BOB: = He thinks he's real tough

## Intervals Within and Between Utterances

Untimed pauses heard between utterances are described within single or double parentheses and are inserted where they occur:

REX: Are you ready to order

((pause))

PAM: Yes I think we are

They may also be described by a sequence of three dots. A short untimed pause within an utterance is indicated by a dash:

DEE: Umm—my mother will be right in

In the Sacks–Schegloff–Jefferson system, pauses may be timed in tenths of a second and inserted within parentheses, whether within an utterance or between utterances:

LIL: Whin I was (0.6) oh nine or ten

HAL: Step right up

(1.3)

HAL: I said step right up

## Characteristics of Speech Delivery

A single dash indicates the intonation of a word broken off before it is finished. A comma indicates the intonation of a phrase broken off before it is finished. Speaker's emphasis is indicated by underlining:

ANN: It happens to be <u>mine</u>

Additional symbols are used in the Sacks–Schegloff–Jefferson system to mark details of speech delivery. Colons are used to mark a lengthening of the sound it follows (usually the entire syllable):

RON:  What ha:ppened to you

More colons prolong the stretch:

TIM:  I'm so : : : sorry re : : : ally I am

Doubled letters indicate a lengthening or stress of a single sound.

## Transcriptionist Doubt

Items enclosed within single parentheses are doubted hearings by the transcriptionist.

TED:  I ('spose I'm not)
(BEN):  We all (t-    )

Here, "'spose I'm not," the identity of the second speaker, and "t-" represent different varieties of transcriptionist doubt. When single parentheses are empty, no hearing could be achieved for the string of talk. A segment for which no hearing can be achieved is marked (unclear).

## Explanatory Material

Square brackets are used to enclose explanatory material added by the analyst to specify a reference, expand an acronym, or convey some other information.

## Citation Conventions

Boldface is used to indicate emphasis by the analyst — that is, to indicate the particular section of interest in a transcribed example.

# Life Stories

# 1

# The Creation of Coherence in Life Stories: An Overview

## What Is a Life Story?

In order to exist in the social world with a comfortable sense of being a good, socially proper, and stable person, an individual needs to have a coherent, acceptable, and constantly revised life story. This book describes the ways in which such life stories are created, negotiated, and exchanged. Life stories are of interest both for their own sake and because they can serve as a model for a unified linguistic analysis—one that moves from the level of the individual construction of sentences, through the form of narratives and the social negotiation of narratives, up to the social level of belief systems and their history, and finally to their effect on the construction of narratives. This work attempts a unified description of a particularly important discourse unit whose use constitutes a widespread social practice that has major consequences for the individual and for the group.

Life stories express our sense of self: who we are and how we got that way. They are also one very important means by which we communicate this sense of self and negotiate it with others. Further, we use these stories to claim or negotiate group membership and to demonstrate that we are in fact worthy members of those groups, understanding and properly following their moral standards. Finally, life stories touch on the widest of social constructions, since they make presuppositions about what can be taken as expected, what the norms are, and what common or special belief systems can be used to establish coherence.

In order to study life stories, we must assume that a life story is something most people have, something they have created, and som

thing that, for both personal and social comfort, must be created in a coherent fashion. This is a culturally warranted, nonproblematic assumption in our culture. To examine it, we must investigate the notion of a life story, the notion of coherence, and the ways in which people apply relatively abstract principles for creating coherence to produce accounts, which count as coherent, of such specific portions of their life stories as why someone became a dentist, volunteered for the Marines, got married, or moved to California.

A precise definition of the life story is given in Chapter 2. This section introduces a general discussion of the cultural notion of a life story, in order to specify immediately the subject matter of this study. First, a life story is a social unit. It is exchanged between people, rather than being treasured in solitude in the caverns of the brain. Second, a life story is an oral unit; written autobiographies have a very different character, due to their different purpose. A life story is also a discontinuous unit, told in separate pieces over a long period of time. Since it is a long-term unit, it is necessarily subject to revision and change as the speaker drops some old meanings and adds new meanings to portions of the life story. As one can observe in one's own conversations and in the conversation of others, at different times, on different occasions, and to different people, individuals give different accounts of the same facts and of the reasons why they happened. Stating the observation this way, of course, presupposes the existence of facts, reasons, and accounts. In the course of this study, I shall show some of the major processes by which these common-sense notions are constructed. But taking them as given for the moment, let us turn to an example.

For some people, although certainly not for everyone, a job or profession constitutes a major component of their understanding of their lives. Consequently, they must be able to give some account of how they came to have that profession. There are exceptions, of course. People whose identity is not defined by their work circumstances need not account for their particular job. Thus, for those who are in circumstances where having any job or any job with a sufficient wage to survive, the identity of the specific job does not require an account. Or if as a matter of choice someone's self-identity is as an artist or a psychic, that person's job as a night clerk in a hotel probably does not require an account in itself, but only as it relates to the main significant identity. In addition, the accounts given for professions that are considered socially negative or improper are quite different from those given for socially approved professions. That is, "What's a nice girl like you doing in a place like this?" receives very different kinds of answers than "How'd you come to

be a neurosurgeon?"[1] The accounts for negatively evaluated professions also depend crucially on the relation between the interlocutors, and on the status of the professions that the other interlocutors hold. The present work uses as data accounts of socially approved professions that form a significant part of their holders' life stories.

As an example of the kind of unit under examination, I often identify myself as a linguist, and my profession is important enough to me that I am often asked how I came to have it. I have many stories to account for this. At times I relate my interest in languages to the fact that my grandmother spoke only Yiddish, so that I grew up passively bilingual, replying in English to her Yiddish and trying to understand the Yiddish that my parents used to keep secrets from the children. I sometimes relate it to the fact that my high school had superb language teachers who got me interested in Latin and French and in the differences and similarities between them and English, and to the fact that my mother was interested in language and helped me with my Latin homework, comparing the Latin to the Spanish she had studied. I relate my choice of linguistics as a field of study to the fact that when I was in high school I read a great deal about General Semantics, or to college courses in literary theory and anthropology. I relate my initial choice of research problems to personal questions about how communication is understood—wanting to know what the mechanism of intuition was, after someone told me that it was because of women's intuition that I knew

1. In a discussion of the kinds of accounts given by hospitalized mental patients, Goffman (1972) shows that, even in these desperate circumstances, individuals may use different types of narratives that present the self in very different ways:

> Given the stage that any person has reached in a career, one typically finds that he constructs an image of his life course—past, present, and future—which selects, abstracts, and distorts in such a way as to provide him with a view of himself that he can usefully expound in current situations. Quite generally, the person's line concerning self defensively brings him into appropriate alignment with the basic values of his society, and so may be called an *apologia*. If the person can manage to present a view of his current situation which shows the operation of favorable personal qualities in the past and a favorable destiny awaiting him, it may be called a *success* story. If the facts of a person's past and present are extremely dismal, then about the best he can do is to show that he is not responsible for what has become of him, and the term *sad tale* is appropriate. Interestingly enough, the more the person's past forces him out of apparent alignment with central moral values, the more often he seems compelled to tell his sad tale in any company in which he finds himself. Perhaps he partly responds to the need he feels in others of not having their sense of proper life courses affronted. In any case, it is among convicts, "wino's," and prostitutes that one seems to obtain sad tales the most readily. (pp. 542–43)

that two apparently friendly debaters were furious at one another. I relate my specific field to teachers I encountered in graduate school. These are all accounts I have used on various occasions, and they still seem to be correct and usable when the proper occasions arise.

It might appear at first that, because I have so many accounts, I have failed to find the **real reason** for my choice of profession. But as such accounts work within my understanding of my life story, the more such accounts I am able to give, the more I make my being a linguist coherent with the entire fabric of my life. The existence of so many multiple accounts seems to assure that the choice of profession is well-motivated, richly determined, and woven far back in time. Indeed, there is a sense of satisfaction in discovering a new account—particularly if it does not contradict an earlier account—as there is also satisfaction in having many reasons for the major choices in one's life. It helps guard against the chilling possibility that one's life is random, accidental, unmotivated.

Like many other people, I have certain parts of my life story for which this strategy of multiple accounts would be difficult, because the possible accounts that I can give might be viewed as contradictory. For example, I must account for the fact that I founded and ran my own business, contracting to NASA and other government agencies, since this is not a career path that can be expected of a linguist. (In contrast, there would be no need to account for a choice of being a professor, although some account might be given about how one came to have a position at a particular institution.) To account for this aspect of my life story, I have two stories, which cannot be told on the same occasion as the sole reason, since they rely on different forms of causality. One is that it was an accident—not my doing at all. (What accident can mean in a life story is extremely interesting; we will consider it in Chapter 5.) This story recounts that when it started I was a university professor. One of my colleagues was giving a public and widely advertised lecture on the language of psychoanalysis. The university public relations officer heard about it, and asked her if she would like a press release sent out on it. When she refused, the P.R. person asked her if there was anything else going on in the department that might be newsworthy. She told the P.R. person that I had just finished some work on small group planning, using the Watergate tapes as data. That clearly sounded like news, so the P.R. officer came to me and asked if I would like a press release. I said, "Sure, why not?" and a press release went out. By chance, it was sent out the week before the David Frost interviews with Richard Nixon were aired, so it was picked up by many newspapers, radio stations, and news services. The release was run in the *San Francisco Chronicle*, where it was seen by someone at NASA who was working on small group planning in aviation crews. He asked if I had anything to say to them, I did a seminar, the group at NASA asked me to work on a contract with them on aviation communications, and that's how it all began. Since I had never before thought of the possibility of a linguistics company, and since the sequence of events depended on a number of unpredictable and unlikely events beyond my control, it clearly can be construed as an accident.

Another version of the story is that I have always felt that linguistics should be concerned with the **use** of language as well as its structure and that, therefore, linguistics itself should be a useful science to other academic disciplines, as well as to a wider world. Therefore, my running a company specializing in applying linguistics to real-world problems is a clear consequence of my long-standing views on the nature of linguistics, which go back to my choice of sociolinguistics as a subfield, to my dissertation topic, and so on.

With a great deal of work in the telling, I could relate these as mutually supporting, noncontradictory stories. But in fact, I tend to tell one or the other to them; on the face of it, they are contradictory, since they appear to use different types of causality that I have not attempted to reconcile. I am willing, as many people are, to live with contradictory accounts that I may bring out on their appropriate occasions.

Appropriateness is not merely a matter of how the teller happens to be feeling that day; it is primarily a social matter. The exchange of life stories is a social process, and there are social demands on the nature of a life story. One is not simply free to construct a life story in any possible way. Addressees make a number of types of social demands on the nature of the teller's story.

One such demand is that we expect our degree of intimacy with a person to correlate with our knowledge of their life story. In other words, as we get to know a person, we expect successively more detailed life stories to be exchanged; and thus we will learn of our friends what has happened to them and what sort of people we are to understand that they are. As our level of intimacy increases, we expect to know more and more about the other. (In fact, what and how much we know about the other may define the notion of a level of intimacy.)

One simple way of demonstrating the existence of this expectation is to look at the meta-comments people make about their grasp of another's life story. One example indicates an expectation about facts. In talking to a new friend, I interrupted a story about his sisters to complain, "You never told me you had sisters." Our degree of acquaintance was such that I could expect to have known this fact already. He said, "Oh I'm sure I told you," a response that implicitly accepted my assumption that he should have told me this fact.

Another example indicates expectations about chronology. I heard a complaint made about a close friendship that, although the speaker knew many things that had happened to her friend, she did not know when any of them happened or in what order. She found this disturbing and felt that it might indicate secretiveness on her friend's part. Knowledge of sequence and chronology can also be expected, and its absence is reportable. This is true because a life story does not consist simply of a collection of facts or incidents. It also requires sequence, since from sequence causality can be inferred; and notions like causality, accident, and reasons are crucial in shaping the meaning of a life story.

Another social demand on life stories is that certain kinds of facts are expected to be integrated into a life story, while others cannot be. Profession has been chosen as the research topic of this study exactly because, for middle-class Americans, one's profession is expected to form part of one's life story. To check this assumption, try to imagine a close relationship in which you did not know your friend's profession. After a short period of time, this ignorance would come to indicate something troubling: absence of knowledge would suggest that the profession is being concealed, possibly for some sinister or disgraceful reason.

It is completely reasonable, in this culture, to ask what someone's profession is. In fact, "What do you do?" is a common and almost always acceptable opening topic of conversation, and one for which a person must have an answer. There are, of course, people who are defined as not "doing" anything, and this question (and the assumption behind it) then becomes problematic and often a source of difficulty. Women who work at home, or whose primary work is taking care of children find that they must answer this question, "Oh, I don't do anything; I'm just a housewife." This answer presupposes that certain kinds of activities do not count as "doing" something, and that not doing something is a matter for apology.

Here is another example of problems in formulating one's activities as "doing something": I was once at a dinner party where all the participants were known to one another except the hostess's new boyfriend. At first the topics of conversation were general, until the newcomer mentioned something about some work he had done on computers. The two other men present, both computer professionals, immediately took interest and asked him, "Oh, what do you do?" A long dead silence followed, broken finally by the hostess asking if anyone wanted dessert, and the topic changed to the excellence of the pastry.

What had gone wrong was that the newcomer did not "do" anything; he lived on an inherited income. And within current social conventions, he could find no way to express this acceptably. His avocation was photography, but since he was not paid for it, he did not feel that he could claim to "do" photography. I later spoke with him about this, and he said that in fact he often had this problem and had not come up with any workable answer. Just a hundred years ago, however, his situation would have been presupposed to be the norm for a gentleman, and the question "What do you do?" would have been deemed as socially problematic as his current situation is today.[2]

At present, not only may a person's profession be asked, but also the reason for it. Thus we may certainly ask someone "Why are you a physicist?" or "How did you come to work for NASA?" This seems obvious, until we consider that other kinds of facts exist that are unlikely to form a focus of a life story, that are hard to give accounts of, and that cannot be questioned socially. In contrast to a socially permissible question like "Why are you a physicist?" it is only marginally possible or intelligible to ask someone "Why are you blue-eyed?" and it is clearly impolite to ask "Why are you intelligent?" (It might be possible to ask a

---

2. As Veyne (1987) notes in discussing the history of this issue of career versus independent income:

> Around 1820 an astrologer says to the young hero of Stendahl's *Charterhouse of Parma*: "In a century perhaps nobody will want idlers any more." He was right. It ill becomes anyone today to admit that he lives without working. Since Marx and Proudhon, labor has been universally accepted as a positive social value and a philosophical concept. As a result, the ancients' contempt for labor, their undisguised scorn for those who work with their hands, their exaltation of leisure as the sine qua non of a liberal life shocks us deeply. Not only was the worker regarded as a social inferior, he was base, ignoble. It has often been held, therefore, that a society like the Roman, so mistaken about what we regard as proper values, must have been a deformed society, which inevitably paid the price of its deformity. The ancients' contempt for labor, the argument goes, explains their economic backwardness, their ignorance of technology. Or, according to another argument, their reason for one deformity must be sought in another: contempt for labor, we are told, had its roots in that other scandalous fact of Roman life, slavery.
>
> And yet, if we are honest, we must admit that the key to this enigma lies within ourselves. True, we believe that work is respectable and would not dare to admit to idleness. Nevertheless, we are sensitive to class distinctions and, admit it or not, regard workers and shopkeepers as people of relatively little importance. We would not want ourselves or our children to sink to their station, even if we are a little ashamed of harboring such sentiments. (p. 118)

third person a question like, "Why is Leslie so dumb when the rest of the family is so intelligent?") Additionally, other kinds of facts exist that need not and cannot be accounted for, and therefore do not form part of a life story, even though they may have an extremely important effect on someone's life course. An example of this sort would be the social incoherence of asking someone "Why are you male?"

The particular conventions governing what can and cannot form part of a life story are obviously not universal, as indeed the notion of a life story is not universal; rather, they differ by culture and subculture. For example, the fact of being male may be accounted for in a culture whose belief system includes the idea of reincarnation into a life situation that is determined by actions in a previous life. In such a system, good deeds in a previous life may have resulted in a male birth in this life. This kind of expected sequence may be taken as a cultural given, known to everyone. Shweder and Miller (1985) give an example of this kind in their discussion of the beliefs of the Oriyans, a community of Brahmans and temple priests in Bhubaneswar, Orissa, India. The Oriyans believe that the natural order is also a moral order, the order of karma, in which events have an ethical meaning. The current situation of one's life reflects one's past deeds; therefore, being born a woman is not random, but a sign of sin in a past life.

In addition, if one is a member of a class of persons who have access to knowledge of past lives (and such membership is a matter of great social significance), one may be able to give a coherent account for one's sex or for the identity and status of one's parents—matters that in a Western belief system must remain unaccountable points of brute fact. Hallowell (1955) gives a very interesting example of this, citing an account by Sleeman (1893) of a low-caste Hindu woman who convinced the family of a deceased Brahmin that she should be allowed to die on his funeral pyre because she had been married to him in a former life. Although at first skeptical, they were eventually convinced by her account that she had been born in a low caste because as a Brahmin in a previous life she had committed a serious but unintentional religious violation. The fact that it was serious led to her current birth; the fact that it was unintentional allowed her to retain the memory and thus bring an end to the violation by dying on his funeral pyre. This is a very elaborate account for kinds of facts that in our belief system need not and cannot be accounted for at all. Clearly this example involves not an idiosyncratic and private account of the speaker alone, but an account that was negotiated between the participants and had the real-world consequence that the family of the deceased Brahmin paid for the woman's funeral expenses and thereafter considered her as part of their family.

Finally, a third demand on the formulation of life stories is that the account the speaker gives must not challenge—and must support, if possible—the addressee's own life story. For example, in the early stages of a romantic relationship, I identified myself as a linguist to someone who identified himself as an artist. He interpreted my being a linguist to mean that I was a scientist—and hence one of **the enemy**—and found it difficult to reconcile this with a close relationship with me. He cleverly solved this dilemma by creating an alternate life story for me that was compatible with his. His formulation was: You are not really a scientist. In fact, you have the talent to be a witch. But in this society, where it is so difficult to get proper witch training, you did the best you could and trained as a linguist—that is, a word-witch. This reformulation solved his problem. I was actually charmed by this entirely unexpected reworking of my story and decided that, yes, what I really am is a word-witch. I even tried this account out on a number of people in my professional world, but it was too contradictory to their stories and so proved to be useless beyond the bounds of a single relationship.

In summary, a life story is an oral unit that is told over many occasions. Conventionally, it includes certain kinds of landmark events, such as choice of profession, marriage, divorce, and religious or ideological conversion if any. Both in its content (the items that it includes and excludes) and in its form (the structures that are used to make it coherent), it is the product of a member of a particular culture. Other cultures may include different items and use different forms. Indeed, the notion of a "life story" itself is not universal, but is the product of a particular culture. Considerable evidence suggests that many groups' members do not conceive of themselves as having a life story (Frank 1979; Langness and Frank 1981; see Chapter 2 for a further discussion).

Although the life story is a linguistic unit crucially involved in social interaction, it is also related to our internal, subjective sense of having a private life story that organizes our understanding of our past life, our current situation, and our imagined future. This inner life story is accessible only to introspection; any attempt to tell it immediately brings it into the daylight world of talk to some audience. Indeed, when one asks people whether they are conscious of having an inner story, and (if so) what it is like, one gets a wide variety of responses. Some people report that they experience it as a narration, often in the third person. Some people see it unfolding like a movie. Some people have an ongoing fantasy life story that continues for years with ramifying events and details, related to the outer, social life story in a parallel or symbolic way. We may call this the Walter Mitty phenomenon. Although it would be extremely difficult to study this inner story, studying the ways in which we make spoken, public life stories coherent also reveals something about the ways in which we create our private universe of meanings.

## What Is Coherence?

This study investigates the ways in which we attempt to make life stories coherent; having reviewed a nontechnical description of what is meant by life story, we may now turn to the question of what is meant by coherence.

Coherence is a property of texts; it derives from the relations that the parts of a text bear to one another and to the whole text, as well as from the relation that the text bears to other texts of its type. For example, a text may be described as coherent if two sets of relations hold. One is that its parts—whether on the word level, the phrase level, the sentence level, or the level of larger discourse units—can be seen as being in proper relation to one another and to the text as a whole. The other is that the text as a whole must be seen as being a recognizable and well-formed text of its type. Thus, a cowboy movie is understood both because its internal structure is understandable—that is, the shootout follows rather than precedes the explication of the problem over the ownership of the ranch—and because it stands in a tradition of prior texts recognizable as cowboy movies.

Coherence must also be understood as a cooperative achievement of the speaker and the addressee; it is not an absolute property of a disembodied, unsituated text. The speaker works to construct a text whose coherence can be appreciated, and at the same time the addressee works to reach some understanding of it as a coherent text and to communicate that understanding. The coherent text that the addressee constructs may not, of course, be the same as the text that the speaker believes was constructed. As long as the gap is not too great, the discrepancy will probably not be noticed. But if it becomes very large, further negotiation about the meaning of the text may be necessary. The following, from Polanyi (1989, pp. 95–96), is an example of such negotiation, involving possible evaluations of a narrative about fainting during rush hour on the New York City subway. The speaker compares conditions on the subway to the Nazi treatment of the Jews:

1. Yeah, the closest thing I can compare it to, and I never experienced that . . . and it's probably a <u>fraction</u> of what <u>that</u> experience was . . . but I think . . . of the way the Jews . . . were herded into the cattle cars . . . [material omitted] And it's just as dehumanizing.

This is an extremely strong claim about the meaning of the narrative, which the addressee refuses to accept, commenting on the speaker's earlier account of how she was treated:

2. But people were pretty nice, hm?

The speaker must then re-form the meaning she claims for her narrative into a mutually acceptable one. (Chapter 3 presents a fuller discussion of this process and this example.)

Within linguistics, a number of complementary approaches can be taken to the investigation of text structure, and together these give a rich understanding of how a text is structured and what linguistic forms and strategies make it coherent. These approaches include discourse analysis, which involves studying the structure of units such as stories, jokes, and descriptions (Labov 1972*b*; Linde 1981); the study of particular lexical and grammatical properties of a language and how they are used to create cohesion of larger textual units (Becker 1979; Halliday and Hasan 1976); and the ethnomethodological school of conversational analysis, which examines the ways in which the structure of an interaction is created by the moment-to-moment work of its participants. (For a review, see Moerman [1987] and Goodwin and Heritage [1990].) This study applies techniques and insights from all of these approaches in exploring the different levels of coherence present in life stories.

Let us make a preliminary examination of the ways in which a text is constructed coherently. The very notion of a life story requires a notion of sequence. A life story is not merely a collection of events that happened in some unknown or irrelevant order. To be a life story at all, an account must have an order that both the speaker and the addressee take as significant. For example, we may know of someone that she worked as an actress and that she got a degree in social work; but we still feel that we do not really understand her life story until we know the order in which she did these things. We feel warranted in drawing certain kinds of conclusions from sequence that are impossible to obtain in the absence of sequence. In English, as we will see in Chapters 3 and 4, temporal ordering is a fundamental device for making a text coherent.

*[handwritten margin notes: events are connected to real world referent: Thus, is what where's their authual referent?]*

Let us take as a fundamental question about the coherence of any text why part B follows part A. A principle of interpretation such as temporal ordering can give a very strong answer for the texts to which it is applied. Temporal ordering allows us to give as an answer that the text in question is coherent — that is, that the relation of A and B in the text is significant because the order of A and B in the text can be taken as a statement about the order of their referents in a presumed past world of real facts and real events. Thus, in the hypothetical example of the actress/social worker, the principle of temporal ordering allows us to assume that she first worked as an actress and then got a degree as a social worker. Once we make this assumption of sequence, many other cultural assumptions can come into play about why the sequence happened as it did: she did not like being an actress; she could not get work; she became too old; and so on. The opposite ordering (first being a social worker and then being an actress) will lead to very different narratives. Detailed interpretations like this are possible only after we recognize that sequence is the major structuring device of the text.

## Sidestepping the Issue of Truth

In focusing on coherence, we concentrate on the life story as a text, rather than on either the speaker of the text or the relation of the life story to some supposed set of facts in a postulated real world. A good deal of previous work on life stories has considered one of these two other aspects. Either the life story is examined as one means of discovering the facts about what really happened (and criticized if it fails to conform to a set of facts that the investigator has determined by other means — usually written forms of information, which are held to be more trustworthy) or it is taken as an indication of the personality, cognitive structure, social situation, or psychopathology of the speaker — a sample in the sense of a urine sample. Both strategies treat the life story not as an object of study in itself, but as an object in partial and rather fragile correspondence to some area of greater interest, which is held to have more factual validity. This study will not be concerned with whether the life stories considered are true to some postulated actual facts of the speaker's life. Rather than making claims about the existence and nature of raw facts, this study assumes that all we can ever work with is texts of one sort or another. Certain kinds of texts such as official written records are treated as having automatic priority, because they represent what will be treated officially as the facts. Smith (1984) has shown that the peculiar characteristic of bureaucratic records is that they process and convert a version of the actual events into documents that possess official endorsement of their supposed status as facts. Various studies show that the social production of medical, legal, and bureaucratic records is not a simple matter of recording facts; instead, it is the result of social processes, negotiations, and rules of thumb to be followed when standard procedures cannot be applied, as is often the case (Garfinkel and Bittner 1967; Zimmerman 1969; Meehan 1986). Let us consider a simple example that makes the same point.

Someone may tell us that he was born in Livorno, and this may seem to constitute a fact with a status independent of the text in which it is told—a fact that can be verified independently of the speaker's bare assertion (viewed as a text). We might attempt to verify it by checking the person's passport or birth certificate, or by asking relatives or friends. But each of these attempts at verification involves consulting a text that is itself subject to the process of interpretation; no such source can be treated as though it were the fact it purports to record.

A common assumption, based in practices of the legal and governmental system, is that certain types of texts such as birth certificates have a privileged status and are more trustworthy than other texts. Birth in Livorno was chosen as an example to show just one of the problems with this assumption. Since much of Livorno was destroyed during World War II and is known to have been destroyed, foreign nationals desiring Italian citizenship can claim to have been born in Livorno before the destruction of its records. Knowing this fact, we may begin to place less reliance on a passport with a prewar Livorno birthplace, and value more highly as evidence a casual remark about the passport's bearer that he does not look Italian.[3]

A classic case of this sort is found in Cicero's *Pro Archia*, which concerns a dispute over whether Archias actually is a citizen of Heraclea, a confederate city of Rome. The argument turns on the relation between documentary evidence and testimony. The public registry of Heraclea had been burned in a war, and the Roman census reports of the relevant years had been so badly maintained that they could not be credited. Therefore, Cicero argues, the oral testimony of reputable witnesses— and the plausibility that Heraclea would have given citizenship to so eminent a man—should take precedence as evidence over the absence of any mention of Archias in incomplete or unreliable documents.

Clanchy (1979) shows that written records are not inherently prefer-

3. I am indebted to Professor Gerald Prince for the Livorno example and to Professor Robin Tolmach Lakoff for the example of Cicero's *Pro Archia*.

able to unwritten ones, and he argues that our current preference in
Anglo-American law (as opposed, for example, to Islamic law), is rooted
in a complex political process arising from differences in the Norman
and Anglo-Saxon legal systems. Clanchy describes the process, which
took place over more than a century, by which the new Norman government succeeded in replacing personal testimony with documents as the
preferred form of evidence for land ownership in England.

Much of the detailed work of history and biography consists of evaluating different types of evidence with regard to their reliability as sup-
ports in establishing possible facts. However, such an evaluation of factuality is not at all the concern of the present work. The processes for
constructing a life story as coherent may be analyzed independently of
the truth or falsity of the particular events, characters, and feelings that
are used to constitute the story. It would be difficult or impossible to
evaluate the factuality of the stories told, and the evaluation would add
little or nothing to our understanding of the creation of coherence.
Nor is it the concern of this study to use a life story to formulate
claims about the speaker. Doing so would involve postulating entities
such as personality types and intrapsychic processes, which would move
the investigation far from the text itself. By remaining within the text
and focusing on its structure, the investigation can determine a great
deal about processes that are common to the entire culture, as well as
some that appear to be particular to individual speakers. We do not yet
know enough about the construction of narratives to make well-founded
judgments about individual differences on the basis of narrative style.

## The Social Demand for Coherence

As we have already discussed, coherence is not an absolute property of
texts, but rather is created by speaker and addressee. The process of
creating coherence is not a light matter; it is in fact a social obligation
that must be fulfilled in order for the participants to appear as competent
members of their culture. In the case of narratives that form part of a
life story, this demand amounts to an obligation to provide coherence —
usually in the form of a chain of causality that is neither too thick nor
too thin. If (in the estimation of a given addressee) this obligation is not
met, the speaker is liable to be criticized or corrected by the addressee.
Such examples are rather rare, since we are excellent at the task of
constructing coherence and normally accomplish it unnoticeably and
without difficulty.

One example I observed of a complaint by a hearer came in a conversation between two people who had been friends for at least twenty years. One of the friends corrected the other's account of how his life had gone, complaining that it sounded too fatalistic. To his surprise, he found that his friend indeed did think that this life course was predestined. In this case, the correction was attempted (and failed) because the participants were operating, unknowingly, with different beliefs about the world, and so could not agree on what constituted adequate coherence.

Another example was a situation in which I was corrected by a friend for producing a story that he judged to be too accidental, because I did not create coherences that he knew I could have drawn. I was attempting to give him an account of how I became involved in Buddhist meditation. The story I told was that I had met someone who invited me to a Buddhist institute where he was teaching for the summer; and since I wanted to spend time with him and had no other plans for the summer, I went. There I began meditating, and that was how I got started. My addressee was a close friend of twelve years' standing; he thus had had both the opportunity and the right to have his own account of my life. He refused to accept my account as I gave it, reminding me that I had always been interested in such matters, citing a number of books on mysticism that I had lent him years before as evidence that my account as given could not be completely correct. My failure to include a coherence that we both knew I could have constructed was an error, subject to social correction. This process of social correction of the coherence furnished by an individual is an extremely important aspect of discourse as a socially constructed rather than an individually constructed phenomenon. It will not be discussed systematically in this study, however, since data of a different sort would be needed to study it.

In addition to being a social demand, adequate coherence is also a personal demand that we make on ourselves. Just as the life story as a social unit has some correspondence to an internal, private life story, so the coherence that we produce for social consumption bears a relation to our own individual desire to understand our life as coherent, as making sense, as the history of a proper person. The internal demand for coherence is accessible only to introspection, and indeed is rarely accessible even in this way, since most of the time we manage to maintain coherence—even if it is a painful coherence—quite adequately. Nonetheless, we can become aware of this personal demand for coherence in situations where some new event has happened that we do not know how to form into narrative, since it does not seem to fit into our current life story. We can observe a great deal of confusion and uneasiness until

Note: a) compares both social life stories e private life story.
(b) to part of our personal ety: "How am I understood by others?" to what extent this remains personal?

we somehow make the new event fit the ongoing story, or until the
story has been changed to accommodate the new event. Although the
postulation of an internal life story is plausible, it raises methodological
problems. Other than by introspection (which is currently unacceptable
as a scientific practice), how can it be studied reliably? This work will
not attempt to consider the internal life story or the personal demand
for its coherence. It may be, however, that the findings on the social
demand and achievement of coherence are also relevant to the personal,
internal sense of having a life story.

## Coherence Systems

Thus far, we have discussed coherence as a personal demand and as an
interpersonal demand and achievement. But although the coherence of a
text results from the conditions of how the text is created and negotiated,
there is also a cultural basis for any such negotiation. First, there is the
basis of what is called "common sense," which is the system of assumptions and beliefs that are assumed to be shared by all competent members
of the culture. Common-sense beliefs are so obvious and transparent
to members of a given culture that they have difficulty perceiving them
as assumptions. There are also special coherence systems that a given
speaker may choose to use. Such systems are popular versions of expert
theories and systems. Examples include versions of Freudian psychology,
behaviorism, astrology, Catholic confessional practice, and feminism.
   To demonstrate the notion of coherence systems, let us first consider
a (constructed) example:

3a. How did you come to be an accountant?
3b. Well I guess I have a precise mind and I enjoy getting all the
    little details right.

The response in 3b relies on common-sense beliefs about character and
ability as a good basis for career choice. Now consider example 4:

4a. How did you come to be an accountant?
4b. Well, my mother started toilet-training me when I was six
    months old.

In contrast to the common-sense coherence presupposed by 3b, 4b requires that the hearer know (if not share) the popular Freudian coherence
system, which attributes the real causes of events to experiences in early

childhood. Notice also that 4b can be uttered as a joke, while 3b cannot. This itself is an indication of the marked nature of the coherence system on which 4b relies.

In later chapters, we will consider a number of coherence systems, including common sense, in detail. At present it is sufficient to remember that, although the coherence of a given narrative in a given conversation is the creation of the participants in that conversation, they have a cultural supply of expected events in a life course, commonly recognized causes, and shared possible explanations from which to construct individual coherences.

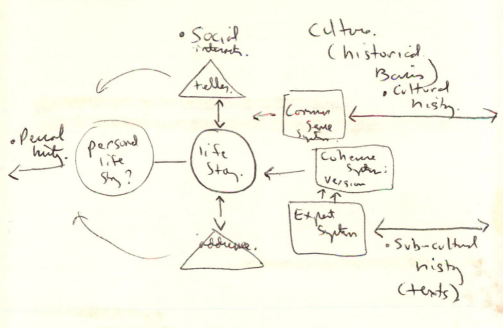

# 2

# What Is a Life Story?

### Definition of a Life Story

In this chapter, I will define the life story as an oral unit of social interaction and indicate how it differs from other revelations or constructions of the self (autobiography, journals, psychological life history, and so on). In defining the life story, I am attempting to render precise and accessible to analysis the common-sense notion of a life story discussed in Chapter 1 — a notion that is already in use by members of this culture, and that describes part of their social practice. Such a work of definition is a common practice in the history of linguistics. Just as "sentence," "story," and "argument" were folk notions before being investigated and described by linguistics (or her older sister, rhetoric), so "life story" is also a folk notion. Part of the interpretive equipment furnished to us by our culture is the idea that we "have" a life story, and that any normally competent adult has one. In this nontechnical use, the notion of the life story means something like "what events have made me what I am," or more precisely, "what you must know about me to know me," where knowing a person specifies a range of linguistic and social activities and relations by the knowers.

This nontechnical definition of the life story bears the same relation to the technical definition that I am about to propose as the various technical definitions of the sentence or the story bear to the common-sense notions that their authors have attempted to capture. Typically, in attempting to render precise some common-sense notion that seems sufficiently important in one's thinking to deserve formalization, one manages a partial match between the intuitive notion one began with and the constructed item that one's definition picks out. But the match

20

is never complete. A glance at the history of definition of the sentence or of the story shows this clearly. If all grammars leak, as Sapir claimed, one of the places where they are most likely to spring the leak is in their definitions. However, even a partial match between the definition and the initial intuition can be extremely illuminating.

The technical definition of the life story that will be used in the present work is as follows:

> A life story consists of all the stories and associated discourse units, such as explanations and chronicles, and the connections between them, told by an individual during the course of his/her lifetime that satisfy the following two criteria:
>
> 1. The stories and associated discourse units contained in the life story have as their primary evaluation a point about the speaker, not a general point about the way the world is.
> 2. The stories and associated discourse units have extended reportability; that is, they are tellable and are told and retold over the course of a long period of time.

We will consider these in turn.

The first criterion a story must satisfy to be included as a part of the life story is that it must make some evaluative point about the speaker or about some event framed as relevant specifically because it happened to the speaker. This criterion depends on the notion of the evaluative point of the story, which will be precisely defined in Chapter 3. For the present, let us say that the evaluative point of the story is roughly the understanding that the addressee must agree to about what the protagonist's actions mean—that is, the general, moral communication of what kind of a person this is and what kinds of actions these are.

Let us consider possible types of evaluative points a story can make. In this discussion, we will look at first-person narratives; the case of second- and third-person narratives is similar but more complicated, and the complications are not relevant to this discussion. One type of evaluative point illustrates something about the character of the speaker. Stories with this type of point convey, directly or indirectly, the information "I am such and such a kind of person, since I acted in such and such a way." Another type of evaluative point a story can convey illustrates one of the ways that the world is. Stories of this type make points like "That's what dealing with the IRS is like" or "You can't trust used car dealers," proving these points by the example of the speaker's experiences with such people or circumstances.

The first criterion for the inclusion of a story in the life story is that it be a story of the first type—that is, that its evaluative point primarily be to show something about the kind of person the speaker is, rather than to demonstrate something about the way the world is. This distinction arises from how the story is constructed, not from the particular type of events narrated. For example, I can tell a story about what happened to me in the hospital in a way that shows what kind of person I am in dealing with difficult circumstances, or in a way that demonstrates a point about what's wrong with hospitals. Only a story of the first type would form part of the repertoire of my life story. (However, the same events may be told at different times to make either of these points—or some other point entirely. The events we use to construct stories are not limited to, or frozen into, a single type of telling.)

The second criterion for including a story in the life story is that it have extended reportability. Reportability is a notion that forms a part of evaluation. An event is not reportable if it is something that happens every day; to be turned into a story, an event must either be unusual in some way or run counter to expectations or norms. (Labov 1972*b*, p. 390) Thus, seeing a parade of elephants marching across the bridge as you drive to work is reportable because it is unusual. Seeing someone killed on the street is reportable because it is both unusual and counter to our norms regarding how things should be. Being cheated by a used car salesman may not be unusual, and indeed may be the sort of thing that one expects will happen in dealings with used car salesmen. Such an event may still be reportable, however, because we believe that it should not happen—that the world should not be that way, although it really is.

The reportability of a given event or sequence of events is not fixed; it depends not only on the nature of the events, but on the relation of the speaker and addressee(s), the amount of time that has passed between the event and the telling of the story, and the personal skills of the speaker as a narrator. Some events in one's personal life or spiritual development may be reportable to one's best friend, but are too personal to tell to a coworker whom one sees every day. Other events are reportable to someone whom one talks to every day, but are not sufficiently significant to tell to a close friend six months later. For example, a story about the terrible traffic jam I was just caught in may be reportable for a day or two, but it is unlikely to be reportable six months from now (unless it was due to the unexpected presence of elephants on the bridge). Here again, though, we must be precise about the point that the story is framed to make. A story about an ordinary awful traffic jam would have limited reportability as an account of why I am late, frazzled, or the like. Framed another way, it might have extended reportability today as an instance of the general principle that this particular road is terrible and should not be used, or that this whole area is getting overcrowded and unlivable.

The narratability of a given sequence of events is not fixed; rather, it is crucially related to the potential speaker's ability to perceive that a reportable event has happened and that it can be seen as having a particular moral relevance. One characteristic that distinguishes good storytellers from average or poor ones is their ability to construe a moral meaning for events that appear to others to be morally neutral. The best storyteller I have ever known appeared to live in a densely moral world. Confronted, say, with the same event of a bad meal that would have elicited from me the comment "This is inedible" or "This is no good," he would have responded with "It's a crime to do this to a good steak." Such moral sensitivity allowed him to perceive almost all his experience as narratable.

Certain types of stories conventionally tend to have extended reportability. These include stories about career milestones, marriage, divorce, major illness, and religious or ideological conversions. Such matters are relevant and reportable over a major portion of one's life and, indeed, involve just those events that must be communicated in order that one may be known. It should also be noted that the examples given here are culturally defined landmark events, but they are not obligatory events of the life story. They are available for a speaker to use, but any speaker may frame entirely different and unexpected events as the stories to be repeated again and again. This is a matter of individual creativity and personal understanding of the salient events of one's life.

Just as individuals within a culture can be expected to include certain types of landmark events in their life stories, a generational cohort can be expected to include certain public landmark events or experiences: "What did you do in the Great War, Daddy?" "Where were you when you heard that Kennedy had been shot?" "What happened to you in the earthquake/blackout?" These questions are all appropriate ones to ask a speaker of the relevant age, and they can be expected to elicit often-told stories.

This list of landmark events is also relevant to our expectation that any competent adult has a life story. We may ask why this definition is restricted to adults. Such a question amounts to asking at what age the life story develops, or who is entitled to have a life story. Clearly it is socially incoherent to ask a three-year-old what his or her life story is. We do know that, even before the age of three, children can refer to events in the immediate and more distant past (Sachs 1983). And Miller and Sperry (1988) have shown that children as young as two are able to refer spontaneously to past events and to communicate their opinion about these events, including a high percentage of negative evaluations. However, several factors make these stories unlikely candidates for inclusion in the life story. One is that it is unclear whether these children's stories are repeated over multiple tellings over a long period of time. More crucially, it appears that, although evaluation in the form of the speaker's emotional responses to events develops very early, the presentation of self as a good and socially competent person is not a factor in such stories. Additionally, our implicit common-sense theories of what kinds of events are likely to form part of a life story do not, in general, include the experiences of three-year-olds. Therefore, even asking a child's parent to recount his or her life story would not be coherent, unless the child had had unusual experiences not to be expected among members of that age group—a life-threatening illness, escape from a war, or the like.

In fact, it is unclear at what age the life story actually begins to be developed, although some time during early adolescence is a good candidate period. No research has directly investigated the development of the life story, but a number of researchers have reported findings that provide at least indirect evidence relevant to this topic. In his classic paper on the structure of narrative, Labov (1972b) gives an instance of an eleven-year-old boy's narrative about a fight he was in when he was in the third grade—a narrative that shows heavy and skilled presentation of self. The entire narrative was structured to prove that his fight with a boy who stole his glove was well justified and that the speaker was both a good reasoner and a good fighter, while his opponent was not only a cowardly fighter but gave stupid and transparent excuses for his behavior.

Eckert (1989) has given examples of extended narrative exchange among a group of girls who are juniors in high school, ages 15 through 17. The examples make it clear that effective presentation of self is a crucial issue for them, both in their narrations and in their attempts to forge an identity for themselves. These narratives focus on the social careers that the girls have had in high school since the time when they all knew each other in junior high school. The issue of social career and the choices that have entered into it play a crucial role in the formation of a distinctive adult self. Conventionally, our notions of what things count as landmark events do not necessarily involve our high school social careers; details about which clique we hung out with or our participation in the cheerleading squad, the football team, or the school newspaper are considered trivial (although memorable) once we become adults. But

Also, — Presentation of Self in Society.

Story: A' → B interrel. reld.

26

as Eckert has shown, decisions about our high school
activities can crucially affect our tracking into the career
lead to adult membership in quite different social classes. ...
although these narratives are not usually recognized conventionally as
involving serious choices with lifelong consequences, they may in fact
involve just such consequences. This lack of recognition of these consequences may be caused, at least in part, by the tacit prohibition in
middle-class American discourse of any overt discussion of social class.
We will discuss this avoidance further in Chapter 5. Indeed, the very
fact that the significance of such choices cannot be directly discussed
may help explain why so many people show enormous zest for discussing
their experiences in high school, however horrific the stories they tell
may be. (You can easily check this assertion by asking a group of people
about their experiences in high school, and observing how long and how
loud the conversation is.)

In summary, little or no research has thus far been done on this topic
directly—not surprisingly, since the present study is the first to focus on
the definition and structure of the life story as a linguistic unit. Stories
that can form part of the life story (as defined here) probably begin to
develop in early adolescence, since this is exactly the period when a
distinct sense of social identity begins to be formed. Network

A final point about the definition of the life story is that it does not
refer exclusively to a particular subset of stories, but also includes the
connections that are created within each story and between the stories of
the life story. This creation of coherence is the subject of Chapters 5, 6,
and 7. The important point here is that a life story is not simply a
collection of stories, explanations, and so on; instead, it also involves
the relations among them. Thus, when any new story is added to the
repertoire of the life story, it must be related in some way to the themes
of the other stories included in the life story, or at least it must not
contradict them. This means (as will be discussed more fully later) that
the stories included in the life story constantly undergo revision, to express our current understanding of what our lives mean. This property
permits the life story to express our entire sense of what our lives are
about, or our sense of what kind of people we are, without ever necessarily forming a single narrative that organizes our entire lives.

## Temporal Discontinuity and Structural Openness

As a linguistic unit, the life story is a rather odd unit: it is temporally
discontinuous; and at any given telling of one of its component parts, it
is incomplete. A common and usually unquestioned assumption is that

units of language are primarily continuous in time; that is, a unit of any size is thought of as having a beginning, a middle, and an ending, with no interpolated material that does not belong to the unit. In practice, however, there are many exceptions to this assumption. At the level of morphology, we find discontinuous constituents. Some English examples are **not only . . . but also, if . . . then,** and **on the one hand . . . on the other hand.** At the level of sentences, we recognize interruptions by others and parenthetical remarks by the speaker. At the discourse level, we can observe both side sequences by addressees (which temporally interrupt the speaker's ongoing discourse, but do not take command of the floor from the speaker) and actual interruptions, either linguistic or nonlinguistic (which temporarily or permanently stop the speaker's ongoing discourse) (Jefferson 1972).

Although such cases of interruption can be found, we as analysts (and as speakers of the language) assume that this is unusual—that proper, prototypical instances of sentences or stories are not interrupted. And indeed, we can observe that participants in a conversation do tend to perform the work required to achieve a resumption of the narrative after an interruption. A speaker may take up an interrupted story with a marker like **Well, anyway,** or the hearer may prompt the resumption with a marker like **So you were saying.** Such markers indicate the work necessary to achieve resumption, and they also indicate that resumption is desired by the participants. Narratives, in particular, are robustly resistant to interruption. I have observed interrupted narratives resumed after breaks of as long as 45 minutes, by a prompt from an addressee, without any of the participants remarking on this as a socially anomalous (or even particularly skilled) procedure.

The assumption of continuity of linguistic units at the level of discourse makes sense in environments where talk is either the main work or the main amusement. This is the case for the situations in which life stories are exchanged, as it is for almost all instances of the discourse units that have been studied to date. But there are also situations of task-driven talk—that is, work settings in which talk is primarily organized by the demands of the task to be accomplished, the physical environment, or the like. Thus, a conversation may be interrupted by the needs of a crying baby, a boiling-over pot, or a ringing telephone; but these are seen as interruptions to a unit that would have worked better if it had been uninterrupted. In contrast, in task-driven talk, the talk itself is organized by the demands of the task, for example, in fixing an automobile, it is not turn-taking rules for speech alone that occasion the utterance "Pass me that wrench" but rather the immediate demand of the task. One very striking example is the talk of helicopter crews. All talk between members may be suspended in order to attend to radio communications from the ground, which are timed by their speakers' needs and task demands and cannot take account of the state of talk in the cockpit, or to attend to physical objects on the ground that need to be tracked or to devote full attention to flying the aircraft when the demands of that task become so great as to prevent ongoing talk. During low-workload segments, talk-driven talk that follows the conventions of ordinary conversation is possible; but even this is assumed to be a filler until some more salient demand occurs, and so is interruptible without the social expectation of resumption (Linde 1988*b*, 1991).

The preceding discussion attempts to show that the unexamined assumption that discourse units are properly continuous in fact holds only for some environments for talk. However, the types of unit that constitute the life story almost always occur within environments that do permit the assumption that the talk is properly continuous.

Thus far, we have considered interruptions of continuity and their status in various types of talk. When we consider the life story, though, we confront a unit that is **necessarily** discontinuous. As we have already seen, parts of it are told on different occasions to different addressees. And since we have defined it as the total of all the stories of a particular kind that are told in the course of the teller's lifetime, it would be impossible to tell the entire life story, even on one's deathbed.

In addition to being a discontinuous unit, the life story is also an open unit—one that is begun and continued without a clear notion at any given time of what its final shape will turn out to be. An open unit is one whose structure is not tightly constrained, and hence the beginning of the unit does not fully predict the possibilities of what the middle and end may be.

To clarify the distinction between open and closed units, let us consider a variety of art forms. For example, Wagner's Ring Cycle is a discontinuous unit but not an open unit. The component operas may be performed on different days, distributed through a given opera season, or even presented over several opera seasons. However, it is a closed unit, consisting of a known number of operas that have a specified order. In contrast, a soap opera is both a discontinuous unit and an open unit. It is discontinuous because it is performed for an hour once a day or once a week. It is open because, when it is begun and as it proceeds, its writers do not have a clear picture of how or when it will end. Its content changes as it proceeds, depending on audience preferences, the availability of actors, changes in popularity of themes in other

*N.b: she ~~too~~ makes life story a unit extending over time to dill audience. I don't know the benefit of saying there is one life story -- because she doesn't go look at period stays.

soap operas, changes in public tastes, important public events, fads, and so on. Such changes also require retrospective rewriting—for example, the revelation that some character did not actually die in a car crash, to explain the reemergence of a character whose actor had previously left the show. Thus, the beginning of a soap opera is not sufficient to allow us to predict what the shape of the story will become.

To some extent, in literary theory, the distinction between open and closed units corresponds to a distinction between certain genres. For example, the classical tragedy is structurally closed: it has a prescribed beginning, middle, and end. In contrast, the romance is episodic: it may be as long or as short, as simple or as ramified as the author chooses to make it, without losing its character as a romance. Auerbach (1957) discusses this distinction in the works of Homer. The *Iliad* tells a single story, with a single shape; while the *Odyssey*, being episodic, has no internal necessity to end at a given place. Perhaps the most striking example of an open literary unit is the serial novel *Les Mystères de Paris*, by Eugène Sue, in which not only the shape of the novel but also the shape of the novelist changed in the course of its writing. This novel, an investigation of the condition of the city's poor, was published by the *Journal des Debats* from June 9, 1842, to October 15, 1843. Brooks (1984) describes its development:

> At its outset, Monsieur Rodolphe—otherwise Son Altesse le Grand-Duc Rodolphe de Gerolstein—is on one of his errands of general and incognito mercy in the social depths of Paris when he meets Fleur-de-Marie, and hears her story in a typically sordid *tapis-franc* or cabaret, in the company of assorted thieves, murderers, pimps, stool pigeons, and other recruits for the guillotine. The destiny of Fleur-de-Marie, prostitute with a heart of gold, is our principal guiding thread through the labyrinth of multiple plots and realms which constitutes *Les Mystères de Paris*. . . . [Sue's point of departure was that of] the fashionable *dandy*, read by a bourgeois audience with aspirations to gentility, who sought a *frisson nouveau* in the novelistic exploitation of the social underbelly. Sue at the inception of *Les Mystères* can validly be accused of slumming, and with less benevolent curiosity than his hero Rodolphe. Yet as he went on, not only did he become the slave of a popular audience which waited eagerly to read—or to hear read—each of the 147 installments of the *Journal des Debats*, he also developed a new concern with documenting, understanding, and dramatizing the miseries of the people. Sue began to imitate his fictive hero Rodolphe, to put on worker's clothes and to visit garrets and work-shops and prisons. He began to inquire into the causes of misery, prostitu-tion, and crime. . . . Sue's friendship[s] with such socialist writers as Felix Pyat were a factor in his conversion, so were the enthusiastic reviews in

the reformist and socialist press that greeted the early installments of the novel; and also Sue's vast fan mail which, along with letters pleading that the novelist alleviate Fleur-de-Marie's sufferings or that he dispatch Rodolphe to succor some real-life victim, included urgings from reformers to persist in the exploration of this new terrain and testimonials from the people themselves, recounting anecdotes of their lives. (pp. 147–52)

While many other artists have attempted to include audience participation in the shaping of their pieces (particularly in the case of performed works), few have sparked so large a public response.

In addition to structural openness, there is also interpretative openness. For example, although Wagner's Ring Cycle is structurally closed, it remains open to different interpretations of its meaning. For example, in his television performances, Boulez has given a twentieth-century socialist reading to the work, which is at least partially based on Shaw's nineteenth-century socialist reading. Indeed, it may be argued that any performed unit is necessarily interpretive; even an attempt to reproduce the original performance represents an interpretation of what that performance was, and a judgment that such a reproduction is currently relevant and valuable. This interpretive component of any performed unit is all the more true for oral, unscripted units. For example, Kirshenblatt-Gimblett's (1975) study of the telling of folk tales shows that they are told with reference to a particular context of current activities and that they gain their relevance by the connection their hearers draw between their content and the circumstances of their telling. The following (translated) narrative told by a Yiddish speaker illustrates the use of a traditional parable with reference to a specific social situation:

1. DVORA: I have to tell you something and this was a true fact. Once I was at my brother's and the atmosphere was tense. My brother had promised the kids to take them to a show over and over again and he was busy in the office and he had no time. Are you listening?

   AL: Yea.

   DVORA: Next time. And he was busy and each time he made an appointment something else come up and the kids were disappointed. It was an afternoon show, a morning show. Nothing worked.

   I come in and my sister-in-law, Ruth, was upset and the kids were crying and my brother says, "O.K." This was nine o'clock. "We can go to a show now." Nine o'clock nobody wants to go to a show. It was late and there was just no point. So I saw there was going to be a revolution because he couldn't understand why they can't go to a show. The kids realized that he should have gone when he made the promise to go so many times. Ruth felt that he was unfair and I thought at this point they need something to break the ice because the atmosphere was just too thick. So I says, "You know, this reminds me of a story."

No. My brother comes up and he says, "Dvora, tell me, what is wrong with a father wanting to take his children to a show? What have I done? Have I committed a crime? I want my children to go with me to a show. They all say I'm doing something wrong. What's wrong?"

So I says, "I'll tell you. It reminds me of a story my mother used to tell me."

A man once came to a rabbi to ask a *shayle* [question regarding ritual purity], forgiveness.

He says, "What is it? What did you do?"

He says, "I didn't wash, I didn't say the prayer before the meal."

He says, "How come?"

He says, "Because I didn't wash my hands."

He says, "Well, why didn't you wash your hands?"

He says, "Because I wasn't eating Jewish food."

He says, "How come you weren't eating Jewish food?"

"Because I was eating in a Gentile restaurant."

He says, "How come?"

"Because it was *Yonkiper* [Yom Kippur, the Day of Atonement, most solemn Jewish holiday and fast day, when every man's fate for the coming year is said to be decided] and the Jewish restaurants were closed."

So this, I said, reminds me of my brother. "Why can't I take them to the show?" Here he had made so many promises and so many disappointments. He couldn't understand how come the kids didn't want to go to the show. (pp. 109–10)

In its context, this tale was extraordinarily effective, causing everyone — even the rebuked brother — to laugh and leading to a family reconciliation about the father's string of broken promises. The tale is a traditional one, and thus, in the terms we have defined, it is structurally closed. Yet the particular choice of the tale for a specific context of telling involves an interpretive openness; the known structure of the tale acquires a new and immediately relevant meaning because of its implied relation to the current situation.

Kermode (1966) relates the characteristically interpretively open character of many Western fictional forms to the pervasive influence of apocalyptic thought, which considers the movement of history toward the end of time. Apocalyptic thought in this sense means a linear rather than a cyclical view of the world—that is, as a directed series of events moving toward a final moment, the end of time. Such a sequence is interpretively open, since the end of time has not yet come; consequently, any sequence is subject to interpretation with regard to its relation to prior and subsequent understandings of the progress of the divine plan. Thus, for example, the story of Abraham and Isaac is interpretively open; it can and must be continually reinterpreted in light of each reader's understanding.

Continuing this account in relation to the life story, the interpretive endpoint corresponding to the Last Days is the proposition that, in the final analysis, the speaker is a good person who behaved correctly. As we will see, all personal narratives are shaped to make some version of this point, and therefore all such narratives must be changed or replaced as the speaker's understanding of what a good person is changes.

The life story is a unit which is thus both structurally and interpretively open; it is much more like a soap opera than it is like a cycle of operas or, *a fortiori*, like a single opera or play. The properties of temporal discontinuity and structural and interpretive openness mean that a life story necessarily changes constantly—by the addition of stories about new events, by the loss of certain old stories, and by the reinterpretation of old stories to express new evaluations. We change our stories at least slightly for each new addressee; we change a given story for a given addressee as our relation to that addressee changes; we reshape stories as new events occur and as we acquire new values that change our understanding of past events; and we change our stories as our point of view, our ideology, or our overall understanding changes and reshapes our history.

I will give here several examples of changes in the formulation of elements of a life story, to illustrate why we must necessarily recognize this unit as temporally discontinuous and open in order to capture its complexity.

During our first social meeting, the speaker, a close friend of a close friend of mine, gave me an account of why he had left a career in science

to become an editor of technical publications, a job which he construed
as not "being in science." He told a story of working in a research
laboratory where his job was to expose mice to strong radiation, and
then kill and dissect them, in order to replicate some result that had
already been established. This horrible and unnecessary task led him
to reject science as a fundamentally inhumane and repulsive activity. I
interviewed him for the current study several years later, when he had
just decided to return to graduate school in geology, a move that he had
formulated as being a return to scientific work. As we shall see from his
account, he relates his new career choice to his original interest in science. Nowhere in the course of the stories he tells does he mention the
details of the job he had once described so vividly when explaining why
he left science. His new account of that period follows:

> 2. And I did that for a year, and for about the last three or four
>    months I, you know, I was just sitting around figuring out how
>    I was going to get out of there. Cause it was boring. (Pause) I
>    worked in science during that time too and I didn't like it too
>    much.

At this point in the interview, I remembered his striking story of
mouse murder and was curious to see whether he would tell it again and,
if so, how he would transform it. So in an attempt to elicit the story, I
asked why he had not liked that job. He made the following reply:

> 3.    SPEAKER: I dunno, just didn't like it. No accounting for
>                 taste, you know.
>   INTERVIEWER: No, no, what were you doing?
>       SPEAKER: I was working in a, let's see, I worked several
>                 jobs, one I was working in a infrared radiation
>                 lab and then I was working in a laser lab, and
>                 finally let's see, I was also working in radiation,
>                 what would you call it? I dunno, radiation biol-
>                 ogy or something like, like that. It really wasn't
>                 very interesting. It was mostly electronics. And
>                 I wasn't too interested in that.

I continued to probe several times but never elicited the story, even
though the account he gave mentioned its setting—the job in the radiation laboratory. Apparently, the story of mouse murder was too violent
a contradiction of his changed view of his life, which anticipated his
return to work in science, and it could not be adapted to form a part of

the new view. Therefore, this story dropped out of the current version of his life.

An even more dramatic example is given by Turner (1980), which contains autobiographical accounts by Doug, a man in his mid-thirties who had lived for 17 years in board-and-care facilities for retarded adults. Initially, the investigator elicited from Doug an account of himself as a retarded person — an account structured around a demonstration that retarded people are indeed human and that he could do many things that normal people might not believe a retarded person could do. The investigator had him retested and found him to be of average intelligence. At this point, in addition to the other changes and obligations Doug faced, he also faced the task of making sense of what had happened and what his life story now was.

Each version of Doug's life story had a different theme. The theme of the first version was identification with the mentally retarded. The speaker used his own experiences and competencies to prove that "we mentally retarded people can do a lot more than most people think we can." He took himself as a representative illustration of what happens to the retarded. The theme of the second version was entirely different. In this version, the speaker asserted that he was always certain that he was not retarded and that there was nothing wrong with him. The competencies and achievements that Doug cited in the first version to show the widespread public misunderstanding of the capacities of the retarded were invoked in version two as proof that Doug knew all along he was not retarded.

In addition to recasting the evaluative point of many of his repeated stories, Doug also began to tell new stories about his efforts over the years to demonstrate that he was not retarded. As part of this, his interest in rocks and fossils, which he had earlier downplayed as "just my hobby" became part of a conscious strategy to demonstrate his competence to the world. This strategy not only affirms his nonretarded status, but makes the sudden dramatic shift in his position in the world an achievement, rather than an incomprehensible and bewildering accident.

The investigator then indicated to Doug that he had provided two incompatible sets of stories, one of which accepted his retarded status and the other of which did not. His response was as follows:

4. I was pretty sure all along that I wasn't retarded but I guess in a way I had two different ways of thinking about it. On the one hand, I was pretty sure there was nothing wrong with me but there was always that doubt, that one percent chance that I was

Example of retarded-label.
1) Stories organized thematically.
2) Explanation harmonizing contradictions.

wrong and they were right. I tried to put forth evidence that I had capabilities but it didn't seem to be affecting the courts or my social workers and I didn't seem to be getting anywhere. They wouldn't really give me a chance to express myself and show my capabilities. . . . I guess that's why I kind of gave up the battle to prove myself. (p. 7)

This explanation shows that Doug is not only capable of reinterpreting his life story to fit his current circumstances, but that he is capable (as we all are) of creating an explanation that harmonizes discrepancies and inconsistencies.

Turner's collection of a meta-account, as he calls it, is a valuable research strategy, given the dramatic shift in his speaker's circumstances and status. In collecting the data for the current study, I at first attempted to collect such meta-accounts, by bringing to speakers' attention discrepancies between their different accounts, but I found that most speakers were so distressed by the revelation of the discrepancies that it seemed unethical to continue collecting data in this manner. In fact, in the course of several interviews conducted in this way, I found it necessary to feed back to the speaker one of his or her prior accounts of why the life presented was coherent, in order to alleviate the pain of the challenge to the coherence of the account.

A particularly complex example of a revaluation of a story in a life story is given by Sacks (1972). The teller of the story holds a relatively low-ranking position in an insurance company; the addressee is a fellow employee who is leaving to go back to school. The story is as follows:

5. TONY: I met a guy in Jersey. — (3.0) — I wz working inna department store in New Jersey, — for a short while. Right In Newark New Jersey. Right on Broad Street. — Big department store. — (4.0) — and uh. I was a trainee there. A manager trainee. — But che hadda learn the business. Y'unduhs- They putchu in sto:ck. -work. Yihknow, the k- behind the counter I mean uh- to learn the business.

JAY: Mm hm.

(2.0)

TONY: And this- this guy wz selling us, insurance. — He was, he- he wen' aroun'tuh all the employees sellin insurance. En 'eez a nice lookin guy. Jewish fella, -about, oh I guess he ez about, — oh about, thirdy five, — sum'n like dat. Said he wentuh acting school with Kirk Douglas. —

En I believe 'im. — So I sez "What happena you" I sez uh "How come you didn' make it." He siz "I got ma:rried I gotta a couple kids," — he sz "I hadda struggle", — he sz the — he sz "The interest was there" he sez "but — then the kid came along, I bought a nice home out here, in Jersey," he sz "I gave it up." He sez "Kirk stuck it out." — I seh "Well that's the way it goes." He wz, selling insurance.

(3.0)

JAY: ((clears throat))

TONY: Maybe he wasn' happy but he's doing it. — A lotta people by- sometimes by circumstances. — Circumstances prevail where you haf to, do something, — not exacly to your liking. — (4.0) — I know it'd be a real catastrophe if all the people in the worl' did that. I unnuhstan'that. — Somebody's gotta do it. (pp. 458–65)

This is a story within a story. Tony, the speaker, recounts a story that an insurance salesman told him about the insurance salesman's failed prospects as an actor. At the time the insurance salesman told him the story, Tony himself, as a management trainee, had prospects for the future. On the occasion when the story is told, however, he no longer has future prospects, but his hearer does, as he is about to return to school. The evaluative point of the story is that one is not always in control of one's life — that sometimes circumstances prevail over what one would have preferred.

Sacks analyzes this as a story with a delayed fuse. Tony might have been able to retell the insurance salesman's story immediately after hearing it as a possibly interesting anecdote about someone who went to school with a celebrity. But there must have been a long delay before he could see the story as being about himself: his circumstances first had to change sufficiently for him to understand himself as someone who had had future prospects that did not mature into a currently desirable situation. Thus the story may now be part of his own life story, as we have already defined the life story, although it was not so when he first heard it.

We have seen some examples of how stories are added to or deleted from the life story, and of how a given story can change its meaning as the circumstances of the teller's life change. We may now consider whether it is meaningful to treat as a unit an entity that is so fluid, and so subject to constant reinterpretation and revision, that it can never be

completed. This issue becomes apparent and problematic as part of the
process of analysis; it is not a problem for us as native speakers, who
believe without question that we have such a thing as a life story.

An image that may clarify the type of entity being defined is a cloud
of butterflies moving across a garden. Some butterflies drop out and
others join in; each butterfly constantly changes its own position slightly
within the cloud, and the entire cloud moves, too. If we can recognize
such a cloud as an entity, we should also be able to recognize the life
story as one.

We may also consider the occasions on which component narratives
of the life story are exchanged. As has already been mentioned, the
stories one tells about oneself are closely tied to the relation one has
with one's addressee. Indeed, the extent to which one knows another
person's life story can be viewed as offering one measure of the intimacy
of the relationship. Therefore, the exchange of components of life stories
is particularly frequent at points in a relationship when intimacy increases. This is a reflection, of course, of our earlier, informal definition
of the life story as "What you must know to know me." In the course of
getting to know someone better, we expect to learn more of his or her
life story.

For example, someone I had recently met told me a story about her
recent divorce and struggles over child custody. I then told a story about
my own divorce. This exchange of stories can be described in a number
of ways. One description is that, by telling the story of my divorce, I established myself as someone who had suffered similarly and so was capable of understanding my interlocutor's situation. This analysis echoes
Sacks's analysis of second stories that are framed to demonstrate the
narrator's understanding of the preceding story (Sacks 1971). Another,
rather common-sense description is that this exchange of personal stories
marked a certain stage of intimacy in our relation. (This is true for the
exchange of stories between speakers who expect that their relation will
continue. It is obviously not true in the case of strangers conversing in
an airplane or waiting room.) A third possible description is that the
exchange created the intimacy, since part of the process of becoming
intimate involves exchanging life stories. Which of the latter two descriptions one prefers depends on one's ontological aesthetics—the extent to
which one chooses to populate one's world with preexisting explanatory
entities like "intimacy." In either case, one can sometimes find markers
in the conversation such as "It's nice to get to know you better" that
indicate the participants' awareness that their level of intimacy has in-
creased.

Another occasion for exchanging stories that form part of the life story involves maintaining a certain state of relationship or degree of intimacy. One may tell an intimate an old story that is part of one's life story but whose telling has never before been occasioned; or one may tell the person a new story, as soon as is appropriate after its occurrence.

Sacks (1971) provides an elegant discussion of the occasions for such new tellings and of the relations between people involved in them. In his analysis, certain types of news must be told to certain classes of people. For example, if any noteworthy item of news has happened, one is expected to tell one's spouse about it as soon as possible. Further, one must notify people such as close friends and relations of any dramatic event such as a death, marriage, or change of job. Such notifications characteristically involve telling a story that is likely to form part of the life story. People in this class can assume that, if they have not heard anything new, one's circumstances (and therefore, one's life story) remain substantially as they were at last report. Indeed, Sacks implicitly treats this type of expectation of being kept apprised of another's life story as a definition of the relation of "being close."

Clearly this discussion of occasions for telling parts of the life story is closely related to our earlier discussion of reportability. A story that is reportable to one's spouse or to the person who works at the next desk may not be sufficiently reportable to justify a cross-country call to one's sister or one's best friend. And yet one's sister or one's best friend can feel confident that, should something occur that is sufficiently dramatic to alter one's life story, it will be reported as soon as possible.

## Relation of the Life Story to Other Presentations of the Self

In this section, I shall attempt to establish the relation of the life story to other forms of presentation of the self—autobiography, biography, journals, and life history as used in anthropology and psychology. I shall attempt only a brief sketch of these forms, since the purpose of this discussion is not to examine them in detail, but simply to clear up the kinds of confusion that can arise between them and the life story.

### Autobiography and Biography

Autobiography is apparently the form closest to life story and is used, like the life story, to constitute the social self. The primary way in which autobiography differs from the life story is that it is a written, not an oral, form. More specifically, it constitutes a literary genre with its own history, its own demands, and its own market. The exact definition of this genre and the tracing of its history require a complex study in literary theory and necessitate the drawing of distinctions between autobiography and such closely related forms as the confession and the memoir. Further, the definition of each of these genres has changed over time.

Misch (1973) details the history of autobiographical writings in antiquity, including such forms as Egyptian tomb inscriptions, monumental records of kings' deeds, Greek and Roman political autobiographies, literary autobiographies, and pagan and Christian religious autobiographies. He ascribes the changes in form to developing notions of individuality.

Bruss (1976) studies four autobiographies, spanning a period of four centuries: *Grace Abounding* by John Bunyan, the *London Journal* of James Boswell, the *Autobiographical Sketches* of Thomas De Quincy, and *Speak, Memory* by Vladimir Nabokov. She shows that the form of each of these autobiographies is shaped not only by the prevailing notions of individuality, but also by the landscape of other current literary genres (such as history, sermon, and novel) in relation to which the autobiography negotiated its own niche. For Bunyan, producing autobiography was primarily an act of religious testimony, and thus the form must be understood in the context of other types of religious texts common during Bunyan's period.

Bunyan published his autobiography, *Grace Abounding to the Chief of Sinners*, in 1666, a time when published autobiographies (as opposed to private journals and commonplace books) were still relatively rare in England. The autobiographies that did circulate were semiprivate documents intended for the authors' family and friends, or perhaps for the members of a congregation. Publication was often posthumous and tended to be initiated by some third party, such as the minister of one's congregation. Only an unusually significant person or experience could justify a claim to wide public attention; and since one could not gracefully claim such significance for oneself, it fell to some third party to decide in favor of publication. The literary community was changing, however, to include authors and audiences who lived outside the decorum of the high culture and who responded to different needs. In the case of Bunyan, as in the case of the religious sectarians, hagiography became autobiography, since saints were no longer distinguished by miraculous works, but by the personal experience of faith.

In contrast, Boswell's eighteenth-century autobiography is not only secular, but to some degree antireligious, reacting against the severe

Knoxist training of his childhood. It thus coexists primarily with such secular texts as the novel and the biography. For Boswell and his literary community, experiences and events were interesting in themselves, without requiring validation through reference to some larger transcendental meaning or as an illustration of exemplary values. The life of a sinner could provide more amusing material for a narrative than the life of a saint, once the act of autobiography no longer required divine sanction.

Bruss's analysis takes Nabokov's *Speak, Memory* as an exemplar of twentieth-century autobiographical writing, in which the very presupposition of an externally existing history is questioned, with the result that autobiography can have no special status of truth to distinguish it from fiction. Autobiographical writers as different as Bunyan, Boswell, and De Quincy at least share the assumption that their writing reflects events, objects, and relationships that exist outside the act of composition. For a twentieth-century writer like Nabokov, however, this view rests on a naive empiricism that assumes a realm of fact that exists independently of description—an assumption that can no longer be taken on faith.

One major distinction between all forms of autobiography and the life story is that anyone—that is, any normally competent adult—can be assumed to have a life story, and indeed is socially required to have one. In contrast, not just anyone can produce a commercially viable autobiography. Typically, one must "be someone" in order to write an autobiography that has any chance of being published. The qualification for being a writer of an autobiography usually involves possessing some form of fame—some already-existing persona that can be assumed to be known to the book-buying public. Thus politicians and generals and writers and actors and athletes write (and apparently sell) autobiographies, since such books continue to be printed and offered for sale.

In addition, however, there are also several ways in which an "ordinary person"—someone with "no claim to fame"—may have an autobiography published. One way is to have been in some way a witness to history, someone who may not have a known persona, but who can add something to our knowledge of already known events. Another way is to frame the autobiography so as to make the author a typical case of a phenomenon of general interest: my struggle to overcome cancer, or my experiences during the war (whichever war is currently of interest.) The following example illustrates this strategy. It is written by the wife of a former government official—someone who is not herself the type of person to write an autobiography, but whose presentation is framed as an example of the prevalent but unspoken problem of spouse abuse in prosperous families. The book jacket copy reads as follows:

Charlotte Fedders' story of her 17-year marriage tells as has seldom been told what it is like to be the victim of physical and emotional abuse, and lays waste the widely held conception that domestic violence does not happen in white-collar homes.

When Charlotte O'Donnell, a doctor's daughter and a good Catholic girl, met John Fedders in 1965, he was a law student at Catholic University—six foot ten, handsome, athletic, smart, and very ambitious. She fell head over heels in love, and when she married him soon after, she could hardly believe her good fortune in making such a catch. Over the next 16 years, John worked his way up to become—at only 39—the chief enforcement officer at the Securities and Exchange Commission, a powerful post at which he earned a reputation for his professional acumen and integrity.

But at home a different side of the powerful executive emerged: he became moody and critical, obsessed with order and discipline. Charlotte, who had never really wanted more than to be a good wife and mother, continued to love him, until finally she found the courage and strength to help herself. In 1985, the marriage ended in divorce court, where the violence became public and Fedders resigned his post. Charlotte has begun the road to recovery and self-esteem; her triumph is truly inspirational.

*Shattered Dreams* tells an intimate and shocking story. Reading it one understands *how* a woman like Charlotte Fedders can become mired in a pattern of abuse for as long as she was, and why it requires such extraordinary courage to break this pattern and begin again. (*Shattered Dreams*, Charlotte Fedders and Laura Elliott, Harper & Row, 1988)

Such a presentation is intended to be exemplary—to show one person's story as an illustration of a problem and as a beacon for others in the same position.

The fact that, in order to write an autobiography, one must be a particular kind of person dictates that autobiographies be organized differently than life stories and that they contain quite different material. Normally, as we have already noted, some public persona or property makes the author's life worth writing about, and this persona or property serves as the theme around which the autobiography is organized. The theme may be developed on the basis of the achievement for which the author is already known, as in the case of many autobiographies of actors and politicians. It may be ideologically based: the development of my thought as an anarchist (Goldman 1931), or the story of my conversion to Catholicism and my decision to become a monk (Merton 1948). Or it may be organized as a defense of some particular action of the author's life. Newman's autobiography (1864) is an interesting example of this—an autobiography intended as an answer to a critic's charges that theological writings Newman published while still a Protestant were cynically intended to encourage his readers to convert to Catholicism. Newman describes these charges as follows:

> He [the critic] desires to impress upon the public mind the conviction that, in becoming a Catholic, I have just found my right place; that I do but justify and am properly interpreted by the common English notion of Roman casuists and confessors; that I was secretly a Catholic when I was openly professing to be a clergyman of the Established Church; that so far from bringing, by means of my conversion, when at length it openly took place, any strength to the Catholic cause, I am really a burden to it, — an additional evidence of the fact, that to be a pure german genuine Catholic, a man must be either a knave or a fool. (p. 5)

Newman then describes his literary plan for refuting these charges:

> I must give the true key to my whole life; I must show what I am that it may be seen what I am not, and that the phantom may be extinguished which gibbers instead of me. I wish to be known as a living man, and not as a scarecrow which is dressed up in my clothes. False ideas may be refuted indeed by argument, but by true ideas alone are they expelled. I will vanquish, not my Accuser, but my judges. I will indeed answer his charges and criticisms on me one by one, lest any one should say that they are unanswerable, but such a work shall not be the scope nor the substance of my reply. I will draw out, as far as may be, the history of my mind; I will state the point at which I began, in what external suggestion or accident each opinion had its rise, how far and how they were developed from within, how they grew, were modified, were combined, were in collision with each other, and were changed; again how I conducted myself towards them, and how, and how far, and for how long a time I thought I could hold them consistently with the ecclesiastical engagements which I had made and with the position which I filled. I must show, — what is the very truth, — that the doctrines which I held, and have held for so many years, have been taught to me (speaking humanly) partly by the suggestions of Protestant friends, partly by the teaching of books, and partly by the actions of my own mind: and thus I shall account for that phenomenon which to so many seems so wonderful, that I should have left "my kindred and my father's house" for a Church from which once I turned away with dread; — so wonderful to them! as if forsooth a Religion which has flourished through so many ages, among so many nations, amid such varieties of social life, in such contrary classes and conditions of men, and after so many revolutions, political and civil, could not subdue the reason and overcome the heart, without the aid of fraud and the sophistries of the schools. (pp. 30–31)

Such thematic organization of the autobiography often means that certain landmark events that we would expect and find in the life story may be left in the background or may be entirely absent from an autobiography. Thus, in reading an autobiography, it is not unusual to discover only upon the marriage of the author's child that the author has been married and had children. To some extent, this appears to be a convention of the form. Jelenek (1980) notes that a majority of autobiographers, both male and female, leave out any extended discussion of such putatively formative subjects as siblings, children, mates, and romantic attachments.

These remarks about autobiography generally hold true for biography as well. Biographies have the additional property that someone other than the person who lived the life is attempting to make sense of it. Consequently, the biographer may approach it with a different set of beliefs than were held by the book's subject and may derive meanings and coherences radically different from those the subject would draw. This can also be true, of course, of an autobiographer looking back at a younger self after the passage of many years or after an ideological conversion. But the autobiographer's task in such a case is to account for the difference between the present writer and the subject of the autobiography. The biographer incurs no such obligation, unless he or she has undertaken to write the life of someone whose motives and actions appear so wholly unsympathetic or incomprehensible to him or her that the reader is justified in demanding some account of why the biographer chose such an uncongenial subject.

The biographer may also have the advantage of writing about a dead subject, which means that the person's entire life course is available for interpretation. An autobiography, unless written in the author's extreme old age, is necessarily incomplete; the back door of "what next" always stands open. In contrast, a biography can pretend to completeness; temporally, at least—if not in terms of access to all materials—the biographer can claim to have the whole story.

## Journals and Diaries

Of all written presentations of the self, private journals and diaries bear the greatest resemblance to the life story as investigated in this study. A journal is a private work; it may be written for the author alone, for a small audience selected by the writer, or for an imagined audience. Unlike the writer of a publishable autobiography, one need have no exceptional qualifications to write a journal: one need not "be somebody."

Indeed, this feature of the journal has led feminist critics to view the journal as an exemplary women's genre. Since the journal as a form is particularly suitable for recording and understanding the events of everyday life, it is a form at which women who are given no access to a broader world may still excel. This understanding has permitted scholars to rediscover many forgotten or unpublished journals as works of literature. Jelenek (1980) notes that women are more likely to write journals, diaries, and notebooks, whereas men are more likely to write autobiographies proper. She attributes this difference to the difference in the literary forms: the discontinuous form of the journal or notebook is analogous to the fragmented, formless, and interrupted quality of women's lives.

Unquestionably, the kind of work of self-understanding and self-presentation that takes place in telling a life story also takes place in writing a journal. However, I have omitted the journal from my discussion of life stories for a number of reasons. First, journal writing is not universal. While every normal adult in this culture engages in telling a life story in a more or less elaborated form, not everyone writes a journal. Second, the journal is a written, rather than an oral form. Although the private journal may function as part of the process of creating a presentation of self, the necessary analysis of the parallel relation between written and spoken texts and the establishment of the relation between the two modalities are tasks beyond the scope of this work. Nonetheless, once the structure of the oral life story is established and understood, a study of the relation of the journal to the rest of the life story would be an extremely rewarding enterprise.

## The Life History in Psychology

The notion of "life history" is used in both psychology and anthropology, with slightly different meanings; neither of these meanings, however, matches the meaning of the term "life story" in the current study. In the remainder of this chapter, I will attempt to sketch the meanings of this term in these two fields and to delineate the ways in which they differ from the life story.

In the field of psychology, the notion of a life history is tied to the idea that any individual's life can be viewed according to a theoretically posited developmental course that includes predictable landmark events and developmental stages. Abilities are assumed to develop in a recognizable sequence, as are pathologies. Most forms of psychotherapy require that the therapist learn something of the patient's history. An excellent example of the assumptions about life history underlying psychological practice can be found in Sullivan (1954), which consists of a series of training lectures for psychiatrists. The author discusses in detail how to obtain a life history, what questions to ask, and why these inquiries are therapeutically relevant. The following outline of this history taking should clarify what the author means by "life history":

Disorders in learning toilet habits

Disorders in learning speech habits

Attitudes toward games and partners in them

Attitudes toward competition and compromise

Ambition

Initial schooling

Experience in college

Interest in boys' or girls' clubs

Preadolescent chum

Puberty

Unfortunate relationships in early adolescence

Attitude toward risqué talk

Attitude toward the body

Sex preference

Attitude toward solitude

Use of alcohol and narcotics

Eating habits

Sleep and sleep functions

Sex life

Courtships and marriage

Parenthood

Vocational history

Avocational interests

A number of points can be made about this list. First, the list is necessarily based on a particular theory of human development — one that suggests possibly relevant categories that may differ considerably from the speaker's own categories. Thus, an inquiry about toilet training arises from a theory holding that some adult personality disorders can be traced to problems in toilet training. This is quite different from the common-sense view of landmark events in one's life. In reading an autobiography or hearing someone tell part of his or her life story, we would be surprised if the speaker began by describing experiences of toilet training, and we would probably conclude that the person was currently in analysis and a bit overenthusiastic about it. (See Chapter 6 for a more complete discussion.)

Second, this list appears to contain both what we would normally consider to be temporally located events (schooling, marriage, and so on) and what we would consider to be static, unchanging aspects of personality (attitudes toward competition, solitude, and the like). However, the psychological view claims that apparently fixed aspects of the personality can be traced back to particular developmental experiences and thus must be considered as part of a history.

A more general point—and the foundation for the notion of the life history—is that everyone's life has regular stages and that, therefore, the developmental theory offers a guide for evaluating anyone's life. Much of such work, beginning with the efforts of Freud and his contemporaries, concentrates on childhood and adolescence, since these periods are considered crucial in personality formation. However, some psychologists have begun to focus on stages beyond early development, including young adulthood, mid-life, and old age (Buhler 1933; Erikson 1962, 1969; Sheehy 1977). This kind of developmental or social psychology stands somewhere in the overlap of psychology, sociology, and anthropology in describing what can be expected to happen to a person in a given culture in the process of creating a self.

Such approaches to life history assume that it is a relatively static entity—that is, that the individual has a fixed life history that has caused his or her present personality. But approaches to the life story can be arranged on a continuum of belief about how fixed it is, since there are also more hermeneutic approaches to the life story that view it as a process of interpretation, rather than as a fixed collection of facts. Such approaches take the therapeutic process to be one in which the therapist teaches the patient that it is possible to construct a new life history—one that will cause less difficulty and be more satisfying than the patient's original life history. Such hermeneutic approaches may help the patient to construct a single, more successful new history; at a more abstract level, they may teach new and less rigid processes for constructing a life history (Schafer 1978):

1) *What is the tally that here —th overlap of fields   in creating self.*

One constant point of reference marks the process of change through
which these data are manifest: the analysand progressively recognizes,
accepts, revises, refines, and lives in terms of the idea of the self as agent.
This is to say that, in one way or another and more and more, the analysand sees himself or herself as being the person who essentially has been
doing the things from which he or she was apparently suffering upon
entering analysis, and from many other problems as well that will have
been defined only during the analysis itself. For example, it is established
progressively that it is the analysand who has been fragmenting or splitting
by repressing, projecting, and adopting other defensive measures; who has
been arranging his or her life so that it has been a series of sexual, social,
occupational, financial, or creative failures or traumata; who has been
engaging in wishful thinking and rationalizing; and who has been tena-
ciously and unconsciously insisting on intermingled and conflictual oral,
anal, and phallic views of human existence. Increasingly, the analysand
claims or reclaims as his or her actions what was previously disclaimed.
. . . The analysand learns about the history of his or her unconsciously
elaborated psychic reality, recognized now for what it is. Psychic reality is
interpreted as the construction the analysand has been putting on actual
and imagined situations and events in the course of his or her life. In the
analysis, these constructions are defined through close study particularly
of the transference and resistance. This history of psychic reality amounts
to a special kind of narrative—what may be called *the psychoanalytic life
history*. Far from being a static arrangement of archaeological deposits,
this life history is shown to be always an actively utilized, though self-
contradictory or conflictual, strategy for defining and acting in one's current subjective situation. That is to say, it is a certain kind of incoherent
or compromised history that one has been telling oneself or that has been
implied in the view one has been taking of one's total life situation. And it
is the self-defeating policies and practices one has adopted and has been
following on the basis of that life-historical account. I emphasize that for
psychoanalysis, one *tells* a history; one does not *have* a history. It is a
history of something, however; a fabrication won't do. . . . But it is not
only the unconsciously elaborated fantasy content of this life history that
undergoes change. More important is the change that is wrought in the way
this history is organized, and this change is a correlate of the analysand's
recognition that he or she has been the imperfect, biased, censorious,
revisionist historian of this life. To characterize this change as an altered
mode of telling as well as an altered content of what is told is to give
another account—an action account—of a major aspect of what psychoanalysts are used to calling structural change or change in the ego's intersys-
temic and intrasystemic relations. (pp. 180–82)

As we shall see, there tends to be considerable overlap between what
goes into a life history elicited as part of psychotherapy and what goes

into the life story, since almost all systems of therapy permit patients to recount significant stories. However, producing a narrative in the therapeutic interview and producing it in ordinary conversation are very different social practices. One of the most important differences is the locus of authority; in the therapeutic situation, the therapist tends to have more authority over relevant categories and meanings, as well as over appropriate forms of discourse. In a situation of free narration, as we have already seen, an addressee has some freedom to accept, reject, or alter proposed meanings for components of the life story, but this is far more limited than the authority that the therapeutic situation creates for the therapist. The life story and the life history also differ considerably in the conditions that govern the reportability and relevance of specific kinds of spoken materials. Thus, the practices of free association, dream report, and the like, while defined as suitable for the therapeutic context, are not acceptable discourse activities in situations where life stories are normally exchanged.

## The Life History in Anthropology

Life history has always been used as a method of data collection in anthropology, in spite of doubts about its scientific rigor. In this context, a life history is a subject's account of his/her life, guided by questions from the anthropologist. Such life histories seem to fall somewhere between autobiography and biography, since they are not shaped primarily by the speaker. The intentions and questions of the anthropologist, the effects of an interpreter or of the anthropologist's imperfect command of the subject's language, the differences between the discourse forms appropriate in the subject's culture and those that the anthropologist expects, and the possible interpolations and deletions of editors all mean that this type of life history cannot be considered purely as the speaker's self-report. For example, in working with an adult male member of the Ilongot, a Philippine group, Rosaldo (1976) found that his expectations that Tukbaw, his intelligent and introspective subject, would produce a deep and intricate life story were not fulfilled. Rather, Tukbaw's account focused on his public self and public actions, but hardly touched on what Rosaldo considered a necessary description of his private self. To obtain such material, Rosaldo found himself eliciting narratives of a type that his informant would never have produced on his own. Life story narratives were not familiar discourse types in his informant's culture. Narratives were familiar; so stories of hunting expeditions, raids, and fishing trips were easy to elicit. But narratives about the self—

particularly what we would call intimate or revealing narratives—were simply not known.

Peacock and Holland (1988) have divided anthropological uses of the life history into two types: the portal approach and the process approach. The portal approach attempts to use the life history to learn about some reality external to the story, which the life history is presumed to mirror. There are two forms of this approach. One form views the life history as one type of data for an objective account of history or ethnography (Kluckhohn 1945; Kroeber 1961; Simmons 1942). The other form is subjectivist and treats the life history as a way to understand the subject's inner life, psychological history, and psychological structure, or to identify the psychological forces typical of the culture (Langness and Frank 1981). The portal approach—particularly the subjective portal approach—can be used to suggest to readers what they would do, how their lives would go, and how they would feel if they were members of the culture being studied. As Rosaldo's description of Tukbaw's narrative shows, however, it is perhaps truer to say that such a production suggests to us what we would feel if we were living Tukbaw's life, with his skills and experience, but retained our own categories of thought and feeling.

In the process approach, the narrative process itself is the focus of analysis, and the types of narratives or other discourse forms available in a given culture are emphasized, since these hermeneutic resources significantly influence understandable emotion and behavior in a culture. As Peacock and Holland indicate, this approach is more recent and less fully developed than the portal approach (Erikson 1963; Peacock 1975, 1978, 1984; Turner 1974). Geertz (1983*b*) is, in a sense, the patron saint of this approach, since he has argued that it is in principle impossible to use techniques of empathy enriched by narration to intuit what it actually feels like to be a member of another culture. According to Geertz, the most one can learn about another culture—and it is a great deal—is how to analyze that culture's own symbolic and discourse categories:

> Let us return to the question of what all this [anthropological description] can tell us, or could if it were done adequately, about "the native's point of view" in Java, Bali, and Morocco. Are we, in describing symbol uses, describing perceptions, sentiments, outlooks, experiences? And in what sense? What do we claim when we claim that we understand the semiotic means by which, in this case, persons are defined to one another? That we know words or that we know minds?

In answering this question, it is necessary, I think, first to notice the characteristic intellectual movement, the inward conceptual rhythm, in each of these analyses, and indeed in all similar analyses, including those of Malinowski, namely, a continuous dialectical tacking between the most local of local detail and the most global of global structure in such a way as to bring them into simultaneous view. In seeking to uncover the Javanese, Balinese, or Moroccan sense of self, one oscillates restless between the sort of exotic minutiae (lexical antitheses, categorical schemes, morphophonemic transformations) that make even the best ethnographies a trial to read and the sort of sweeping characterizations ("quietism," "dramatism," "contextualism") that make all but the most pedestrian of them somewhat implausible.

All this is, of course, but the now familiar trajectory of what Dilthey called the hermeneutic circle, and my argument here is merely that it is as central to ethnographic interpretation, and thus to the penetration of other people's modes of thought, as it is to literary, historical, philological, psychoanalytic, or biblical interpretation, or for that matter to the informal annotation of everyday experience we call common sense. In order to follow a baseball game one must understand what a bat, a hit, an inning, a left fielder, a squeeze play, a hanging curve, and a tightened infield are, and what the game in which these "things" are elements is all about. When an *explication de texte* critic like Leo Spitzer attempts to interpret Keats' "Ode on a Grecian Urn," he does so by repetitively asking himself the alternating question "What is the whole poem about?" and "What exactly has Keats seen (or chosen to show us) depicted on the urn he is describing?" emerging at the end of an advancing spiral of general observations and specific remarks with a reading of the poem as an assertion of the triumph of the aesthetic mode of perception over the historical. In the same way, when a meanings-and-symbols ethnographer like myself attempts to find out what some pack of natives conceive a person to be, he moves back and forth between asking himself, "What is the general form of their life?" and "What exactly are the vehicles in which that form is embodied?" emerging in the end of a similar sort of spiral with the notion that they see the self as a composite, a persona, or a point in a pattern. You can no more know what *lek* is if you do not know what Balinese dramatism is than you can know what a catcher's mitt is if you do not know what baseball is. And you can no more know what mosaic social organization is if you do not know what a *nisba* is than you can know what Keats' Platonism is if you are unable to grasp, to use Spitzer's own formulation, the "intellectual thread of thought captured in such fragment phrases as "Attic shape," "silent form," "bride of quietness," "silence and slow time," "peaceful citadel," or "ditties of no tone."

In short, accounts of other peoples' subjectivities can be built up without recourse to pretensions to more-than-normal capacities for ego effacement and fellow feeling. Normal capacities in these respects are, of course, essential, as is their cultivation, if we expect people to tolerate our intrusions into their lives at all and accept us as persons worth talking to. I am certainly not arguing for insensitivity here, and hope I have not demonstrated it. But whatever accurate or half-accurate sense one gets of what one's informants are, as the phrase goes, really like does not come from the experience of that acceptance as such, which is part of one's own biography, not of theirs. It comes from the ability to construe their modes of expression, what I would call their symbol systems, which such an acceptance allows one to work towards developing. Understanding the form and pressure of, to use the dangerous word one more time, natives' inner lives is more like grasping a proverb, catching an allusion, seeing a joke — or, as I have suggested, reading a poem — than it is like achieving communion. (pp. 68–70)

In conclusion, we see that the life story is distinguishable from various other forms of discourse that involve the presentation or construction of the self, such as autobiography, biography, journal, and psychological life history. The existence of this constellation of forms suggests that the construction and the presentation of self indeed constitute a major enterprise for our culture. In Chapter 7, we will consider some of the history of this enterprise. In Chapter 3, we will consider the identity and structure of the particular discourse units that are combined to form the overall life story.

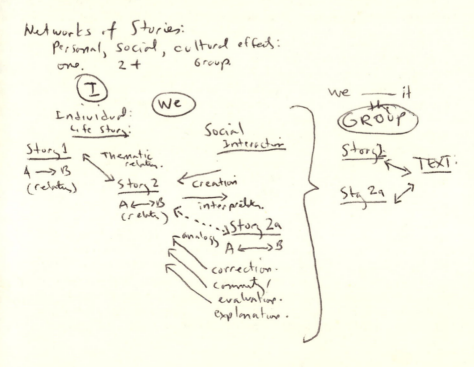

# 3

## Methods and Data
## for Studying the Life Story

*1) On life stories.*
*— may included*
*stories, included*

*Note: Because a life story is open + continued,*
*we can examine the intertextual nature of it.*

As we have defined it, the life story is a temporally discontinuous unit
told over many occasions and altered to fit the specific occasions of
speaking, as well as specific addressees, and to reflect changes in the
speaker's long-term situation, values, understanding, and (consequently)
discursive practices. Studying a unit of this sort poses substantial problems. Obtaining the text of an entire life story would require recording
all the talk ever produced by a given speaker. In principle this is possible,
but both practically and ethically it is not. However, obtaining part of
the life story is sufficient to indicate the nature of this open unit and the
principles of its construction; so we need not be concerned with the entire volume of a lifetime's worth of talk, but only with a selection from
it. Let us now consider how such a selection should be made.

The choice of proper methods for studying the life story depends
crucially on the kinds of questions we want to ask about it. If we are
interested in the relation between the external, socially exchanged life
story and the internal sense of having a life story, we must rely primarily
on introspection of our own internal narratives and of their relation to
our social narrative practices. If we attempted to study the entire life
story or to determine the characteristics of all the individual narratives
that are included in it, as well as of those that are not, we would find
ourselves in the impossible position of requiring a complete recording of
a lifetime of speech. We might attempt to take an extended sample—for
example, recording all the speech produced by a single speaker on one
designated day per month for five years. Assuming that this project had
major appeal to a major funding agency, it could be done, although the
task of data analysis for so large a sample would be heroic and horren-

*Goal!*
*1) construction of narrative*
*2) coherence of narrative*
*3) relation of narrative.*

dous. The approach taken by the present study is that the most interesting and immediate questions — and the ones most important in establishing the study of the life story as a research paradigm — are those that involve the nature of the principles of construction and coherence that speakers use to form the individual narratives constituting the life story, as well as the principles that they use to relate and reconcile these individual narratives. An interview situation can be structured to elicit narratives that form an important part of the life story, often including several narratives on the same topic, as well as explanations and other forms of reflection on and reworking of a narrative.

Because these questions involve extremely general structural phenomena that are present in a great many kinds of narrative, we can use as data a small representative portion of a speaker's life story. A cross section of a life story, taken at a single moment in time, contains a large enough number of narratives and their relations to permit us to study the creation of coherence. Because this method of sampling a cross section of a speaker's life story generates a manageable amount of data, it also permits us to consider a number of speakers and to compare the ways in which they handle equivalent problems in constructing similar types of narratives and in creating coherence for similarly problematic chains of events.

## The Data of This Study

The data chosen for this study come from oral interviews on choice of profession — specifically thirteen interviews with white middle-class American speakers. This is not a statistically balanced sample: there are too few subjects, and they were not chosen randomly, but rather specifically because they were known to have professions that were important to them, and that would therefore form an important part of their life stories. At this point in the development of research into the construction of life stories, a statistically balanced sample is neither necessary nor appropriate. Since this type of research is still in its initial stage, it is not possible to formulate and provide statistical proofs of hypotheses about life stories. Rather, this work attempts to shape a paradigm for studying this previously undescribed phenomenon. At this stage of research, the most valuable form of data consists of central examples of the phenomenon of interest, selected to provide a first description of its form. When that has been accomplished, the methodology of hypothesis testing may become increasingly appropriate.

Choice of profession is used as the interview topic because, at least for middle-class professionals, it is a necessary part of socially acceptable self-presentation. You need only recall how often you are asked "What do you do?" to realize just how necessary an answer to this question is in self-presentation. Or consider a situation in which you are acquainted with someone but do not know that person's occupation. Depending on the circumstances of the acquaintance, after a short period of time, such a lack of knowledge becomes anomalous and, eventually, sinister. This is understandable, since a person's occupation is a piece of information that is expected to be publicly available and that serves as a basis from which many inferences may be drawn about social class, position in the world, education, and so on. These pieces of information must be known in order for an individual to know how properly to interact with someone else. (Compare with this the situation in languages such as Japanese and Tibetan, which have an elaborate system of obligatory markers of social relation. There, in order for strangers to be able to speak to one another at all, they must know something about the other's age, kinship status, occupation, education, or ranking on some dimension that will permit the social relations of the two participants to be established — all before a polite initial sentence can be uttered.)

All of this is true about a specific social world in which occupation plays a major role in self-definition. Such a social world is, of course, quite culturally particular. In some societies there is little or no occupational differentiation, and such differentiation as there is is gender-based. Since all adult males and all adult females are expected to do essentially the same tasks, there are no distinguishable occupations and hence, of course, no account of them. In other societies, occupation is almost entirely determined by one's family of birth, such as the classic caste system of India. Here, of course, we cannot expect to find any personal account of how one came to be a merchant, a shoemaker, or whatever. We might, however, find a more general typology — for example, the characteristics, habits, and preferences of members of various castes.

On the other hand, in many fairly traditional societies that have far less occupational differentiation than do developed Western societies, some specialized occupations do require an accounting. For example, in discussing the ways in which traditional Mayan midwives learn their skills, Jordan (1989) shows that these include a major component of practical apprenticeship, but also a component of learning how to tell the appropriate stories — both practical stories about past experiences of various kinds of births and legitimating stories about their position as midwives:

In addition to this information packaging function, some stories also serve as culturally recognized claims to expert status. There are certain stories the apprentice needs to learn to tell in order to be recognized as a bona fide member of a community of practitioners. Such stories may be quite stereotyped. For example, Lave reports that "every tailor who described his apprenticeship included an account of the day his master left the shop in the middle of sewing a pair of trousers for a customer and told him to finish it." In Yucatan today, midwives tend to tell stories about training they have had with western medical personnel while traditionally (and this is still the case in remote hamlets), midwives told about dreams during which they received their calling and everything they know from "goddesses" (diosas). (p. 935)

Closer to home, many people and groups of people have little choice about their occupation, and consequently it does not play a positive role in their sense of self-definition. In a study of the school experience of English working-class boys and how it leads them into their working lives, Willis (1977) offers an example in which the self is defined more by opposition to the institutions of school and work than by participation in them:

Altogether, in relation to the basic cultural groundshift which is occurring in relation to the school and the development of a comprehensive alternative view of what is expected from life, *particular* job choice does not matter too much to "the lads." Indeed we may see that with respect to the criteria this located culture throw up and the form of continuity it implies, most manual and semi-skilled jobs *are* the same and it would be a waste of time to use the provided grids across them to find material differences. Considered therefore in just one quantum of time—the last months of school—individual job choice does indeed seem random and unenlightened by any rational techniques or means/ends schemes. In fact, however, it is confusing and mystifying to pose the entry of disaffected working class boys into work as a matter of *particular* job *choice*—this is, in essence, a very middle class construct. The criteria we have looked at, the opposition to other, more conformist views of work, and the solidarity of the group process all transpose the question of job choice on to another plane: "the lads" are not choosing careers or particular jobs, they are committing themselves to a future of generalised labour. Most work—or the "grafting" they accept they will face—is equilibrated by the overwhelming need for instant money, the assumption that all work is unpleasant and that what really matters is the potential particular work situations hold for self and particularly masculine expression, diversions and "laffs" as learnt creatively in the counter-school culture. These things are quite separate from the intrinsic nature of any task.

The putative diversity of jobs (and range of qualities necessary for them) presented in the careers programme when it works at its "best" is explicitly rejected—at least as far as their own future is concerned.

> JOEY: It's just a . . . fucking way of earning money. There's that many ways to do it (. . .) jobs all achieve the same, they make you money, nobody does a job for the love of a job (. . .) you wouldn't do it for nothing. I don't think anyone would, you need the bread to live (. . .) there's a difference in the actual ways you do 'em, but it's there like, they all achieve the same end, they all achieve money, they're all the same like.

> SPIKE: Every job is the same. No, I've gone too far in saying that, every job ain't the same, because your job's different, er, a doctor's job's different, a solicitor's job's different. The jobs what are the same is where you've got to fucking graft, when you'm a grafter, see all jobs are the same (. . .) There ain't a variety, it's the same job. There's outdoor jobs, indoor jobs.

The central subjective realisation of the commonality of modern labour and relative indifference to its particular embodiment, is one of the most basic things that "the lads" truly learn at the heart of their culture in a way that is invisible to the school. . . . Basically this concerns an experiential separation of the inner self from work. . . . Satisfaction is not expected in work. The exercise of those parts of the self which might be appropriate to intrinsic satisfaction in work is denied. It is as if one part of the self is detached for a felt greater hold on other parts. . . . Status and identity are constructed informally and in the group, and from the resources of the working class culture and especially its themes of masculinity and toughness—the social region which has made parts of their selves truly active and achieving—as it has grown and taken shape in the school and not from a detailed involvement in work tasks. (pp. 99–102)

Terkel (1972), in a series of interviews about how people feel about their work, covers an extremely wide range of occupations and shows that people in various working-class occupations differ widely in their reactions to them, depending on the characteristics of the job, and on their own assessment of it. (Unfortunately, Terkel does not specify how his transcripts were made or edited, so this extremely interesting material cannot be used directly as data for a linguistic analysis.)

A garbage man speaking about his job achieves a self-definition in spite of his job's being similar in structure to the ones Willis describes (although very different in the kind of self that is defined):

> People ask me what I do, I say, "I drive a garbage truck for the city." They call you G-man, or "How's business, picking up?" Just the standard

. . . Or sanitary engineer. I have nothing to be ashamed of. I put in my eight hours. We make a pretty good salary. I feel I earn my money. I can go any place I want. I conduct myself as a gentleman any place I go. (p. 103)

In contrast, a policeman explains that the job he is doing is exactly the one he wants:

Every child has a dream. I had two. One was to be a Marine and the other was to be a policeman. I tried other endeavors but I was just not cut out for it. I am a policeman. It is one of the most gratifying jobs in the world. (p. 129)

The preceding discussion has attempted to show that choice of profession is not a universally usable question that will elicit part of the life story in all possible circumstances. For the middle-class speakers who are used in this study, however, it is a relevant and revealing question that works brilliantly as an elicitor of a portion of the life story.

We might also ask what other topics would work — what other themes are likely to be included in the life story. Operating from some folk notion of turning points or major landmark events, we might expect education, marriage, childbirth, major illness, ideological or religious conversion, divorce, and major geographical moves to be part of the life story. Such landmark events have, among other characteristics, the property of being used to date personal epochs. Thus, speakers frequently use such events as markers to indicate a relevant time period. Examples include such datings as **Since I came to work at XYZ Co**, **Since I've been out here, Since my operation**, and **Since we had the baby**. Event markings like this serve not only to locate an event in chronological time, but also to indicate the characteristics of the time that are relevant to the statement being made. Hence, the dating **Since we had the baby** is likely to precede some statement about the characteristics of the speaker's life that have been affected by the baby. This type of time anchoring or time identification resembles the structure of reference to places described by Schegloff (1972). This study shows that the ways in which co-conversationalists specify the location of a person, place, or thing is not fixed wholly by geography, but rather is sensitive to the location of the participants, the relevant membership characteristics of the participants, the knowledge of the world that is assumed for members of that class of person, and the topic or activity of the interaction. At the conclusion of an extensive investigation of the formulation of location, Schegloff notes the parallel between place and time specifications:

More directly parallel to discussion of place formulation are temporal formulations. . . . a few observations may suggest that temporal formulations may particularize in their domain in a manner congruent with location formulation. Note that an event may be formulated as occurring at "2:06; about 2, in the afternoon; Monday afternoon; Monday; the third week in January; January; January 23, 1964; January 23, 1964 A.D.," providing a seeming calendrical parallel to what were called G [geographical] terms above. Or an event can be formulated as "before we met," "after the baby was born," "a month after your grandfather died," etc., forms that appear to be temporal formulations similar to $R_m$ [relation to members] terms in place formulations. Formulations such as "the day after the Kennedy assassination," "a week before the election," "the day of the storm," etc., are for various membership groups located by "reference to landmark," in this case "landmark dates." (p. 116)

It would be extremely interesting to investigate the possible list of events that might be included in the life story, and the relation between the events used as dating landmarks and the life story. Such an investigation would reveal the folk notions of the probable developmental course of the human life in a given culture—a folk notion parallel to the list given in Chapter 2 of the developmental events expected by psychological theory. However, this question inquires into the content of a life story rather than its form. The current study is limited to investigating the form of life stories—the ways in which they are made coherent—regardless of their particular component events. For this purpose, it suffices that occupational choice is a major theme for life stories and one that is appropriate for conversation between speakers who are not closely related.

## The Use of Interview Data

In any investigation of the use of language, the question always arises as to the best source of data. Many different types of data sources have been used. One strategy is to record ongoing social situations, either overtly or without the knowledge of the participants. Examples of such investigations include dinnertable conversations (Tannen 1984; Polanyi 1989; Goodwin 1984; Goodwin and Goodwin 1987), therapist-patient interactions (Labov and Fanshel 1976; Krainer 1988a, 1988b), doctor-patient interactions (Frankel 1984), and police helicopter crew conversations (Linde 1988b). In all of these instances, the investigator did not convene the parties to the interaction; rather, they had their own reasons for coming together and talking. The investigator may be present, as in

Tannen's and Polanyi's work, but as a participant, not as an investigator who stands apart from the course of the social event. Alternatively, with even less intervention, only the investigator's recording device may be present.

Another version of this technique involves using data that have already been recorded by the participants. One example is the Watergate tapes, recorded by the decision of President Nixon and used in studies of small group planning (Linde and Goguen 1978) and of a variety of syntactic constructions (Prince 1979). Another example is the recordings made of cockpit conversations in commercial aviation — the so-called black box tapes. By law, these tapes are erased after a successful flight, but they are transcribed and made publicly available when accidents occur. These have been used in a study of discourse forms and of the relation between patterns of social mitigation and the status relations of the participants (Linde 1988*a*).

A different strategy consists of obtaining data by interviewing people, either singly or in groups. This technique allows the interviewer to elicit a particular discourse unit or topic of speech that is not so common that it can be expected to occur in almost any interaction. For example, if one is interested in the rules of turn taking, a conversation on almost any topic will be satisfactory as data, since any conversation must have some kind of turn-taking organization. In contrast, if one is interested in somewhat less pervasive but still ordinary discourse phenomena, such as apartment layout descriptions (Linde 1974; Linde and Labov 1975), explanations of income tax decisions (Weiner 1980; Goguen, Weiner, and Linde 1983), fight narratives (Labov 1972), or birth narratives, one must ask about them directly, unless one is willing to wait with tape recorder poised for an impractically long time. Although these types of discourse do appear in spontaneous conversation, they are sufficiently rare that one cannot simply tape conversations at random and wait for them to occur.

These two strategies of data collection are appropriate for different kinds of investigation. The strategy of recording some type of spontaneously occurring social interaction is suitable for investigating a fairly general phenomenon such as therapeutic discourse, the use of evaluation in narrative, subcultural differences in conversational style, or the effect of rank on the use of mitigation. These are global phenomena and are necessarily present in any instance of the appropriate speech situation. The strategy of using interview data is suitable for eliciting a particular discourse unit or, more specifically, for raising a particular topic of discourse.

In using interview data for linguistic analysis, one must always inquire about its relation to spontaneous conversation. In its strongest form, the question is whether the investigator may be inducing the speaker to produce a kind of speech unlike anything that would be produced under any other circumstances. We have already seen, in connection with the life history method in anthropology, that such abnormal production is quite possible (Chapter 2). To understand this problem, we must make a number of critical distinctions.

The first distinction has to do with the nature of the interview situation. It is certainly possible to structure an interview in a way that demands a type of speech that would not be produced in any other context. One form of this type of elicitation consists of requesting speech on a topic that would not normally be explained linguistically. For example, we might ask someone to explain how to tie a pair of shoelaces without using hand gestures or a shoelace. Another form of this type of unnatural elicitation involves requesting that the speaker produce some sort of verbal output, without the interviewer's offering any contribution or feedback. For instance, in the oral IQ or fluency test, a child is shown an object or a picture and asked to tell everything he or she can about it. Another example is the psychotherapeutic technique of free association. A third is the investigation of problem solving or some other mental activity in which the subject is asked to describe the mental process as it occurs. All such tasks produce socially aberrant verbal output that is structurally extremely different from nonelicited speech. The bizarre nature of such productions comes from the experimenter's attempt to make speech into a trace of an autonomous mental activity, divorcing it from its primary interactional and social function.

The interview situation does not intrinsically exclude the social nature of language, however. Most forms of interview do involve some exchange between the interviewer and the subject, some admission that the interviewer is also a participant. Further, the linguistic or social science interview is not the only form of interview; the interview is an existing social form used as a technique to achieve all kinds of social purposes. The doctor–patient interview and the lawyer–client interview are familiar examples. Others, such as the hairdresser–client interview or the decorator–homeowner interview, may not immediately come to mind as interview situations, but they constitute interesting instances in which the authority relations are reversed — that is, instances in which the expert is of lower status than the nonexpert.

Therefore, it is a mistake to try to make a sharp distinction between the interview situation and so-called real life, or between the interview situation and noncontrived social interaction. The interview is part of real life, too. What is important is to attend to the details of the structuring of the interview and the relation between the participants, to ensure that the interview conditions do not prevent the occurrence of the very phenomenon one hopes to collect.

A second point in the use of data from interviews relates to whether the data are taken as representative only of the interview situation or whether they are viewed as exemplifying a phenomenon that happens in other situations as well. In the first case, of course, there is no problem: any interview is an excellent example of itself. One such example is the psychotherapeutic interview, since this situation is (or at least is claimed to be) unique in its structure. In other words, the kind of discourse present in the therapeutic interview is claimed to be particular to that situation, as are the transformative possibilities inherent in such a situation.

A more complicated analytic problem is the situation in which data taken from an interview are used as an example of a more general social or linguistic phenomenon. The question is whether such a generalization is legitimate — whether the data gathered in the interview situation are the same as data produced in a related but nonelicited speech situation, whether the data are wholly different, or whether the interview data bear some partial but regular similarity to nonelicited speech. One way to tell which of these possibilities holds in a particular case is to observe our own spontaneous speech and that of others. If, for example, we want to use apartment layout descriptions in an investigation, we can listen to determine whether they occur in spontaneous speech and whether they are the same as or closely similar to instances gathered in the interview situation. Such informal checking requires observation **after** some elicited data has been recorded and analyzed to suggest the structure of the discourse of interest. We cannot rely on our memory of nonelicited observations, since memory is extremely unreliable for this kind of detail about discourse structure. In practice, I have found that such observation included developing an extreme interest in the adventures of friends who were searching for apartments, and following strangers down the street as their conversation turned to such adventures. Such are the exigencies of empirical research.

Another check is to compare the interview data with recorded, nonelicited data. If instances of the phenomenon in question have been recorded, they can be compared with elicited instances to see whether they are the same, closely similar, or quite different. The term "closely similar" means usably similar for the type of study we wish to do or for the type of analysis we need to perform. For example, Wolfson (1982) has shown that elicited narratives and spontaneously produced narratives differ from one another on an extremely fine level of detail—specifically, in the use of the historical present tense. This is not an arbitrary difference; it arises because one condition that encourages heavy use of the historical present is the feature of the narrative's being performed—that is, being acted out to give the addressee an opportunity to experience the event. Performed narratives are much more likely to be produced when the speaker and addressee share characteristics such as age, occupation, or ethnicity, or when there is a relation of friendship between speaker and addressee. These characteristics are not likely to be shared by the participants in an interview situation, so the use of the tense system tends to be at least slightly different in elicited narratives. Similarly, as we shall see, the form of evaluation in elicited narratives may differ from that in spontaneous narrative, since spontaneous narrative may include a component of negotiation between the primary speaker and the other interlocutors—a negotiation that an interviewer may be unwilling to engage in, since it involves a direct effort to bias the data the speaker may give.

Whether such differences matter depends on the nature of the argument. If the analysis we wish to make requires data at this level of detail, elicited narratives cannot be taken as identical to spontaneous narratives. But if the argument involves a less detailed or higher level of structure, the two types of data can be taken as identical for the purposes of a particular analysis. Therefore, the issue of whether results from interview data can validly be generalized depends crucially on the particular nature of the investigation and must be decided individually for each investigation. In the case of the life story, interview data can be used because the life story, as a major means of self-presentation, occurs naturally in a wide variety of contexts (including interviews) and is thus quite robust.

## The Analysis of Discourse Data

As discussed in the preceding section, the interview form was chosen as a suitable source of data for this study. The data consist of a number of discourse units: the narrative, the chronicle, and the explanation. We will first consider the general question of how discourse data are to be analyzed, and then study the particular structure and function of each of these discourse units.

We must begin by considering what a discourse unit is. As Chapter 1 shows, the narrative is certainly popularly considered to be a unit. That is, speakers in the culture can recognize a stretch of talk as a story, can identify a type of talk as "telling stories," and have names for these units and activities. From the viewpoint of the ethnography of speaking, this is sufficient to establish the cultural existence of such units (Hymes 1964, 1972). However, we also want to know what kind of units these are from an analyst's point of view, to determine what kind of analysis is best applied to them. The two extreme possibilities are to treat them as units of formal linguistic structure, or to treat them as functional units of social interaction. Both approaches have been tried as exclusive modes of analysis. I will consider each approach separately and then attempt to show that a union of both approaches is necessary if we are to understand how these units function as components of the entire life story.

Treating narrative as a unit of formal linguistic structure is a classic move in the tradition of American structural linguistics. This structuralist approach begins with the assumption that any object of study can best be understood by identifying its component parts and the rules for properly combining them. In the case of linguistic units, the structuralist approach further assumes that there is a hierarchy of levels of linguistic units, organized by a principle of inclusion; that is, units at a given level of structure are composed of several units of the immediately preceding level of structure. This view is summarized by Lyons (1968):

> The relation between the five units of grammatical description (in the languages for which all five are established) is one of *composition*. If we call the sentence the "highest" unit and the morpheme the "lowest," we can arrange all five units on a scale of *rank* (sentence, clause, phrase, word, morpheme), saying that units of higher rank are composed of units of lower rank. Alternatively, we can say that units of higher rank can be analysed (or "decomposed") into units of lower rank. (p. 171)

This assumption of a hierarchical organization of linguistic units is common to American structural linguistics of the 1930s, 1940s, and 1950s, as well as to the many varieties of tranformational and generative grammar that stem from Chomsky's initial work.

Until quite recently, however, both the existence and the position of the discourse unit in the linguistic hierarchy have been problematic. Most theories of syntax did not consider units larger than the sentence. For example, Bloomfield (1933, p. 170) defines the sentence as "an independent form, not included in any larger (complex) linguistic form." This definition was the result of analytic convenience: it was felt that the majority of linguistic regularities could be described at the sentence level and that describing these regularities provided problems sufficient to occupy as many linguists as cared to participate. For Chomsky, the restriction goes further: the sentence is the basic unit of a formal system whose task is to account for all the sentences and only the sentences of a given language (Chomsky 1957, 1965). Even working within this approach, however, linguists found relationships between sentences that must be considered in order to understand all the semantic relationships in a text. One classic strategy for dealing with this is to view an entire text as a single long sentence composed of shorter sentences joined by **and** or other connectives (Katz and Fodor 1963). Although there have been classic discussions of the structure of the folktale at the level of plot, for example (Propp 1968), these discussions have not been joined to linguistic analyses at the sentence level.

Related to these schools of syntax are approaches that assume that the sentence is the highest level of linguistic structure, and that consideration of anything beyond the boundaries of the sentence is to be treated as the study of context or of pragmatic rules. Both of these approaches are explicitly not structuralist, in that they are not concerned with **units** of linguistic structure, but with rules or principles governing the use of linguistic units described elsewhere. The most influential of these theories is Grice's theory of conversational implicature (Grice 1975, 1978), which holds that a set of assumptions exist that guides people's use of language, and that these assumptions arise from rational considerations that promote efficient communication. Grice's assumptions are expressed as the following four maxims of conversation, all of which are subsumed under the single principle of cooperation that precedes them:

> *The co-operative principle:* make your contribution such as is required, at the stage at which it occurs, by the accepted purpose or direction of the talk exchange in which you are engaged.
>
> *The maxim of Quality:* try to make your contribution one that is true, specifically: (i) do not say that which you believe to be false (ii) do not say that for which you lack adequate evidence.
>
> *The maxim of Quantity:* (i) make your contribution as informative as is required for the current purposes of the exchange (ii) do not make your contribution more informative than is required.
>
> *The maxim of Relevance:* make your contributions relevant.
>
> *The maxim of Manner:* be perspicuous and specifically: (i) avoid obscurity (ii) avoid ambiguity (iii) be brief (iv) be orderly. (Levinson 1983, pp. 101–2)

These maxims are not intended to describe the actual ways in which people speak, since the next linguistic exchange you have will very likely demonstrate that they do not. Rather, the maxims are intended to provide the principles to which speakers orient in attempting to understand apparent violations. Grice (1975) gives an example of how understanding such violations can be explained by these maxims:

### A Flouting of the First Maxim of Quantity

A is writing a testimonial about a pupil who is candidate for a philosophy job, and his letter reads as follows: "Dear Sir, Mr. X's command of English is excellent, and his attendance of tutorials has been regular. Yours, etc." Gloss: A cannot be opting out, since if he wished to be uncooperative, why write at all? He cannot be unable, through ignorance, to say more, since the man is his pupil; moreover, he knows that more information is wanted. He must, therefore, be wishing to impart information that he is reluctant to write down. This supposition is tenable only on the assumption that he thinks Mr. X is no good at philosophy. This, then, is what he is implicating. (p. 52)

Within the last ten or fifteen years, the discourse level has been admitted into linguistics proper as recognition has grown that some questions at the morphological and syntactic levels of linguistic structure can be answered only through consideration of relations between sentences. The recent interest in machine parsing and understanding of text has confirmed that discourse-level investigations are essential in order to account for a wide array of phenomena such as pronominalization, reference, and deixis. (For discussions of this endeavor, see Joshi, Webber, and Sag 1981; Schank and Burstein 1985; Polanyi 1990.)

The most relentlessly structural approaches to the description of discourse involve a direct attempt to use the methods of generative grammar, using the same kinds of rule structures to generate texts rather than sentences. One example of this strategy appears in Van Dijk (1972), who proposed that a well-formed discourse must have an abstract deep structure that defines its coherence. A discourse grammar would then have a series of transformational cycles at both the discourse level and the sentence level, to convert this deep structure into a linear sequence of coherent, grammatical sentences.

Such an approach is entirely top–down: it starts from a postulated macrostructure, and then describes how it can be broken down into its component parts; further, it describes the nature of the dependency relations that hold between these parts. No successful instance of such a grammar has yet been written; it remains a hypothetical possibility.

In contrast, other structuralist methods use a bottom–up approach. These start with the smallest parts, and then they describe the relations that hold between them to form larger units. The classic example of this approach is Halliday and Hasan's study of cohesion (1976).

Such structuralist methods can yield a skeleton of a given discourse unit, but they cannot show how these units function as part of the social practice of speakers. For this kind of approach, we must turn to functional accounts of discourse. The contrast between these approaches to the analysis of discourse has been described by Levinson (1983) as an opposition:

> *Discourse analysis* (or DA) employs both the methodology and the kinds of theoretical principles and primitive concepts (e.g., *rule, well-formed formula*) typical of linguistics. It is essentially a series of attempts to extend the techniques so successful in linguistics, beyond the unit of the sentence. The procedures employed (often implicitly) are essentially the following: (a) the isolation of a set of basic categories or units of discourse, (b) the formulation of a set of concatenation rules stated over those categories, delimiting well-formed sequences of categories (coherent discourses) from ill-formed sequences (incoherent discourses). There are a number of other features that tend to go with these. There is typically an appeal to intuitions, about, for example, what is and what is not a coherent discourse. There is also a tendency to take one (or a few) texts (often constructed by the analyst) and to attempt to give an analysis in depth of all the interesting features of this limited domain. . . .
>
> In contrast, *conversation analysis* (or CA), as practised by Sacks, Schegloff, Jefferson, Pomerantz and others, is a rigorously empirical approach that avoids premature theory construction. The methods are essentially *inductive*; search is made for a recurring pattern across many records of naturally occurring conversations, in contrast to the immediate categorization of (usually) restricted data which is the typical first step in DA work. Secondly, in place of a theoretical ontology of *rules* as used in syntactic description, we have an emphasis on the interactional and inferential consequences of the choice between alternate utterances. Again in contrast to DA, there is as little appeal as possible to intuitive explanations and they certainly do not circumscribe the data; the emphasis is on what can actually be found to occur, not on what one would guess would be off (or unacceptable) if it were to do so. Intuition, it is claimed, is simply an unreliable guide in this area, as indeed it may be in other areas of linguistics (see, e.g., Labov 1972*a*). There is also a tendency to avoid analyses based on single texts. Instead, as many instances as possible of some particular phenomena are examined across texts, not primarily to illuminate "what

is really going on" in some interaction (a goal judged impossible, such illuminations evading participants as well as analysts on many occasions), but rather to discover the systematic properties of the sequential organization of talk, and the ways in which utterances are designed to manage such sequences. (pp. 286–87)

The most active and interesting example of the interactional or functional approach to discourse is conversation analysis, which attempts to view discourse as an arena of social interaction rather than as a formal unit of linguistic structure. Within conversational analysis, the paradigmatic example of the attempt to study the use of language without relying on preexisting categories is the study of turn taking (Sacks, Schegloff, and Jefferson 1974). This study attempts to describe the moment-by-moment work that participants in a conversation do in order to achieve an orderly transition between speakers. Even here, however, units of linguistic structure must be used, if only covertly, to specify exactly what a transition relevance place is, and how it can be recognized by speakers.

Similarly, the exemplary work on narrative done by Goodwin (1984) and by Goodwin and Goodwin (1987) uses the categories provided by discourse analysis for the internal structure of narratives, to describe the ongoing work by which participants collaboratively construct these units. For example, Goodwin and Goodwin (1987) make use of such subunits of narrative structure as preface, background, climax, and parenthesis sections as part of the task of the participants, who must exhibit different types of reactions in different sections.

These studies show that a purely structural approach to discourse is possible but barren, while a purely functional approach is not possible at all, since some form of internal linguistic structure must be posited (if only covertly). A combination of the two can provide extremely rich and fruitful results. Adopting this perspective, we shall now consider the types of discourse found in the data of this study.

For the purpose of this study, the relevant unit is the discourse unit — the unit directly above the sentence. Common and extensively studied examples of the discourse unit include the oral narrative of personal experience (Labov 1972; Linde 1986; Polanyi 1989), the joke (Sacks 1974), the explanation (Goguen, Weiner, and Linde 1983), the description (Linde 1974; Linde and Labov 1975), and the plan (Linde and Goguen 1978). As a structural unit, the discourse unit has two criterial properties: defined boundaries and a describable internal structure.

The property of definable boundaries means that the discourse unit is a bounded unit; with some interesting exceptions, we know when a speaker is or is not engaged in telling a narrative. There may, of course, be boundary disputes — either at the beginning, when the speaker negotiates with the hearer whether the narrative shall be told, or at the end, when the speaker negotiates with the hearer what the proper response to the unit is (Sacks 1974; Polanyi 1978, 1989). However, the existence of such negotiations does not mean that the unit is structurally unbounded. Rather, it means that the establishment of such boundaries has serious social consequences for how the interaction can proceed.

Perhaps the most important effect of establishing the boundaries of the discourse unit has to do with the structuring of turn taking. As we have seen, all other things being equal, the sentence is the potential unit of turn exchange; that is, a second speaker may begin to speak at a point when the first speaker has reached a syntactically permissible end for the ongoing sentence. However, if the first speaker has negotiated permission to produce a recognizable discourse unit such as a joke or a narrative, that speaker has the floor until the unit is completed. A second speaker may contribute questions, appreciations, side sequences, and so on, but the discourse unit and topic in progress will not be changed until the unit is completed.

The other important property of the discourse unit is that it has a precise internal structure. Just as sentential syntax is describable, so is the syntax of larger units. Examples of such descriptions will be given later in this chapter. As we shall see, a description of this internal structure is necessary if we are to understand the interactional process of constructing a discourse, since the task of hearers is quite different (for example) in different sections of a narrative.

We turn now to a discussion of the particular discourse units in the data used for studying the life story. Three major discourse units are present: the narrative, the chronicle, and the explanation.

## The Narrative

The narrative is perhaps the most basic of all discourse units; it certainly has received the most study. Thus far, this work has used terms like "story," "narrative," and "autobiographical account" as if their meanings were obvious — and indeed these are popular as well as technical terms. But it is now time to formulate technical definitions for these terms. The account I shall give of narrative is based on Labov's analysis of the oral narrative of personal experience, since of all the analyses suggested for the understanding of narrative, it provides the most useful skeleton for studying naturally occurring oral data (Labov and Waletzky 1967; Labov 1972*b*).

The oral narrative of personal experience is defined as "one method of recapitulating past experience by matching a verbal sequence of clauses to the sequence of events which (it is inferred) actually occurred" (Labov 1972*b*, p. 359). A number of general points can be made about this definition, before we go on to the specifics of the definition. One point is that, as Labov defines it, the narrative is concerned with personal experience and thus is taken to be a representation of an actual occurrence. The relation between the clauses of the narrative and the inferred actual events corresponds to the distinction — drawn by a number of narrative theorists studying literary narrative — between histoire or fabula (the content of the narrative, which consists of the chain of events, plus the characters and the setting) and discourse or plot (the expression by means of which the content is communicated). The order of events of the histoire need not entirely match that of the plot. The plot is the order in which the reader or listener becomes aware of what happened — that is, the order of appearance. This need not match the actual order of occurrence. It is possible to have a matching order (abc), a flashed-back order (acb), or an order *in medias res* (bc) (Chatman 1978).

In considering oral narratives of personal experience, Labov assumes the factuality of the events described or takes the degree of factuality as a problem for the analysis. The present study, however, is not concerned with postulation of the independent existence of the actual events of the speaker's life or with the study of their relation to the narrated events. We are not primarily concerned here with whether the narratives of the life story describe events that actually occurred, or whether they describe actually occurring events accurately. More important to us are the fact that the speaker presents such events as having occurred and the ways in which this presentation is made.

A second important general point in Labov's definition is that it relies on the narrative presupposition — that is, the assumption that the order of clauses in the narrative can be taken to mirror the order of events in some postulated real world. This is an important characteristic of the English language, and one that has major consequences for the interpretation not only of sequence but also of causality. We shall discuss this further in Chapter 4.

Labov's definition of narrative establishes the spine of the narrative, so to speak, as a sequence of simple past-tense main clauses. Under extremely unusual circumstances, we may find narratives that are composed solely of ordered past-tense main clauses. The following, from Labov (1972*b*, p. 360), is such an example:

*Labov: abstract is optional.*

1. Well this person had a little too much to drink and he attacked me and the friend came in and she stopped it.

Such minimal narratives are extremely rare. They seem to occur when the speaker is for some reason obliged to tell a narrative that is unpleasant or painful to recount, and so tells it in as short and limited a form as possible. Example 1 was offered in answer to an interview question about whether the speaker had ever been in danger of death. Having answered that she had, she was then socially committed to backing up this claim. This example of the minimal narrative is clearly an artifact of the interview situation, since it is in the interview situation that a speaker is most likely to be put on the spot by a direct question of this sort, where the authority of the interviewer severely constrains the possibility of answering "None of your business." The minimal narrative may also exist in spontaneous conversation, however, functioning as a bid for permission to tell the full narrative.

The aberrant flavor of example 1 indicates that most narratives consist of a great deal more than simple past-tense narrative clauses. There are four ordered structural parts of a narrative: the optional abstract, the orientation, the narrative clauses, and the optional coda. The unordered part of the narrative—that is, the portion that may appear anywhere and may indeed form part of some other structure—is the evaluative material. Let us discuss these parts in turn.

The optional first part of the narrative in Labov's analysis is termed the **abstract**. It has also been called the *announcement* (Wald 1978) and the *preface* (Sacks 1971; Goodwin 1984). Since the abstract is an optional element of narrative structure, it may or may not be present. It has a number of functions. First, it may serve to summarize the narrative:

2. I once had to have my number changed because someone was bothering me. They were very good, they did it very quickly.

Alternatively, it may offer an evaluation of the narrative to come, enabling the hearer to understand what kind of a narrative it is to be or how to understand and respond to it:

3. That was more or less an accident.

Since the abstract occurs at the boundary of the narrative, it serves a particularly interactive function. It may constitute a bid for an extended turn in which the speaker will have the floor for the course of the narrative, or it may form the basis for negotiating whether the narrative is to be told, whether it is relevant, and so on. Goodwin (1984, pp. 225–26) provides a simple example of such negotiation:

4. ANN: Well - ((throat clear)) (0.4) We could used a liddle, mari-
    juana. tih get through the <u>weekend</u>.

   BETH: What h⌐appened?

   ANN:                Karen has this new <u>hou</u>:se . . .

In this simple negotiation, Ann offers an abstract, which Goodwin calls
"a preface offering to tell the story," and Beth accepts the offer by
requesting that the story be told.

The abstract may even be provided by someone other than the speaker
of the narrative, as in the following exchange taken from Polanyi (1985):

5. BILL: I heard secondhand or whatever that you got robbed.

   SUSAN: Yeah.

   BILL: That's distressing. What happened?

   SUSAN: We were parked down at the hill . . .

After the abstract, if it is present, almost all narratives then contain
orientation clauses. These clauses establish the characters, the time, the
place, and the circumstances of the narrative. Orientation clauses may
be placed at the beginning of the narrative, or they may be interspersed
with the narrative clauses. Indeed, skillful placing of orientation material
is one feature that distinguishes good storytellers from clumsy ones. The
following are some examples of orientation clauses:

6. Karen has this new <u>hou</u>: en it's got <u>a</u>ll this like- (0.2) ssilvery : :
   g- gold wwa:llpaper (Goodwin 1984, p. 225)

7. It was last weekend on the Promenade. They had a Promenade
   art show. (Linde 1981, p. 85)

8. Yeah, you know, I was sittin' on the corner an' shit, smokin' my
   cigarette, you know I was high and shit (Labov 1972*b*, p. 357)

The **narrative clauses** then follow, forming the skeleton of the narrative. These are, as we have said, simple-past tense main clauses, whose
order is taken as the order of events. Let us review example 1, the
example of a minimal narrative:

1a. Well this person had a little too much to drink

1b. and he attacked me

1c. and the friend came in

1d. and she stopped it.

Clause 1a may be seen as being a rather minimal orientation clause; it gives almost no information about who the character is, but it does indicate the person's condition, which provides an explanation for the following events. Clauses 1b, 1c, and 1d all contain simple past-tense verbs: **attacked, came, stopped.** A more complex series of narrative clauses can be seen in example 9, which is excerpted from an elaborate narrative about triumphing over the difficulties of finding an apartment in New York City. (The relevant verbs of the narrative clauses are indicated in boldface.)

9a. we **stumbled** into a house that belonged to U, who was one of the first people to start the brownstone renovation, as it turns out, in Brooklyn Heights

9b. and she **took** an interest in us and **began** to make phone calls about finding a place to live

9c. and we **tried** a couple of them out and they were both very expensive and not very attractive

9d. and so about five we **settled** down for a cup of coffee in a drugstore

9e. and the pharmacist **strolled** over

9f. and we **told** him our problems

9g. and he **said** he knew of an apartment. (Linde 1981, pp. 101–3)

The final narrative clause may be followed by a coda, signaling the end of the narrative. This may be a purely formal marker, like "that was it," to announce that the ending has been reached. Or it may give the effects of the events narrated, as in example 10, or it may bring the sequence closer to the present, as in example 11:

10. And it worked out very well. (Linde 1981, p. 96)

11. We really didn't intend to live there very long but we lived there four and a half years, I believe, it was before we moved. (Linde 1981, pp. 102–3)

Either form of coda serves to indicate the end (or at least a possible end) of the narrative.

Thus far, the structural units we have considered are all sequential: it is possible, with some reversals and overlaps, to establish their position within the narrative. They can thus be viewed as syntactic units of the narrative. But narratives also crucially contain evaluations, which do not have a standard position in the structure of the narrative. The **evaluative** sections of the narrative represent the means that the speaker uses to convey the point of the story or to show why it is worth telling. Viewed interactionally, the evaluation is the part of the narrative that conveys to its addressees how they are to understand the meaning of the narrated sequence of events and what kind of response the speaker desires. Thus it is socially the most important part of the narrative. The minimal narrative given in example 1 lacks any evaluation, and this is what gives it much of its odd effect. Although the events are dramatic, the narrative is not, since the speaker gives no indication of what her attitude toward them is (other than reticence) or of how she wants the addressees to understand these events.

Unlike the other components of narrative structure, the linguistic forms that express evaluative structure cannot be specified simply, since evaluation can be indicated by a wide range of linguistic structures and linguistic choices. It may be overtly and externally expressed, as in the clause "I think that's pretty good." It may be expressed through specific choice of words. For example "We went home to my house" is purely a narrative clause, but "We all finally made it home to my house" clearly has evaluative force as well. The words **finally** and **made it** presuppose that the deed took a long time to accomplish and was difficult enough that it might not have been accomplished. Even simple repetition can have evaluative force, as in "He looked and he looked and he looked for her," which is clearly more evaluative than the sentence "He looked for her." Evaluation may also involve a contrast of linguistic form with the surrounding forms; thus, a switch from direct to indirect discourse or from indirect to direct discourse may indicate a heightening of action. Finally, evaluation may be accomplished by paralinguistic features such as pitch or tone of voice, and by nonlinguistic features such as gesture and facial expression. (See Wolfson 1982 for a discussion of the use of paralinguistic features in performed narrative.)

Achieving agreement on evaluation is perhaps the most interactionally important part of the process of narration. It is the outcome of a process of negotiation between the participants, rather than being exclusively the achievement of the speaker. It is the task of the speaker to construct a narrative with an acceptable evaluation, and to give the addressees sufficient cues to understand this evaluation; simultaneously, it is the task of the addressees to give a response that either indicates that the evaluation is understood and accepted or expresses disagreement with it in a well-founded way. Goodwin and Goodwin (1987) give a number of examples of both successful and unsuccessful negotiations of agreement, indicating the extremely fine-grained work necessary from all participants in order to achieve such agreement. Here is a simple example from their study:

> 12. EILEEN: This beautiful, (0.2) Irish Setter
>     DEBBIE: Ah : : :
>     EILEEN: Came tearin up on ta the first *gree*(h)n an tried ta
>     steal Pau(h)l's go(h)lf ball. ·hh

By placing an assessment [evaluation] in her talk speaker secures an immediate subsequent assessment from a recipient. Moreover, through the way in which she pronounces her "Ah : : :" Debbie coparticipates in the **evaluative loading** of Eileen's talk, and indeed matches the affect display contained in Eileen's assessment with a **reciprocal affect display**. The talk marked with the assessment is thus not treated simply as a description, but rather as something that can be responded to, and participated in, in a special way. (p. 11; emphasis in the original)

Such agreement, though apparently simple, is not automatic; rather, it constitutes a social achievement on the part of all participants. The recipient may misunderstand what kind of response is required and may produce a response that is locally coherent but turns out not to be appropriate to the rest of the narrative. Or the recipient may in fact disagree with the proposed evaluation and refuse to ratify it. Here is another example from Goodwin and Goodwin (1987):

> 13. CURT: *This* guy had, a beautiful thirty two O:lds
>     (.05)
>     CURT: Original
>     MIKE: ((Nod))

By providing further information about the car being described Curt shows that he is still awaiting a response to his earlier talk. Moreover **the word chosen is informative about the type of response he is seeking.** Specifically this term provides recipient with further grounds for treating what has just been described as something to be assessed. . . . Mike's nod receipts Curt's talk but in no way assesses it. Rather the nod seems to constitute a kind of continuer, an action which deals with the talk which has just been heard as preliminary to further talk, rather than as something to be appreciated in its own right. . . . Thus by responding in the way that he does Mike shows that he has dealt with what Curt has said, without however treating in the way that Curt proposed it should be treated. (p. 44)

Another very striking and extended example of the social negotiation of evaluation is given in Polanyi (1989, pp. 94–96). The text was collected by Deborah Tannen as an answer to the question "Have you ever had any interesting experiences on the subway?"

14. A: I just had . . . two p . . . particular incidents that I remember . . . and one- uh- . . . [I] neither one of them really had . . . any kinds of endings or anything, that you know resolution, they just happened

   . . . um . . . <u>one</u> of them was- uh- . . . back in . . . what 66? . . . 67 . . . when [?] I (?) <u>fainted</u> on the subway . . . It was very um . . . uh . . . <u>frightening</u> experience . . . I had <u>don't</u> even remember <u>fainting</u> before in my life let alone on the subway . . . and uh- . . . it was a h . . . very hot . . . August day . . . and I was going into the city . . . from Queens? . . . A-nd . . . I was standing . . . in a very crowded car . . . And I remember standing . . . I was standing up . . . I remember holding on to the . . . center pole . . . and . . . I remember (chuckle) saying to myself . . . there is a person over there that's falling to the ground . . . And that person was me . . . And I couldn't . . .

   B: Oh, wow

   A: . . . put together the fact . . . that . . . there was someone fainting and that someone was me . . . And I just fell down . . . (clears throat) then all of sudden there was a lot of space and . . . people . . . helped me up, and . . . someone sat me down . . . a-nd then-uh . . .

   B: It wasn't rush hour

   A: Yes it was . . .

   B: Yeah?

   A: That's . . . partly why I fainted

   B: Mm

   A: Uh . . . I was under . . . tremendous . . . emotional pressures at the time . . .

   B: Mm

   A: and personal . . . pressure . . . and . . . the crush . . . of the <u>bodies</u> . . . and the no [?] <u>air</u> in the <u>car</u> . . . and everything just kind of combined . . .

   B: Mm

A: A-nd um- . . . it was incredibly <u>hot</u>, . . . a-nd uh- . . . we just waited . . . until the next stop, (low pitch and amplitude -----------) which was just a few minutes away . . . and then . . . someone took me off . . . the car and (sighs) he got a policeman . . . and . . . he came over . . . and asked what was wrong, and he asked me just two questions. "Are you pregnant?" . . . to which I said no. I mean they . . . like he was told that I had fainted . . .

B: (chuckle)

A: A-nd uh, . . . uh he said . . . in a very embarrassed kind of way do you have your period now . . .

B: (laugh)

A: And I said no . . . A-nd then he said OK and he sat me down, and they got an ambulance . . . and the ambulance ca-me, and took me to . . . a nearby hospital . . . A-nd u-m . . . I just stayed in the . . . emergency room . . . for . . . I guess an hour . . . It was it was heat prostration . . . A lot of it . . .

B: Mm

A: Having eaten . . . having . . . having not had . . . not . . . <u>eaten</u> . . . for several <u>da-ys</u> . . .

B: uh

A: and . . . I was job hun [glottal stop] it was just . . . a whole mess . . . <u>but</u> . . . u-m . . . <u>after that</u>, . . . I could not . . . ride . . . on the subway . . . And to this day I have trouble riding on the subway . . . If I'm with someone I feel OK . . . If I'm alone, . . . <u>in</u> rush ours . . . I c . . . I . . . c-an't. If . . . I'm very very scared of . . . fainting again . . . Um . . . I don't know if you've ever

B: Um

A: experienced . . .

B: I haven't

A: . . . There is <u>no</u> experience in the <u>world</u> . . . like experiencing . . . rush hour . . . in the subway . . . Uh- . .

B: Oh, rush hour. Not fainting

A: Yeah. The closest thing I can compare it to, and I never experienced <u>that</u> . . . and it's probably a <u>fraction</u> of what <u>that</u> experience was . . . but I think . . .

B: Mm

A: of the way the Jews . . . were herded

B: Mm

A: into the cattle cars . . . Tsk and that's . . . you know . . .
maybe . . . maybe part of <u>that</u> ties into that . . . kind of
. . .

B: Yeah

A: thing . . . and I just panic . . . I mean . . . everything in
me . . . freezes up, and I can't do it . . .

B: Mm

A: And it's just as dehumanizing . . .

B: But people were pretty nice, hm?

A: People . . . are . . . Always nice when there's a crisis like
that . . . And . . . and the context was right . . . I was
<u>white</u>, . . . I was a young woman . . . I was w-ell dressed,
I was . . . obviously not . . . pervert, or a deviate . . . or a
criminal . . .

B: (laugh)

A: <u>Had I been</u> . . . had I been . . . anything <u>other</u> than that
. . . I could've fallen . . . and they would've stepped <u>over</u>
me . . . Or perhaps <u>on me</u>

B: (laugh)

A: you know cause that's the way people in New York <u>are</u>.

C: Didn't you used to grab the strap . . . in the subway?

A: I was just saying . . . I . . . yeah . . . But I was . . . standing in the center of the car, holding onto the center <u>pole</u>,
. . . and I just slid down the pole . . .
A-nd uh- . . . it was funny because . . . in my <u>head</u> . . .
I said . . . <u>awareness</u> was such . . . that . . . that I said to
myself . . . gee wizz there's a <u>person</u> over there, falling
<u>down</u>. and that person was me.

B: It's weird . . .

A: Ok that was . . . that experience.

Polanyi (1989, pp. 64–73) offers an extended analysis to show that
this narrative contains a negotiation about evaluations that both speaker and addressees can accept. The most critically contested part of
this narrative is the implicit claim that rush hour can be compared to

the Nazi concentration camp horrors — this claim is not accepted by the audience:

> A: Yeah. The closest thing I can compare it to, and I never experienced that . . . and it's probably a fraction of what that experience was . . . but I think . . . of the way the Jews . . . were herded into the cattle cars . . . Tsk and that's . . . you know . . . maybe . . . maybe part of that ties into that . . . kind of . . . thing . . . and I just panic . . . I mean . . . everything in me . . . freezes up, and I can't do it . . . And it's just as dehumanizing . . .

The essence of this proposal is that, during rush hour in the subways, people are so deprived of their basic needs of air, space, and individuality that they become like beasts. But one of the addressees rejects the proposal by asking a question that contradicts this proposal:

> B: But people were pretty nice, hm?

This response expresses disagreement with the speaker's evaluation of the people who ride on the subways during rush hour as **dehumanized.** The use of **but and the question form using hm** propose a very different evaluation of the events in the narrative. In response, the speaker agrees that people acted nicely:

> A: People . . . are . . . Always nice when there's a crisis like that

However, the reasons she then gives for why they acted that way suggest that they were not *truly* nice:

> And . . . and the context was right . . . I was white, . . . I was a young woman . . . I was w-ell dressed, I was . . . obviously not . . . pervert, or a deviate . . . or a criminal . . . Had I been . . . had I been . . . anything other than that . . . I could've fallen . . . and they would've stepped over me . . . Or perhaps on me

The argument here is that the people on the subway would only act nicely to members of a privileged group, which is not evidence of niceness, but rather of bigotry. However, at the end of this argument, the speaker also offers a further evaluation:

> A: . . . that's the way people in New York are.

This is a promising move in the negotiation, since debate about how New Yorkers are is always popular, particularly with New Yorkers. But the addressees do not pick up this evaluation. Instead, C enters the conversation and provides the basis for a new evaluation:

> C: Didn't you used to grab the strap . . . in the subway?

This is an implicit evaluation of the speaker as an inept subway rider. The speaker's answer to this charge of incompetence is first to emphasize that she was a fully competent subway rider who was holding the pole rather than the strap:

> A: I was just saying . . . I . . . yeah . . . But I was . . . standing in the center of the car, holding onto the center pole . . . and I just slid down the pole . . .

She then presents an evaluation of the strange perceptual quality of fainting—an evaluation entirely unrelated to the previous argument about Nazi cattle cars and people in New York:

> A: A-nd uh- . . . it was funny because . . . in my head . . . I said . . . awareness was such . . . that . . . that I said to myself . . . gee wizz there's a person over there, falling down. and that person was me.

This evaluation suggests that the narrative can be understood as a recounting of an interesting experience—a much weaker evaluation than the previous proposals. B accepts A's proposed evaluation by offering a somewhat sympathetic comment:

> B: It's weird . . .

The speaker then accepts B's acquiescence and closes the negotiation by adding a coda:

> A: OK, that was . . . that experience.

Having seen these examples of the negotiation of evaluation, we may now consider what the task of the participants is in an actual situation of narration. As the simple instances of negotiation in examples 12 and 13 show, the work of coming to a group agreement can be so skilled and subtle that it is too small for us to notice easily. In fact, in the telling of most narratives, agreement is so successfully negotiated that the possibility of disagreement either does not arise or is folded back into the narrative. A situation like example 14, in which active disagreement is expressed, is extremely rare. It is not surprising that the disagreement erupts over the narrator's use of the Nazi concentration camps as a comparison, since culturally the Nazis and everything associated with them have been placed in a category so extreme as not to be human, and thus not available for comparison to everyday human experiences.

Narratives request agreement on their evaluation. If they do not receive this as a matter of course, an agreement is negotiated. Eventually, as in example 14, agreement may be reached. (Of course, such agreement is verbal, not necessarily psychological; that is, one of the participants may make the concessionary moves necessary to allow the narrative to continue, without actually being convinced.) If disagreement escalates further, the participants may not be able to negotiate an agreement. In such cases, the participants may agree to disagree and go on with the narrative; or the narration may break down, and the participants may move on to some other form of talk; or the entire speech situation may break down, with one or more participant leaving; or one of the participants may be discredited as drunk, stoned, crazy, or in some other way incompetent.

Goodwin (1986) presents a complex example of disagreement on the evaluation of a narrative being told to a group of two to four addressees. The number varies because the story, which involves what may have been a fight between racers at a local auto race, is framed as being specifically relevant to the two men in the audience, while the two women present move in and out of participation as addressees. In this situation, two alternate evaluations are proposed—one by the speaker, and one by two of the other participants. The narrative is prompted by the primary narrator's wife, Phyl, who offers the abstract: **Mike siz there wz a big fight down there las'night.** This abstract provides a prospective evaluation of the event as a big fight but distances the speaker from responsibility for the characterization, since it is presented as Mike's evaluation and not her own. Mike, the primary speaker, then begins to recount the events at the race track. Early in Mike's narrative, before the orientation section is completed, Phyl provides an alternative characterization of the events of the possible fight as an empty show put on by participants who threaten and bluster but do not actually fight: **Yeh they'd be doin'it en den ney go down'n ney *thr*row their h*hel*mets off'n nen n(h)ey j's l:*l*ook et each other.** Later in the narrative, as Mike gets to the actual events of the fight, Gary, one of the addressees, produces an evaluation that is consistent with Phyl's characterization of the protagonists as producing aggressive displays but not actually fighting.

15. MIKE: settin there en'e takes iz helmet off'n *clunk* it goes on
top a the car ge gets *o*ut'n goes up t'the trai*ler* 'n gets

that god damn iron *b*a:r?, 'hhh *rraps* that trailer en
a*way* he starts t'go en evrybuddy seh 'know, seh he:h
yer right'n 'e throws that son'vabitch down ·hhhh So
they all go dow n
                     [      [

GARY:                  A:*ll All* show

                                              (p. 294)

This evaluation proposed by Gary as the way to understand Mike's story
is accepted by a number of participants, as indicated by their actions.
The two women present agree with Gary's evaluation—Phyl by nodding,
and Carney (the other woman) by producing a further example of the
same phenomenon of aggression as **all show**: **It reminds me to those
wrestlers on television.** Gary treats his own evaluation as the completion
of the story by turning away from Mike and requesting a beer from
Curt, the other member of the audience.

At this point, Mike could have agreed with this evaluation of his
narrative, or he could have attempted a negotiation on the evaluation.
But in fact, neither of these moves occurs. Rather, the narrator attempts
to continue his narrative as a narrative about a fight; and eventually he
does complete it, albeit with a reduced audience. In fact, his final audience consists only of Curt, the other racing aficionado, who is willing to
agree with his assessment of the events as a big fight.

The difference in outcome between this narrative and the one in example 14 is interesting. In the subway narrative, disagreement by the audience with the narrator's evaluation of the events eventually moves the
narrator to change her evaluation. In the racing narrative, disagreement
by the audience leads to a reconstitution of the audience, which is possible since one member of the audience is in agreement with the speaker's
initial evaluation. This constitutes an alternative strategy for proceeding
with a narrative in the face of disagreement. However, it accords with
the original claim: a narrator cannot simply ignore disagreement about
the meaning of the events narrated and blithely continue with the narrative. Some social action must be taken to manage disagreement.

The preceding two examples of managing disagreement raise an interesting question about possible differences in men's and women's strategies in this area. It might be argued that women's discourse, much more
than men's discourse, exhibits a strong social demand for agreement
between the participants. Arguments (sketched in Chapter 4) have been
put forward that women tend to define themselves relationally, while

men define themselves individualistically and oppositionally, and these would suggest that this demand for agreement might be the case. (On the other hand, see Goodwin (1982) for a discussion of women's conflictual discourse.) In any case, this is a question for further research; it is too important to be decided either *a priori* or on the basis of two examples.

We have now seen what evaluation is and how it functions interactively in the production of narrative. To understand the role of evaluation in narratives that form part of the life story, we must distinguish between two major kinds of evaluations that can be made. One kind serves to establish reportability, while the other is intended to demonstrate that the events and characters of the narrative conform to norms shared or negotiated by speaker and addressees. Reportability has been discussed in Chapter 2. Briefly, it involves the contrast between completely ordinary and expected events, which are not narratable, and events that are sufficiently unusual or unexpected to justify the speaker's holding the floor with them.

In addition to being made coherent by the relative reportability of their events, narratives are also made coherent by the moral comments they offer on the way things are, the way things ought to be, and (most especially) the kind of person the speaker claims to be, as demonstrated by the actions of the protagonist. In examining narratives that form part of the life story, we will find that this kind of moral evaluation, particularly of the character of the speaker, is among the most powerful tools we have for understanding what speakers do as they construct their narratives and what is at stake for them in narrating parts of their life story. Once again, narratives involve (among other things) a negotiation between speaker and addressees about what their values are and about how actions are to be understood. This negotiation is part of an attempted proof by the speaker of the following high-level claim: "I am a good person, a proper person, a competent person; I did what any good person or what any extraordinarily good person would do in this situation, or as much as a good person could do when blocked by extraordinarily difficult circumstances" (see Polanyi 1989). Thus, narrative is a presentation of the self, and the evaluative component in particular establishes the kind of self that is presented.

Let us now consider some examples of this kind of evaluation. Example 16 makes an unusually explicit statement of the speaker's good qualities, directly claiming that, when he was in school, he was good at every kind of sport because of his natural ability:

16. So it was kind of funny. I became, very suddenly, when I was
    eight years old, uh, in grade eight, uh . . . I discovered <u>sports</u>.
    And it was just because we were having uh, a . . . uh high
    school required sports thing, and everybody had to run and
    jump and all of this. And, I won every race, and I jumped the
    <u>far</u>thest and the <u>high</u>est, and threw the <u>far</u>thest, and all of this
    and I had inherited my father's tremendous strength. And that,
    'gain, changed everything because I then became the leader in
    high school on <u>sports</u> and was (unclear) through high school. I
    managed the teams I was <u>on</u> most of the teams. I refereed the
    teams. I was very proud of the fact that in grade twelve, I
    succeeded in getting the three hundred and ten students in the
    school, every single one of them, involved in some form of
    sports, including the kid in the wheelchair refereeing the table
    tennis matches. <u>Everybody</u> was involved in sports. I . . . made
    a list and checked them <u>all</u> out, very careful.

Interestingly, in addition to the explicit and relatively morally neutral
claim of sports ability, this narrative also makes an indirect claim of the
moral value of caring for people. The speaker presents himself as being
a good person not only because he exploited his physical ability, but also
because he attempted to bring to others with lesser abilities the benefits
of participation in sports.

Let us now consider a somewhat more complex example. This narrative shows the speaker's cleverness in using his understanding of the
principles of currency exchange, gained through his work at a bank, to
live for free in Europe:

17. And so, uh uh I went to Europe. What the hell. Had a sister in
    Europe whose husband was a NATO . . . fighter pilot, and
    they said, "Come and stay. No cost. All the food you like.
    You cn-" we lived in Baden Baden. Which isn't a bad place in
    Europe to live. So, I went over and spent a year there. And I
    traveled to Paris, and to Frankfurt and Rome and Venice,
    Vienna and Venice and London. I had a very good time. And
    it didn't cost me anything. Though, as a matter of fact, my
    foreign exchange was what <u>saved</u> me. I only had . . . a few
    hundred dollars, but I discovered that they had fixed the ex-
    change rate on the base of four marks to the dollar. And
    downtown you would get 3.87 marks to the dollar. So I'd buy
    four hundred dollars worth of marks, go downtown, get three
    eighty, three, four hundred marks worth of dollars, make thir-

teen dollars profit and that was enough for the day. I didn't spend that much. This went on day after day and I (unclear) to keep myself in the same amount of money. The thing that killed me was Christmas, of course, which used up all the capital and then I didn't have enough to exchange. So I came back in February and I'd been there just over a year at that point.

The evaluation of the speaker's cleverness in living in Europe for free is obvious. A somewhat subtler aspect of the evaluation is the way the speaker shows that the reason this system ultimately came to an end was beyond his control. Although the working of the scheme is framed as redounding to his credit and occurring because of his agency — **I discovered, my foreign exchange** — the failure of the scheme is framed passively, as a fault of the calendar rather than of the speaker for not foreseeing it — **The thing that killed me was Christmas, of course, which used up all the capital.**

We have now discussed all the parts of a narrative. To flesh out this description of narrative structure, let us examine a narrative that was offered in one of the interviews on choice of profession. The speaker has already explained her choice of English literature as a profession. The interviewer then asks her about her choice of specialization:

18. Q: And how bout the particular field?

    A: That was more or less an accident. Uh, I started out in Renaissance studies, but I didn't like any of the people I was working with, and at first I thought I would just leave Y and go to another university, uh but a medievalist at Y university asked me to stay or at least reconsider whether I should leave or not, and um pointed out to me that I had done very well in the medieval course that I took with him and that I seemed to like it, and he was right. I did. And he suggested that I switch fields and stay at Y and that's how I got into medieval literature.

Although relatively short, this narrative is extremely rich and indicates a great deal about the speaker's beliefs about the world. We will examine it in greater detail in Chapter 5. But here, we will begin by dividing it into the parts of narrative structure discussed previously, in order to show the internal structure of the narrative and how the parts fit together.

| The Clause | Structural Type |
| --- | --- |
| And how bout the particular field? | Abstract furnished by interviewer's request |
| That was more or less an accident. | Evaluation of entire narrative |
| Uh, I started out in Renaissance studies, | Orientation |
| but I didn't like any of the people I was working with, | Orientation/Evaluation |
| and at first I thought I would just leave Y and go to another university | Narrative (main verb **thought**) |
| uh but a medievalist at Y university asked me to stay or at least reconsider whether I should leave or not, | Narrative (main verb **asked**) |
| and um pointed out to me that I had done very well in the medieval course that I took with him and that I seemed to like it, | Narrative (main verb **pointed out**). Absence of subject indicates that the verb is closely tied to the previous verb, and may be simultaneous with it. Also evaluation of speaker's university career. |
| and he was right. | Evaluation |
| I did. | Evaluation |
| And he suggested that I switch fields and stay at Y | Narrative (main verb **suggested**) |
| and that's how I got into medieval literature | Coda: summarizes the narrative and marks the ending |

This is a relatively simple and undramatic example of the narrative of personal experience, but formally its structure is quite clear and should serve to indicate what a narrative looks like, what its parts are, and how they fit together.

The preceding discussion has dealt with the structure of the oral narrative of personal experience. This structure is one of the primary discourse units and forms the basis for the structure of many derivative units: the pseudo-narrative description (Linde 1974; Linde and Labov 1975); the habitual narrative of typical rather than specific event sequences; and the hypothetical or future narrative of events that may take place under specified conditions. Each of these discourse units shares some but not all of the defining conditions of the narrative. None plays a major part in the life story. Now, however, we turn to a discourse unit related to the narrative that does play such a role.

## The Chronicle

Thus far, we have considered the narrative — the discourse unit that plays the greatest role in the construction of the life story. A discourse unit related but not identical to the narrative is the chronicle, which may also form part of the telling of a life story. The chronicle has not previously been discussed by other researchers in discourse analysis, and therefore our understanding of it cannot be as rich as our understanding of the narrative, which has been widely studied. It is a fairly common unit in the data of this study, though, and therefore it must be examined.

The discourse unit that I here call the chronicle consists of a recounting of a sequence of events that does not have a single unifying evaluative point. The term *chronicle* has been taken from the usage of historians, who distinguish between a chronicle (a document recounting events temporally, usually year by year) and a history (a document recounting events not only by time but also by theme). Thus a report of the history of a monastery year by year is a chronicle; the events of one year may include the election of a new abbot, the death of a cow, and an invasion by Vikings. If one wants to know the results of the Viking invasion, one may have to wait until the next year's entry. In contrast, a discussion of the events leading to the decline and fall of the Roman Empire is a history; it will discuss the reasons underlying events and those events' relation to other events, rather than being limited to a purely chronological presentation (White 1973, 1987).

White (1987) offers the following example of a chronicle and discusses the ways in which it is unlike a history:

> I take as an example of the chronicle type of historical representation the *History of France* by one Richerus of Rheims, written on the eve of the year A.D. 1000 (ca. 998). We have no difficulty recognizing this text as a narrative. It has a central subject ("the conflicts of the French"); a proper geographical center (Gaul) and a proper social center (the archepiscopal see of Rheims, beset by a dispute over which of two claimants to the office of archbishop is the legitimate occupant); and a proper beginning in time (given in a synoptic version of the history of the world from the Incarnation down to the time and place of Richerus's own writing of his account). But the work fails as a proper history, at least according to the opinion of later commentators, by virtue of two considerations. First, the order of the discourse follows the order of their occurrence and cannot, therefore, offer the kind of meaning that a narratologically governed account can be said to provide. Second, probably owing to the "annalistic" order of the discourse, the account does not so much conclude as simply terminate; it

merely breaks off with the flight of one of the disputants for the office of archbishop and throws onto the reader the burden for retrospectively reflecting on the linkages between the beginning of the account and its ending. The account comes down to the writer's own "yesterday," adds one more fact to the series that began with the Incarnation, and then simply ceases. As a result, all of the normal narratological expectations of the reader (this reader) remain unfulfilled. The work appears to be unfolding a plot but then belies its own appearance by merely stopping *in medias res*, with the cryptic notation "Pope Gregory authorizes Arnulfus to assume provisionally the episcopal functions, while awaiting the legal decision that would either confer those upon him or withdraw the right to them." (p. 17)

In White's view, then, the chronicle provides the raw material of a story, which it is the historian's task to shape. For oral conversation, the chronicle has something of the same character, but it provides materials for the participants, rather than for a historian who takes a meta-stance toward the materials used. In ordinary conversation, we are most likely to find chronicles used when the speaker needs to fill in temporally organized information that is unknown to the addressee. Thus, at the reunion of friends, we hear chronicles used to answer questions like "I haven't seen you since July; what have you been doing with yourself?" They are also exchanged when people are getting to know one another and want to learn something of the basic chronology of one another's lives.

Example 19 is an example of a chronicle. It immediately follows a narrative about how the speaker left college and began working in a bank, and it ends with a strong evaluation that taking that job was the wrong decision to have made. The chronicle then identifies what the speaker did in the intervening period between leaving that job in order to enter the army and the time of the interview. This chronicle is cast in terms of decisions about events rather than in terms of events directly, because the speaker was incorrectly informed by the person who arranged the interview that my interest was in how people make life decisions. In spite of this unusual factor, I have chosen example 19 as a representative chronicle because it is quite short. Other chronicles in the data, such as example 20, relate the sequential events directly, without the overlay of ascribed motives for their occurrence. Here is example 19:

> 19. Uh, the other decisions, I made a decision out here [in California] to, to, to not go into the theater uh out, here, in Asia. Went into the service and then went a year abroad. Decided

while abroad not to go into movies or the theater. And so made the decision there and came back and didn't know quite how to get into city work, so in terms of decided to be a teacher, again, it was the first and most realistic avenue I saw of getting into poverty work at all. Wasn't, it certainly wasn't that I wanted to be a teacher. I always saw it as a temporary thing, and never more then when I got involved in it. But um then I made a very deliberate decision to get out of teaching and into the community housing group, and a ver- a very wrenching decision to leave the community s- group and join the city bureaucracy. And then a very easy decision to get the fuck out of the city bureaucracy.

A number of the structural characteristics of this chronicle define the chronicle as a discourse unit. First, it makes use of the narrative presupposition; that is, the order of narration is to be understood as the order of events. Thus, in this chronicle, we are to understand that entering military service preceded teaching, teaching preceded work at the community housing group, and work at the community housing group preceded employment in the city bureaucracy.

A second characteristic of the chronicle is that the other elements that constitute a narrative are absent. There is no abstract, no orientation section, and no coda or conclusion. The structure consists entirely of the narration of events in sequence.

The third and most striking characteristic is the treatment of evaluation. This chronicle does contain evaluative material, but its use is very different from the use of evaluation in a narrative. In a narrative, the evaluative material is used to indicate the point of the narrative as a whole. This means that all (or almost all) of the evaluation makes the same point or helps the speaker to build toward that point. In contrast, the chronicle contains evaluations of individual events but not of the sequence as a whole.

Arguably, we might find a chronicle that has a unified evaluation. This would involve an account structured as follows: "It's been a terrible year: Example 1, Example 2, Example 3." Such a unit can be analyzed in two different ways. One way is to see it as a chronicle, in spite of the overall evaluation, since each of the examples could function as a part of a table of contents of potential narratives. The other way is to see it as a reasoning structure (rather than as a chronicle) designed to establish the proposition "It's been a terrible year" by the support of three examples. The decision about which is the correct approach must be based on close analysis of actual instances of this structure. Since no such instance occurs in the data of this study, the question remains open.

In the case of unevaluated chronicles, an important interactive reason explains this absence of evaluation. In telling a narrative, unless the narrative has been explicitly requested, the speaker must offer some justification for telling it; that is, the speaker must demonstrate why it is legitimate to hold the floor for an extended turn. In contrast, a chronicle is used to give information that has already been demanded, either by the addressee or by the speaker's and addressee's mutual understanding of the situation. Therefore, the purpose of telling the sequence is already established. Further, because the chronicle may imbed narratives, the addressee can request amplification of any event mentioned in the chronicle, based either on personal interest or on the evaluation given. Such an amplification is likely to come in narrative form, and this narrative will have its own evaluative structure. In effect, the possibility of imbedding narratives means that the chronicle can serve as a table of contents of potential narratives that will be told or not told depending on the response of the addressee.

As a further illustration of the chronicle, let us consider example 20, which is a fragment of an extremely long chronicle detailing the speaker's development as a professional musician — a chronicle that was not specifically requested by the interviewer, but that forms the core of a long monologue and was immediately prompted by the speaker's reflection about how teenagers have the time to get into anything that interests them:

20. And when you're a teenager you know you can give all the time you want to any obsession, that's a great time to do it. So. So I really picked up a lot of technical skills in those years. And I started playing immediately in a, in a bluegrass band with some friends of mine who got interested in it and a friend of mine uh had gone back to the South in his last year of high school cause his folks had moved back there and he wrote me about this fiddler that he had met and there were maybe two fiddlers in LA at that time so this, so he brought my friend Brantly out from North Carolina and we started a bluegrass band. And, and that was, we, we played in all the clubs and here, and that was when I was about seventeen, sixteen, seventeen. And then uh we all went our separate ways, we went to college, but I immediately fell into, you know, in that scene, into other, well I met all these other musicians. That's w- I met Jody immediately, when I moved to Berkeley, and Sandy

Rothman, who'd just got off the road with Bill Monroe, who was the father of bluegrass, and that was very impressive to me. So. And I fell in with a bunch of those people. We had lots of bands going back and forth. Shall I, do you know all these (unclear)? //Interviewer: Yeah// OK. In Berkeley a couple, after a year or so, um, the, you know Beatles and, and the whole psychedelic rock thing was taking place and uh, I got an electric guitar and, and started uh practicing with some people, and pretty soon I was in one of those bands that played "Gloria" and "Satisfaction" and all those songs. At fraternity parties. So. I did that for a while and you know a lot of stuff about electric guitar. I just, I got, what I did was I got um started studying Chuck Berry and B. B. King and uh and then a lot of the more derivative guitar players that followed them, you know, and but mainly they were the ones that I listened to to cause every guitar player sounded to me either like B. B. King or Chuck Berry. And I, and they still do.

And, and, uh, and while I was doing that, an old high school buddy of mine who was uh, was writing songs, and in, living in Santa Barbara and playing with a band and taking drugs and getting crazy and uh when when everybody in this band either flipped out or killed themself or got drafted, he moved up to Berkeley and checked out what I was doing and and we started getting together and and ah we, we formed a sort of partnership that kept up for about eight years when we, the two of us were the core of a band that kept changing you know exc- personnel except for us two, for that length of time, and we wrote all these songs, and, and played 'em and, and uh recorded 'em and toured and you and so on. And we did that through most of the sixties. And I kept on playing bluegrass through that time too, but mostly just for fun. You know. It, well, we had a lot of discouraging things happen to us, and eventually split up as a, as a group, but before we did we started playing pop music to, to survive and you know finance the project, you know, playing top 40 bands in bars and stuff like that. And uh, which culminated in a six month long engagement at the Condor Club in San Francisco in which I MC'd for Carol Doda [a well-known local stripper].

Clearly this chronicle contains material for many narratives, which would have emerged had the addressee requested them.

*[handwritten: Life Sty = a) narrative b) chronicle c) explanation]*

## The Explanation

A third important discourse unit that forms part of a life story is the explanation (Goguen, Weiner, and Linde 1983; Weiner 1980). In the discussion that follows, the term *explanation* is used to describe the linguistic structure of a particular discourse unit; it is not used to describe the social function of explaining, which may be realized by a variety of discourse structures. For example, a speaker may tell a narrative in order to justify some action, and the narrative thus functions as an explanation. But the explanation as a discourse unit has a particular structure that distinguishes it from other discourse units, and it is this structural unit that the present section describes.

The discourse unit of explanation begins with a statement of some proposition to be proved, and then follows it with a sequence of statements of reasons (often multiply embedded reasons) why the proposition should be believed. Schiffrin (1985), in studying the structure of spontaneous rhetorical argument, has called these elements **position** and **support**. In example 21, we see a typical example of such an explanation — one that is by no means as long or as logically elaborate as many found in these data. It follows the narrative given in example 16 about the choice of medieval literature. Immediately after the speaker told this narrative, I asked her "Do you think it [medieval literature] was the right choice?" She then answered this question with an explanation showing that the choice between medieval literature and Renaissance literature, which she had at first considered, in fact made no real difference. Thus, we may view this explanation as a logical proof of the equivalence of medieval and Renaissance literature:

21. Sometimes I don't think it makes any difference. Uh I don't think I could've ever specialized in a very late field and been happy. I mean, I think if I had been in the nineteenth or twentieth centuries I would've gotten bored and probably turned in desperation to literary theory, which is what a lot of people do. Um, now that seems to me like a horrible sin, but it might have happened.

    As for the difference between medieval or Renaissance or seventeenth century, I don't think it makes much difference. Um I'm very happy being a medievalist and I now couldn't imagine switching, but if I had liked the people in the Renaissance and had stayed in it I would never have imagined switching either. So, um, you know, I mean it was a right choice because it led to a job and it led to good friends and it led to a good career and a lot of satisfaction, and uh in other circumstances I think staying in the Renaissance would have led me to the same place.

The proof begins with the statement of the proposition to be proved, which is an equivalence: **(Sometimes) I don't think it** [the choice between medieval and Renaissance literature] **makes any difference.** The speaker then establishes that this is the correct equivalence to be proved, by showing that other apparently possible alternatives need not be considered: a choice of nineteenth- or twentieth-century literature would have led to the sin of despair and literary theory. The speaker then restates the equivalence to be proved: **As for the difference between medieval or Renaissance or seventeenth century, I don't think it makes much difference.** She then shows that in two particular respects the choice of either field would have led to the same result:

1. She cannot imagine switching from medieval literature to Renaissance literature; but in the alternative world of the other choice, she would have felt the same way about Renaissance literature.
2. The choice of medieval literature has led to a satisfying life, but the choice of Renaissance literature would have led to the same sort of life.

Thus, the equivalence of the choices in these two relevant respects establishes that the two choices are in fact equivalent.

As we have seen, one form of the discourse unit of explanation consists of presenting the structure of a statement followed by reasons why this statement should be believed, using markers such as **because** or **so.** Another form of this structure involves giving the reasons in the form of specific examples. Example 22, taken from a discussion of how the speaker chooses whether to do a long form or a short form for federal income tax, shows a statement followed by a sequence of examples illustrating that the statement is true.[1]

1. For readers who are not familiar with American income tax law, here is a summary of the portions relevant to these examples. Estimated income taxes are deducted from each salary check. At the end of the fiscal year, the taxpayer files a claim form, listing income, taxes already paid, and expenses that the law permits as deductions from taxable income. Depending on the extent of these expenses, the taxpayer may either receive a refund from the government or be required to pay additional taxes. Someone who does not wish to do the complex record-keeping and calculations that the process requires may choose to fill out a "short form," which assumes certain standard deductions for each particular income level. The long form offers a greater opportunity to reduce the amount of taxes paid, while the short form offers the convenience of a much simpler calculation.

22. Well I, I know most of my own deductions, myself. What
    deductions are good, like the depreciation of my property, uh,
    maintenance of my property, certain sorts of things like that,
    the deduction I got from interest

Another form of justification of a statement relies on eliminating all
relevant alternatives. We have seen an instance of this in example 21.
Now we shall consider a simpler example, also from the domain of
income tax choice:

23. I calculated my deductions and they were nowhere close to the
    uh (pause) standard so I took the standard so I probably could
    have filled out a short form if I wanted to but I'm so used to
    filling out the long form that I did that

The speaker here shows that he has considered the alternatives of itemiz-
ing deductions on the long form and of filling out a short form, and he
demonstrates that his decision to do standard deductions on the long
form was a considered choice rather than a mistake.

Having investigated the structure of the discourse unit of explanation,
let us turn to the issue how such units are used as part of social practice.
When logicians who are unfamiliar with informal oral argument look at
explanations like the ones given in examples 21, 22, and 23, they are
often shocked and horrified by the combination of mechanisms of formal reasoning with reasoning that they deem appallingly bad. (This is
not a thought experiment; I have performed it with a number of logicians.) The shock comes from the logicians' belief that the function of
logical reasoning is to discover or establish truth. However, the use of
such explanations by speakers in social practice has very little to do with
the establishment of truth by formal means.

When we look at the ways in which explanations are used in these
data, we find that speakers appear to use explanations to establish the
truth of propositions about which the speakers themselves are uncom-
fortable, or to defend propositions whose validity they feel their addressee has in some way challenged. This follows from the structure of
explanation itself, which first states a proposition and then enumerates
the reasons for believing it to be true. Such a structure would not be
relevant in the absence of some suggestion that the proposition might
not be believed.

Thus, in example 21, the explanation follows a narrative in which the
speaker states that her choice of professional field was more or less an
accident. And although the speaker does not indicate that she finds

anything wrong with an accidental choice of field, our knowledge as members of this culture tells us that this is somewhat problematic, going against our belief that a competent person is an active agent in charge of his or her own life. (The question of how the meaning of accident should be interpreted in this example will be discussed in Chapter 5.) Consequently, if the speaker presents some choice of event as an accident, this account must be remedied in some way. Explanations are used to plug a leak in the account that the speaker wishes to construct, rather than to do the primary work of constructing a solid account.

In this regard, consider the sequence of examples 24 and 25, which begins with the speaker stating that going into the Marines was a waste of time. When I questioned him about this evaluation, the sequence in example 25 followed. (The boldfaced portions are marked to indicate the analyst's analysis of doubt or discomfort by the speaker; they do not indicate the speaker's emphasis.)

24. INTERVIEWER: How'd you get into the Marines?
    SPEAKER: I (pause) volunteered. But uh --
    INTERVIEWER: Yeah, I know, that's how it's done.
    SPEAKER: (Laughs) Yeah, well I wanted to be with the best, or **some bullshit** reason. I had a roommate in high school that did it. **I'm very uncomfortable about it.**

Immediately following this question-and-answer sequence, the speaker gives an explanation that attempts to demonstrate that his time in the Marines was not wholly without value to him:

25. It was a m- **it was a mistake** but you know, you can't spend two years anywhere and not learn something. So there are always, you know, I learned how to program a computer and I learned what a really <u>horrible</u> bureaucracy can do to people, and I learned what the military machine is all about, at one level, at least, first hand. And all of that uh all of that was extremely valuable stuff.

Example 25 is a very clear case of an explanation being given in a situation in which the speaker has ambivalent feelings, to establish a point that the speaker himself doubts.

The general pattern that emerges from these data is that the form of logical reasoning found in explanation is not our first mode of presenting unproblematic experience; that is the place reserved for narrative. Rather, explanation is a remedy that we employ once things have begun to go wrong in some way. In other words, the form of logical reasoning is used not to arrive at the truth—the role that formal logic claims for itself—but as a rhetorical form to demonstrate that propositions that may appear dubious, false, problematic, or stupid do in fact have justifications that should lead to their addressee's believing them.

## Discourse Analysis and the Issue of Interpretation

Thus far, this chapter has discussed the issues involved in choosing appropriate data for various questions of discourse analysis, shown the data chosen for the present project, and illustrated the structure of the major discourse units that are found in these data. We must now consider briefly the question of the status of such analysis—that is, what an analyst does in interpreting discourse units.

Questions that arise in any analysis of discourse include the degree of precision such an analysis can claim and the possible independence (or lack thereof) of the analysis and the analyst. More pointedly, one may ask whether the structures that the analyst claims to have discovered are rigorously determined by markers in the test, or whether they are due, partially or wholly, to the desires and biases of the analyst.

Although I have stated this position in perhaps its most extreme form, it actually is posed this way by proponents of content analysis and by other researchers who hold to similar theories about what scientific objectivity requires of the social sciences. Such theories specify that any contribution on the part of the experimenter represents a defect in the method; any such contribution must be viewed as experimenter bias and must be eliminated. For meaning to be scientifically valid, it must be communicated by a fixed set of markers in the text that invariably correspond to a portion of the meaning. The analyst's task, then, is simply to discover these markers and to make explicit their correspondences. As might be expected, no actual attempt to analyze discourse within such constraints has been made—or at least reported as successful. The approach that comes closest is Bales's interaction process analysis. Significantly, this technique was developed before reliable and accurate tape recorders became widely available and therefore it relies on a coder's real-time count of categories of utterance that would give indications of the attitudes and motivations of the speakers (Bales 1950). This model of coding has remained popular in social psychology, even after technological developments have rendered the limitations within which it functions obsolete.

Recent developments in pragmatics and semantics have shown that, even at the sentence level, no invariant relation exists between linguistic form and interpreted meaning. Thus, not all utterances that we understand as having the force of questions have the form of questions, nor are all utterances that have the linguistic form of questions to be interpreted as questions. For example, "Could you pass the salt?" has the form but not the force of a question, while "You had poached eggs for breakfast this morning" may have the force but not the form of a question.

More generally, language does not possess rigid correspondences between form and meaning in either direction. No given form invariably signals a given meaning, and no given meaning is signaled exclusively by a single fixed form or set of forms. Between the text and the meaning, an interpretation must always be interposed, and this must be done by a human interpreter. (Attempts have been made in the area of artificial intelligence and machine translation to automate this act of interpretation. Such limited success as has been achieved—primarily in texts with extremely limited semantic domains—suggests that a mechanical interpreter must be supplied with an analogue of a human's world knowledge, as well as an analogue of human inferencing and reasoning processes.)

This gap between text and meaning has been widely discussed in the literature of hermeneutics, particularly as part of the notion of the "hermeneutic circle," which refers to the relation between the text and the interpreter. The interpreter can never come to a text with an entirely open mind, but must have some preunderstanding of the text—some expectations about the kind of text it is and the kinds of things it says. Otherwise, the interpreter will be unable even to enter into the act of interpretation. This is a necessary part of the process of understanding. It can never be eliminated by more rigorous methodology or more clever experiment design; it can only be acknowledged or swept under the rug. (See Palmer [1969] for a history of hermeneutics and a discussion of the varying definitions of its scope.)

If we admit that no one-to-one correspondence exists between linguistic form and meaning, and that a relation always exists between the interpreter and the interpretations that he or she can make, we are faced with the fact that texts admit of multiple interpretations. This poses a serious question for the interpreter: What do I mean when I describe a structure and say that it is the structure of a narrative, or when I give an interpretation of a pattern of evaluation and say that it is the evaluation of the narrative?

First, we must realize that all texts, spoken as well as written, admit of many readings and are socially expected to admit of many readings. To take a simple example, we recognize that, in any three-party conversation, any two participants will differ at least slightly in their interpretations of what the third party has said. In fact, this is a social resource, since it permits interaction to continue without exact agreement, which is certainly a rare commodity. In the area of written language, for example, my reading of the poem "Sailing to Byzantium" will not be the same as yours, and we may derive pleasure and profit from a comparison of the differences. Literary theory has, at this point, entirely exploded the possibility or even the desirability of arriving at an interpretation that can be said to be the author's intended meaning. In the area of psychological interpretation, Freud has spoken of the "overdetermination" of utterances as the property that permits puns, jokes, dreams, slips of the tongue, and psychoanalysis.

We may then ask what can keep us from drowning in a sea of equally possible interpretations of any text. What prevents this is the fact that, as social actors, we make interpretations for a particular purpose within the constraints of a particular social world. As analysts, we might wish for an absolute standpoint from which to interpret, but because we are members of a social world, our interpretations must be shaped by our needs and intentions. "So sor- so very glad to be here" will be interpreted in one way by a hostess who believes that she needs to keep her party going, and in another way by a psychoanalyst who believes that she needs to understand her patients' "deep" motivations. Neither interpretation is more privileged than the other, and neither interpretation invalidates the other; both are valid within the social world and the necessities of their interpreter.

What is true for the participant in a social situation is equally true for the investigator studying a text now abstracted from its original social context. The investigator cannot hope to come up with a single correct interpretation, but can attempt to produce one or more interpretations that will be adequate for the analytic purposes of the investigation. Furthermore, the situation of an academic interpreter who studies a text now abstracted from its social context differs less than one might think from the situation of a participant who produces interpretations within the social context. Even for the academic investigator, the process of interpretation is part of an ongoing process of social dialectic. Any interpretation I propose is open to the criticism, revision, and destruction of other workers who are sufficiently interested in the questions I have proposed or the texts I have offered to engage themselves seriously with those texts. Such criticism will be based on principles that can be used more or less objectively to judge potential interpretations: internal consistency, plausibility, faithfulness to evidence, and coherence with other texts of the same sort. Therefore, although many interpretations of a text are possible, not all interpretations can withstand the process of criticism. Moreover, not all interpretations are equally rich in interesting directions for further research. But although this process will eliminate some interpretations, we cannot expect it to enable us to select a single correct interpretation.

Even though we have abandoned the notion of a single correct interpretation, we still have recourse to principles of interpretation. Our interpretations are constrained by the text and by specific features of it; they are not solely produced by the whim of the investigator. As interpreters, we can be precise about the description of what in the text suggests a particular reading; here, all the resources of linguistic theory are potentially of use for discourse analysis. We can also be precise about the scope of a particular claim: is some interpretation to be taken as true of this narrative, of all narratives about professional choice, of all middle-class American narratives, or of all possible narratives?

This precision on the part of the investigator is possible exactly because interpretation is equally possible and necessary for the speaker and the addressee in a given social situation. Discourses are structured in order to communicate and to allow for the negotiation of multiple meanings. And to the extent that they succeed, they succeed both for the participants, who are imbedded within the speech situation, and for the investigator, who steps outside the immediate speech situation but necessarily brings along his or her member's competence.

# 4

# Narrative and
# the Iconicity of the Self

Thus far, we have looked at the life story as a common notion in our culture, and we have defined it as a technical term. Subsequently, we considered theories and methods for studying language at the discourse level and for eliciting and studying this particular discourse unit. This preliminary work has laid the foundation for investigating the main issues of this study, which are the questions of how people formulate their life stories in an acceptably coherent way and why the establishment of such coherence is so important. In this chapter, we will discuss the function of narrative in the establishment of the self, laying out the properties of the self that are constructed by various aspects of narrative structure and by the social process of narrative exchange.

Narrative is among the most important social resources for creating and maintaining personal identity. Narrative is a significant resource for creating our internal, private sense of self and is all the more a major resource for conveying that self to and negotiating that self with others. We may now ask why this should be so. Why is narrative so effective in creating and maintaining the self? To sketch an answer to this question, let us begin by considering the nature of the self that is constructed, and then turn to the nature of narrative. In other words, let us first take up the qualities or characteristics of the self that the narrative creates and maintains, and then investigate how various aspects of narrative structure contribute to creating just this type of self. Such an inquiry will lead us to ask, what kind of a self is recognized as a self in this culture, and how do people go about making it?

Again, we are concerned with the self within a particular culture, since different cultures appear to have different resources for creating an approved type of self, and since they seem to use them to create different types of self. For example, in an argument mentioned in Chapter 2, Geertz (1983*b*) discusses differences in the Javanese and Moroccan constructions of self, in the course of arguing that the anthropologist comes to understand other cultures not through a quasi-mystical process of communion with others, but through an understanding of the particular linguistic and cultural resources that each culture deploys. Thus, he shows that Javanese and Moroccan Arabic use different kinds of terms for identifying people, and that these linguistic differences are the building blocks of different understandings of what a person is.

In considering this question of the qualities of the self we create, we will consider theories drawn from psychology and from the theory of autobiography, since these fields have paid closest attention to the nature and structure of the self. We will ask only what kind of self is created by narration—that is, what qualities of the self are supported by language. We will not consider (except to exclude) aspects of the self that are created and maintained nonlinguistically. And being prudent people, we will certainly not discuss here why a self is desired or created at all, since this is a question whose answer must come from philosophical analysis or religious experience—not from an analysis of the language used to create a self.

## Psychological Theories of the Self

We may look to psychology for an attempt at a complete description of the various aspects of the self, both linguistic and nonlinguistic, and of how the self develops over the life course. Stern (1985) discusses the development of the sense of self in the infant, and how its various characteristics develop. The following passage indicates the aspects of the social self, both nonverbal and verbal, and the kinds of psychological disturbances characteristic in the adult who has not accomplished this work:

> Such senses of the self include the sense of agency (without which there can be paralysis, the sense of non-ownership of self-action, the experience of loss of control to external agents); the sense of physical cohesion (without which there can be fragmentation of bodily experience, depersonalization, out-of-body experiences, derealization); the sense of continuity (without which there can be temporal disassociation, fugue states, amnesias, not "going on being," in Winnicott's term); the sense of affectivity

(without which there can be anhedonia, dissociated states); the sense of a subjective self that can achieve intersubjectivity with another (without which there is cosmic loneliness or, at the other extreme, psychic transparency); the sense of creating organization (without which there can be psychic chaos); the sense of transmitting meaning (without which there can be exclusion from the culture, little socialization, and no validation of personal knowledge). (pp. 7–8)

Erikson (1962, 1969) has stressed adolescence as the particular time when a coherent sense of self must be developed, describing this need as the *identity crisis*, a notion and a phrase that has become incorporated into popular psychology. In his 1962 book, Erikson makes the following comments about identity and the identity crisis:

I have called the major crisis of adolescence the *identity crisis*; it occurs in that period of the life cycle when each youth must forge for himself some central perspective and direction, some working unity, out of the effective remnants of his childhood and the hopes of his anticipated adulthood; he must detect some meaningful resemblance between what he has come to see in himself and what his sharpened awareness tells him others judge and expect him to be. . . . In some young people, in some classes, at some periods of history, this crisis will be minimal; in other people, classes, and periods, the crisis will be clearly marked off as a critical period, a kind of "second birth," apt to be aggravated either by widespread neuroticisms or by pervasive ideological unrest. (p. 14)

The sense of identity, which is not wanting in most adults, prevents such feelings of panic [caused by the realization of the possibility of one's own nonexistence]. To be adult means among other things to see one's own life in continuous perspective, both in retrospect and in prospect. By accepting some definition as to who he is, usually on the basis of a function in an economy, a place in the sequence of generations, and a status in the structure of society, the adult is able to selective reconstruct his past in such a way that, step for step, it seems to have planned him, or better, he seems to have planned it. (pp. 111–12)

We turn now to major characteristics of the self that are specifically maintained and exchanged through language. We will consider three such characteristics: continuity of the self, particularly continuity of the self through time; relation of the self to others; and reflexivity of the self, or treatment of the self as other, including moral evaluation of the self.

First, the kind of self we recognize as a self should have continuity through time. There should be a relation, though not a complete identity, between Charlotte in 1965 and Charlotte in 1993. Further, the past should be not only related to but relevant to the present; that is, the

1) Content not mentioned } narrative
    presupposition.

self should be continuous—legato rather than staccato. A proper or comfortable self is *not* a pointillist self, consisting of isolated moments of experience that may be remembered but do not touch or influence one another. As we shall see, this aspect of continuity and relevance of the self through time is established in narrative by the narrative presupposition.

Stern (1985) points out that the sense of continuity is partially created and supported by processes other than language, since what he calls a self-history—a continuity of memory through time—develops very early, as early as three months. However, this is a *sense* of self, rather than a knowledge or awareness that one has a history. The later developmental achievement of a linguistically expressible history is our concern. The more developed adult awareness of one's history and its shape is discussed in autobiographical theory by Olney (1972), who treats it as an achievement of the autobiographer, rather than as a fact about the self that is automatically given. He traces the beginning of this line of thought to the pre-Socratic philosopher Heraclitus, whom he views as anticipating the entire history of autobiographical theory. Heraclitus argues that the world is in flux both internally and externally; the same man cannot step into the same stream twice, and this is true because of changes both in the man and in the stream. But despite this flux, there is a oneness or integrity of the self, and the work of the individual is to come to realize this oneness.

The ability to perceive or create a sense of historical continuity is an achievement of a normal personality. Multiple personality disorders represent an extreme disturbance in the sense of continuity of the self and in the reliability of this continuity—that is, in one's confidence about waking up tomorrow the same person as one was yesterday. In such disorders, continuity of memory of events may extend across several personality fragments, or different memories may be distributed exclusively to different fragments. In either case, what is absent is a sense of the continuity of the self (Braun 1988; Schreiber 1982).

The extent of the continuity of the self is culturally determined. For cultures that believe in reincarnation, the self may be seen as continuous over more than one lifetime, at least for the class of persons who have legitimate access to that kind of memory. (For example, in Indian and Tibetan traditions, while everyone is thought to be subject to rebirth, only persons of considerable spiritual advancement are normally assumed to be able to remember their previous births.)

The second property of the self that is created by narrative is the distinguishability of the self from others, such that it is different and unique but at the same time related to others. This property is established linguistically on several levels and in several ways. At the most basic level, it is created by the existence of linguistic markers that formally establish the distinctions between persons. This is a universal feature of language; all known languages have such markers. The property of distinguishability is also established by the social and interactive nature of narration itself: a narrative is not a soliloquy; it is told to someone, and it must elicit some response from its addressee.

The precise nature of the individual's distinguishability from and relation to others has been radically altered by discussions in feminist psychological and literary theory. Earlier discussions of the nature of the self focused only on the distinction of the self from others—the heroic individual against the world. Weintraub (1978) discusses the historical development of autobiography in Western culture as a move from an exclusive reliance on exemplars of the ideal personality to a conception of the unique individual. The exemplar is an ideal of a great personality that embodies the values of a given culture. The individual model views the self as unique and undefinable by general models of the ideal life. Thomas à Kempis's *Imitatio Christi* assumes that the task of self-formation can best be done by imitating a lofty model. In contrast, modern autobiography employs, implicitly or explicitly, a model of the value of the differences between individuals, so that a person's task of self-formation becomes one of actualizing the only authentic mode of being that is possible for that person.

Gusdorf (1980) makes a more radical point, arguing that only in certain specific historical and cultural situations can a person be said to have a self at all. Autobiography as a genre appears to be a Western form and expresses a Western concern with the singularity of the individual life. In most cultures, he argues, the individual is defined in relation to the community, rather than outside or in opposition to it; thus, the basic unit is not the individual but the community. In such cultures, autobiography is not a conceivable genre, because a sense of the self as such does not exist.

This argument implies that only certain historical and material conditions permit the creation of the individualized self. Accordingly, not all people in all circumstances can attain to the individualized self. Considerable research has been done to show the history of the rise of this conception (Misch 1973; Weintraub 1978; Olney 1972).

More recently, feminist critics have argued that this theory of the individualized self is impossible to apply to women's experience of the self, and that (as Weintraub himself suggests) the theory may be dangerous if it is viewed as the sole tool for understanding men's experience of the self. Specifically, while this view may describe an idealized version of privileged white male experience, it leaves women, people of color, and marginalized groups of all kinds without a self or with a self that is deficient when compared to the normative self. Friedman (1988) summarizes this argument:

> A woman cannot, Rowbotham (1973) argues, experience herself as an entirely unique entity because she is always aware of how she is being defined *as woman*, that is, as a member of a group whose identity has been defined by the dominant male culture. Like Lacan, Rowbotham uses the metaphor of mirror to describe the development of woman's consciousness. But her mirror is the reflecting surface of cultural representation into which a woman stares to form an identity: "The prevailing social order stands as a great and resplendent hall of mirrors. It owns and occupies the world as it is seen and heard." That mirror does not reflect back a unique, a category that is supposed to define the living woman's identity.
>
> The cultural hall of mirrors—the repositories of representation—does not reflect back a unique individual when a man stands before its mirrors either. The cultural categories MAN, WHITE, CHRISTIAN, and HETEROSEX-UAL in Western societies, for example, are as significant for a man of the dominant group as they are for a woman at the margins of culture. Isolate individualism is an illusion. It is also the privilege of power. A white man has the luxury of forgetting his skin color and sex. He can think of himself as an individual. Women and minorities, reminded at every turn in the great cultural hall of mirrors of their sex or color, have no such luxury. Quoting Georg Simmel . . .
>
>> If we express the historic relation between the sexes crudely in terms of master and slave, it is part of the master's privileges not to have to think continuously of the fact that he is the master, while the position of the slave carries with it the constant reminder of his being a slave. It cannot be overlooked that the woman forgets far less often the fact of being a woman than the man of being a man.
>
> The emphasis on individualism as the necessary precondition for autobiography is thus a reflection of privilege, one that excludes from the canons of autobiography those writers who have been denied by history the illusion of individualism. (pp. 38–39)

In an argument in psychological theory, Chodorow (1974) has claimed that the definition of the self differs for women and for men, because women are the primary caretakers of infants and young children in all known cultures. Therefore, girls have the example of their mothers in relation to themselves as a model of how to be, while boys must move away from their primary relation in order to enter into the world of men. Because of this, women form their understanding of the self much more as being based on relations with others and much less as being based on distinguishability of the self from others, while for men it is just the opposite. Gilligan (1982) uses this argument that the understanding of the self and its relation to others differs for men and women to discuss the development of moral understanding in children and adolescents; she argues that this difference leads to important differences in understanding of values, what it means to be a good person. For a woman, she argues, moral value lies in sensitivity to others' needs and others' points of view. This means that women must define themselves relationally, rather than individually or oppositionally. Women have been defined and judged as nurturers, caretakers, and helpmeets of men, but these roles and concerns are seen as secondary in psychological theories of men's development. In these theories, individual achievement is equated with maturity, while concern with relationships is seen as psychological weakness.

Eckert (1990) has discussed these gender differences and the kinds of discourses that arise from them in terms of economic roles:

> The origins of gender differences in styles of interaction can be traced to the traditional roles that relegate women to the domestic realm and men to the economic marketplace, and while these roles have changed to some extent in our society, the social norms and the norms of interaction that they have created remain to complicate and thwart social change. . . . While a man's personal worth is based on the accumulation of goods, status and power in the marketplace, a woman's worth is based on her ability to maintain order in, and control over, her domestic realm. Deprived of power, women can only gain compliance through the indirect use of a man's power, or through the development of personal influence.
>
> Men's power can be used indirectly by winning men's cooperation through social manipulation, or by borrowing men's status through the display and exploitation of connections with men. It is not, therefore, surprising that women are more concerned with the shape of their social networks, with their connections to people in those networks, and with their ability to understand and influence people. While it is frequently said that women are more status conscious than men, it would be more accurate to say that they are more status *bound*.
>
> Actual personal influence without power requires moral authority. In other words, women's influence depends primarily on the accumulation of symbolic capital on the painstaking creation and elaboration of an image of the whole self as worthy of authority. This is not to say that men are not dependent on the accumulation of symbolic capital, but that symbolic capi-

tal is the *only* kind that women can accumulate with impunity. And indeed, it becomes part of their men's symbolic capital and hence part of the household's symbolic capital. While men can justify and define their status on the basis of their accomplishments, possessions, or institutional status, women must justify and define theirs on the basis of their overall character and the kinds of relations they can maintain with others. (pp. 3–4)

We may caricature these two views of the self as Prometheus versus the Angel in the House. Although they have each been assigned as appropriate for one gender, in fact, both are extremes; no individual uses one strategy exclusively. In oral narrative, as we shall see, both properties — distinctiveness and relation to others — are important, and both are established by the characteristics of narrative and the act of narration.

Finally, a self that we can recognize as a functioning social self should have the property of reflexivity. That is, it should function as one self among many similar selves, so that it can be reflected on, or related to as an other.

The nature of the process of narration contributes to the creation of this reflexivity, because one can never immediately speak the present in the present. This necessarily creates a distinction between the narrator and the protagonist of the narrative, and interposes a distance between them. Consequently, the narrator can observe, reflect, adjust the amount of distance, and correct the self that is being created. The very act of narrating creates the occasion for self-regard and editing.

The most pervasive way in which the self is treated as an other is in the determination of the moral value of the self. Not only must the self be related to others, it must be related properly. The classic statement of this aspect of the self is given by Mead (1934), who discusses the ways in which the self incorporates the norms of the society, both in its own self-conception and in its estimation of the probable responses and judgments of others:

> The organized community or social group which gives to the individual his unity of self may be called "the generalized other." The attitude of the generalized other is the attitude of the whole community. Thus, for example, in the case of such a social group as a ball team, the team is the generalized other in so far as it enters — as an organized process or social activity into the experience of any one of the individual members of it.
>
> If the given human individual is to develop a self in the fullest sense, it is not sufficient for him merely to take the attitudes of other human individuals toward himself and toward one another within the human social process, and to bring that social process as a whole into his individual experience merely in these terms: he must also, in the same way that he

takes the attitudes of other individuals toward himself and toward one another, take their attitudes toward the various phases or aspects of the common social activity or set of social undertakings in which, as members of an organized society or social group, they are all engaged; and he must then, by generalizing these individual attitudes of that organized society or social group itself, as a whole, act toward different social projects which at any given time it is carrying out, or toward the various larger phases of the general social process which constitutes its life and of which these projects are specific manifestations. This getting of the broad activities of any given social whole or organized society as such within the experiential field of any one of the individuals involved or included in that whole is, in other words, the essential basis and prerequisite of the fullest development of that individual's self: only in so far as he takes the attitudes of the organized social group to which he belongs toward the organized co-operative social activity or set of activities in which that group as such is engaged, does he develop a complete self or possess the sort of complete self he has developed. (pp. 154–55)

The structure, then, on which the self is built is this response which is common to all, for one has to be a member of a community to be a self. Such responses are abstract attitudes, but they constitute just what we term a man's character. They give him what we term his principles, the ac-knowledged attitudes of all members of the community toward what are the values of the community. He is putting himself in the place of the generalized other, which represents the organized responses of all the members of the group. It is that which guides conduct controlled by principles, and a person who has such an organized group of responses is a man whom we say has character, in the moral sense. (pp. 162–63)

Mead here suggests that being a good self is essential to being a social self at all. As we shall see, this aspect of the self is created by the evaluation component of narrative and through the social negotiation of evaluation.

Let us now consider in detail the ways in which narrative structure gives rise to these desired properties of the self.

### Temporal Continuity of the Self and the Narrative Presupposition

Temporal continuity of the self is built into the very fabric of narrative, since (as we have seen) the defining characteristic of the narrative is its reliance on the principle of narrative order. Hence, the skeleton of any narrative is the sequence of past-tense main clauses, whose order is taken to match the order of events as they are presumed to have happened. This technical definition is completely in accord with the generally held, folk notion of a story: a story has a beginning, middle, and end, and is properly told in that order. Without a sequence of events, we do not have a story. We may have something—a description, an explanation, a mood piece—but we do not have a story.

To illustrate the functioning and the strength of the narrative presupposition, consider the following two examples:

1. I got flustered and I backed the car into a tree.
2. I backed the car into a tree and I got flustered.

In example 1, we as readers or hearers assume that getting flustered preceded backing into the tree, in the actual sequence of events; while in example 2, we assume that it followed backing into the tree.

Narrative is thus structured around temporal sequence and the assumption that temporal sequence is a relevant dimension of understanding. From this, we can easily derive the notion that the past is relevant and connected to the present. This connection of the past to the present may even be established formally by the inclusion of the coda—the optional part of narrative structure that may be employed to bring the story up to the present or up to a later period of time. For example, consider a coda we saw in Chapter 3:

3. We really didn't intend to live there very long but we lived there four and a half years I believe it was before we moved.

Thus we may say that in its mirroring of the characteristics of the kind of self we want to have, temporal continuity—or identity of the self through time—is the most basic form of coherence we can create.

It might be argued that the existence and primary relevance of temporal sequence constitute facts about human thought rather than facts about language or about a particular language. However, we may perhaps more appropriately understand temporal sequence as being a consequence of the morphological structure of certain (but not necessarily all) languages, rather than as being a cognitive universal. Certainly, this is a more parsimonious hypothesis, and it should at least be considered.

At the most fundamental level, the coherence we are able to achieve is dictated by our language and by the resources it makes available to us. This is an obvious statement if we take it to mean that we can most easily recognize objects and events for which our language has names. But a deeper look at the use we make of the resources of our language shows that a direct connection exists between the categories of the language and the ways in which texts can be structured.

Any language contains obligatory morphological categories—categories that must be marked in every sentence. Thus, in English, verb tense and noun number are obligatory categories; all verbs must be marked for tense and all nouns must be marked for singular or plural (with a few exceptions). Other categories, which are obligatory in other languages, such as evidentiality marking of verbs, are not obligatorily present in English. We can indicate the nature of the evidence that leads us to assert a particular proposition, but the grammar of English does not require us to do so. In contrast, many languages require that the speaker mark whether the information being conveyed is a piece of direct experience, of inference, of universally known truth, or whatever the categories of that language may be. (Chafe and Nichols [1986] provide a cross-linguistic survey of this phenomenon.)

The obligatory categories of a language are generally assumed by the speakers of that language to be iconic; that is, we assume that the existence of past, present, and future is a fact about the way the world is, not a fact about the English language. This is the basic argument of the Sapir-Whorf hypothesis: categories that have been assumed by Western philosophy to be universals of human thought are actually categories of the Indo-European languages. (Carroll [1991] offers a review of this hypothesis.) The naive assumption is that, with regard to time, English mirrors the world, rather than creating it. Only when we look at other languages, which have different obligatory categories for verb marking, do we see that this assumption does not hold for all languages.

Of the obligatory categories of a language, some (but not all) are used to structure discourse. These discourse-structuring categories exert the most influence in establishing the epistemology of the speakers of that language. For example, In English, number is an obligatory category of nouns. Whenever we use a noun, we must indicate whether we mean a **book** or **books**, a **child** or **children**. A few exceptional nouns, like **sheep** and **fish**, are not explicitly marked for singular and plural; and a whole class of nouns, called mass nouns, like **rice** and **justice**, can only be singular. But the overwhelming majority of nouns in English must be marked for singular or plural. Nonetheless, number is not a text-structuring device in English: we do not conventionally build discourses with parallel structures exploring the singular and plural aspects of an issue. Number is taken as iconic, that is, the universe is assumed to break naturally into categories of one and more than one, but this fact is not used as a conventional text-structuring strategy.

To see what such an approach is like, let us look at a Burmese example in which number and its subcategorizations are used to structure texts. In Burmese, numeral classifiers are an obligatory category; that is, every time a noun is modified by a numeral, the phrase must include a classifier that indicates what kind of noun is involved. A somewhat analogous construction in English, which may serve to give a flavor of this grammatical form, is the use of classifiers for mass nouns. Thus, if we wish to count mass nouns, we must add a classifier—two chunks of chocolate, three heaps of rice, four acts of justice. The classifiers **chunk, heap,** and **act** form an implicit categorization system for the relevant qualities of mass nouns.

In Burmese, these classifiers are used as the basis for a systematic understanding of what kinds of object exist in the universe (Becker 1975). For example, encyclopedias are published that classify all objects into sets of two, sets of three, sets of four, and so on. These represent a taxonomy of the Burmese universe. The encyclopedias, and the structures they present, are not simply philosophical categorizations; according to Becker, they form the basis of texts, as well:

> Each set in itself is a structure—a kind of plot from a universal plot book—around which to guild a discourse. That is, a sermon is built around, say, the four cardinal virtues (love, attention, happiness, indifference), a political speech around, for instance, the three kinds of mistakes (those resulting from lack of memory, from lack of planning ahead, or from misguided beliefs), and a play around some other appropriate set, perhaps the four false hopes (hoping to get rich by reading treasure maps, hoping to get healthy by reading medical literature, hoping for wisdom by following a learned man, and hoping for a girlfriend by dressing up). These sets are assumed *a priori* to any discourse as impersonal structures to which nature, both human and non-human, properly and appropriately corresponds. A true sermon, a wise foreign policy, or a well-constructed drama will be rooted in one or more of them. (pp. 109–10)

The reader may object that this form of text structuring is found in English and other Western languages, in the tradition of sermons structured around the Seven Deadly Sins or the Seven Cardinal Virtues. But this is a very specialized tradition with a limited number of numbered sets, and it is not available for use by the average speaker. In contrast, the Burmese example forms the basis for a wide variety of texts, usable by a wide variety of people.

In summary, every language has a wide variety of obligatory grammatical categories. Of these obligatory categories, some are generally taken to be iconic—facts about the nature of the world, rather than facts about the particular language. Of these iconic categories, some are taken as the basis for structuring texts. As we have already seen, one of the most basic text-structuring strategies in English is the narrative presupposition of event sequence, which is marked by verb tense.

It has been argued that narrative is, indeed, iconic—that it mirrors the necessary structure of human thought, rather than mirroring the categories and resources of given languages. But we have a report of at least one language that does not rely on narrative presupposition to do the organizational work it does in English and other Western languages. This is Javanese, which uses entirely different principles of text structuring than the ones that some Western theorists believe to be universal. In his study of Javanese shadow plays (*wayang*), Becker (1980) has shown that this art form does not follow the temporal and causal constraints of Western narrative. Rather, it is organized by place and by coincidence. The organizing principles of the plot of a shadow theater piece, stated by contrast to Western expectations, are as follows:

1. The plot can begin at any point in time. It has no temporal beginning, middle, or end. It must, however, begin and end in certain places; it cannot begin and end anywhere, although it can begin and end anytime. It must begin and end in a court—the first the court of the antagonists, and the last the court of the protagonists. The middle section must be in nature, usually in forest or on a mountain but sometimes in or beside the sea.

2. Coincidences, far from being avoided, impel action, for they induce cognitive puzzles or paradoxes. Coincidences are the way things happen, and the way communication between unlikes occurs. In Javanese and Indonesian, the word used to describe what we call a coincidence (a causeless interaction) is *kebetulan*, literally a "truth."

3. Any scene in a *wayang* plot may be transposed or omitted, except for the constraint that the plot begin in a court, have its center in nature, and return to the court. Transpositions and omissions of story material do not destroy or even change the whole; anything can be left out or brought in.

This is clearly very different from any Western notion of a plot. It is true that some experimental writers in the West (for example, Joyce, Faulkner, and Robbe-Grillet) have exploited the omnipotence of the narrative presupposition by bending or even breaking it. But the shadow theater is not an avant garde or even an elite form of entertainment in Java; its position in the culture closer to the position of a soap opera than it is to the position of *Finnegans Wake*. Further, the organization of the shadow play is not an isolated case; similar coherence strategies are used in other traditional Javanese discourse types, although the colonial influence of Dutch (and more recently, English) has relegated these to a position of secondary importance.

Returning to the narrative presupposition in English, we should have learned from our brief trip to Java that this presupposition is not a hard-wired fact about human neurology but rather a language-based strategy. The narrative presupposition also provides another bonus to languages that employ it: not only temporal sequence and temporal continuity, but also causality. From the apparent iconicity of temporal order that the narrative presupposition gives us, we can derive the presupposition of causality. The natural logic of English is *post hoc ergo propter hoc*. To illustrate this, let us return to examples 1 and 2:

1. I got flustered and I backed the car into a tree.
2. I backed the car into a tree and I got flustered.

In example 1, we assume that getting flustered (the earlier event) caused the speaker to back into a tree; while in example 2, we assume that backing into a tree caused the speaker to get flustered. This rather simple example is in fact extremely important, since (as we shall see in Chapter 5) establishing adequate causality is one of the most important tasks for the teller of a life story. In the current discussion, we can see that establishing causality permits the creation of a self whose past is relevant to its present, since events in the self's past can be interpreted as causing present states and events.

## The Self as Separate but Related to Others

Thus far, we have discussed the continuity of the self in time. We now turn to the issues of distinguishing the self from others and of relating the self to others. We will first consider the general properties of language that allow individuals to establish these effects, and then we will turn to the specific properties of oral narrative that fine-tune it.

As we have observed, at the most basic level of the linguistic structure of English, the existence of pronouns establishes the existence of discrete, distinct persons. As far as we know, this is a universal of language; all languages distinguish among different persons who may or may not be participants in the speech situation: the first person (the speaker); the second person or persons (the addressees); and the third person or persons (those not present or not participating in the speech situation). This distinction may be made using pronouns or other forms, such as prefixes or suffixes on verbs; and one of the persons of the system may be distinguished by having no overt grammatical marking. While person systems across languages differ in the distinctions that they make—such as the difference between languages that distinguish between exclusive and nonexclusive "we" and those, like English, that do not—the important point for this discussion is that all languages do distinguish among the persons of the speech situation.

It has been noted, both in psycholinguistics and in clinical psychology, that a crucial stage in the linguistic and psychological development of the child comes with the learning of pronouns (or other markers of person; for convenience in discussion, we will here refer to them as pronouns, since the focus of this study is on English). The critical aspect of person that the child must learn is that pronouns are shifters, in Jakobson's term (Jakobson 1984). That is, **I** is not a name, like **Susie** or **Jack,** that refers to the same person, no matter who uses it. Rather, **I** changes its reference depending on who uses it. To understand this is not merely to understand an arbitrary fact about language use—like the fact that we do not say **childs,** but instead say **children.** To understand the shifter nature of **I** is to come to comprehend that others exist in one's world who have the same nature and who must be seen as separate but fellow beings. This is an important step forward into humanity (Clark 1978). *There are other "I"'s.*

Pronouns are thus a central linguistic resource for establishing the self. Let us now turn to the specific aspects of narrative that further contribute to this process. Oral narrative is an interactive linguistic unit that necessarily requires a relation with one or more addressees. Unlike diaries, narratives are not told for one's own benefit only. (Indeed, even diaries—apparently the most solitary, recipientless form of language use—tend to have an imagined reader: perhaps a friend, perhaps the writer in later life, perhaps some imagined form of posterity. Or the diary itself is sometimes given a name, and addressed as a person.) Narrative as an oral form requires an interlocutor who agrees with the speaker, as we have seen, whether the agreement is immediate or negotiated.

Further, the act of narration itself is a relational act. Even if one is telling a story of one's own life—a story of how, in certain particular circumstances, one acted as a good person or as a person who was wrong but learned what was right—such an act of narration necessarily implicates the addressees. First, narratives of personal experience are frequently told as moral or behavioral *exempla*, suggesting how the addressee should behave in a similar circumstance in his or her life. Studies of women's conversations have suggested that an exchange of narratives constitutes a discussion of different ways of handling a similar situation and may include proposal, argument, and negotiated agreement on the best way to handle a boss, a baby, or a friend who acts in a certain way (Kalcik 1975). (Comparable studies have not yet been done for groups of men, so it is premature to claim, as some have, that this discourse practice is particularly characteristic of women.)

Silberstein (1982) in a study of American courtship stories, has identified the existence of similarities of structure in the way that three generations of a family tell their own and other family members' courtship stories. This suggests that parents' and grandparents' stories serve as a model for children's stories, and possibly even for their behavior in finding a mate. Even when there is no immediate similarity in the circumstances narrated and the addressees' circumstances, the speaker must frame the story in such a way that the addressees feel that they would have acted in the same way, if they had found themselves in those circumstances. In this sense, a narrative that does not immediately bear on its addressees' situation must be framed as the story of Everyman—how any reasonable person would behave—in order to justify taking up the addressees' time and attention with what would otherwise be an alien tale. (I owe this observation to the late Erving Goffman.)

In fact, the types of relations permitted by the narrative are even more complex than this, since they extend not only to relations between the participants in the speech situation, but also to relations reported in the narrative and to relations between the participants in the speech situation and the characters in the narrative. Thus, as we have seen, the narrator is maintaining and extending a relationship with the other participants by the act of narrating. The narrator also indicates his or her relation to the protagonist (of the same name) and to the other characters in the narrative, as well as indicating the relation between these characters. In addition, by their comments on the narrative, the interlocutors may indicate or establish relations with the characters of the narrative.

Thus far, we have discussed establishing relations to others in connection with narratives focused on the actions of the self, which may appear to support the notion of the separate, Promethean self. But other narratives, which may also play a prominent role in one's life story, involve one's actions as a member of a group. Because this constitutes a very important form of establishing relations to others, let us consider some of the ways in which narratives can be used to create group membership for the self and solidarity for the group. To indicate that establishing relations is not exclusively or even primarily a female strategy of narration, I have chosen examples from an entirely male and traditionally masculine context.

These narratives are told during flight missions by the crew members of several different helicopter crews of an airborne law enforcement agency. The data were collected during in-flight video recordings of several weeks of routine law enforcement missions. The participants are the pilot (identified in these narratives as P) and the flight officer (identified as FO). The pilot has control of the operation of the helicopter; the flight officer, who is not a pilot, has control of the police mission. Crew members are not kept together as teams, but since they are drawn from a pool of about eight pilots and eight flight officers, all crew members know one another quite well—especially since many of them participate in a number of popular and well-attended group social activities, such as fishing trips on a chartered boat (advertised as "Pigs at Sea"), that permit all members of the group to create and maintain group solidarity.

These narratives are characteristic of conversation during low-workload periods of the flight missions, such as the return to base after a mission. They are, of course, very different from the entirely operational discourse that characterizes performance of the actual missions (Linde 1988*b*). The examples illustrate progressively more complex and problematic issues in the establishment of group values.

The simplest form of maintaining group values is accomplished through the exchange of narratives about shared interests: fishing, raising horses, vacation plans, and schedule problems:

*narr. exchange of shared interest.*

4. FO: How's uh (pause) Gizmo doin?

   P: Good, good he uh (pause) Sally was gettin' him out ta' exercise him the other day and um get the halter lead rope on him and (pause) comin' through the gate she let the (pause) the uh thing slip you know, and it banged on the on the rest of the corral //FO: Yeah// kinda spooked him and he reared up a little bit and she held him back the first time then um he reared up again and pulled the rope out of her hand and took off a runnin'.

   FO: Oooh.

   P: I was try- we were gonna move him from the little corral over to the dog kennel so he could run around a little bit.

> (pause) And uh I got I got both dogs by the scruff of the neck so they won't take off after him. He comes runnin' by me at a gallop and uh fortunately, neither one of the dogs tried ta' go after him. And uh (pause) I got the dogs put away. (pause) He ran down just about down toward the driveway down toward the r- the road then start comin' back up and was just kinda wanderin' around eatin' at the grass and stuff. I think he was af- he'd stepped on the lead rope a couple of times and was afraid to run //FO: Yeah// cause it was trippin' him up. (pause) Sally got some alfalfa and was trying to coax him over and uh he's keepin' just far enough ahead that you couldn't catch him.

FO: Bein' ornery.

P: Yeah then he uh saw a nice green poisi- poison oak bush and started nibblin' on that so we got him (pause) got a hold of the rope. That's the only, only time he's been real ornery. Sally's been ridin' him bare back 'n . . . (unclear) He's a real good horse so far.

This seems to be a rather simple narrative about a horse misbehaving, rather than a narrative about either the speaker or the addressee. But in spite of its simplicity, it serve to maintain solidarity in a number of ways. First, the flight officer knows that the pilot keeps horses and remembers his new horse's name. This indicates a familiarity and monitoring of the pilot's activities that is characteristic of people in some sort of intimate relation. (*Intimacy* here refers to the intimacy of frequent contact, not necessarily emotional intimacy.)

In addition, the flight officer gives evaluative responses to the pilot's narrative that indicate his own familiarity with horses and demonstrate that he shares this interest: for example, his backchanneled **Ooh** when the horse pulls the rope out of Sally's hand and takes off running; and his evaluation of the horse's running away as **being ornery,** which is an insider's characterization.

At a more complex level of negotiation, team members discuss work-related activities and events and come to immediate agreement on values. For example, a narrative about the difficulty of an airborne pursuit of a plain white car receives an immediate evaluation of agreement from its addressee that that kind of pursuit is indeed difficult. In trying to follow the cast of characters, remember that the second of the following two stories involves both the helicopter crew and several ground car crews:

5a.  P: I think it was me and M were, uh, on a (keeper) out of, uh, (unclear) S County line up by where R lives

FO: Yeah

P: And I . . . It was a, uh, pursuit by the, uh, 281 or 265 from A and, uh, the guy, uh . . . had a, uh, no plates on the, on his Trans Am, rented Trans Am. (They led) him up, then the guy kinda pulled into a, a dirt driveway, parked in a parking lot, uh, a driveway out in front of this guy's house, and then split on foot. So we responded. Last time he saw him he was heading in one direction and he drove around the perimeter, so to speak, to try to head him off at the pass, and, uh, we had evidence that he'd entered into this one house, and they saw that he <u>had</u> been in the house, and they went to the next house and found out that he'd stole a car out of the driveway. We were, we were orbiting for thirty minutes, and no telling when he took that car, ya know. We didn't, we didn't see that car leave, so probably happened while we were en route or-

FO: Yeah

P: Shortly after we got there, ya know, and where we weren't sure of what the location was. That's a problem when you got people living in a place, ya know. You got all those, uh, people moving and vehicles moving. You don't know if it's good guys or bad guys.

FO: Yeah. It's like when you're doing the surveillance with D.O.J.'s [drug surveillance with Department of Justice officers]. You've really got to concentrate to keep, to keep that car

5b.  P: Yeah G was, was funny. One time we were two thousand feet up, you know, and coming through the interchange, 99 and uh 50, and there's . . . we're following a white car, or something incredibly plain like that. G looks down at the . . . looks away for a second, looks back up and there were <u>five</u>, no less than <u>five</u> of the same color vehicle (FO laughs) Same, same basic shape and everything. (FO laughs) He goes "Stop. I, I can't, I don't know which one it is. You, you watch, see which way that one goes. You see which way that one goes," and he managed to get the guys [in a police car] who were following him, one of 'em

in close enough to positively say it was the right vehicle.
(FO laughs) And meanwhile somebody else [in a police
car] is going mach three down (south) with the other one
that looked kind of like that

FO: Yeah, the white one or silver one, it seems like
P: Yeah
FO: (unclear) and stuff

A number of points can be made about this sequence of narratives.
First, both are about the difficulties of pursuit from the air. The first
focuses on how hard it is to pursue a suspect in a peopled area. The
second involves the difficulties of following a common and nondistinc-
tive kind of car. The flight officer agrees with the pilot's evaluation of
both stories. In the first, he offers a comparison to show that he understands how hard that kind of pursuit is:

F: Yeah. It's like when you're doing the surveillance with D.O.J.'s.
You've really got to concentrate to keep, to keep that car

In the second story, he indicates his comprehension of the story by his
laughter and by his indication that the car that "looked kind of like that"
was in fact "the white one or the silver one."

This narrative is not just a matter of abstract agreement on job difficulties, although that would itself have a beneficial effect on group solidarity. Rather, the context of its telling makes it particularly effective
for continuing good relations between the two crew members. It was in
fact told on a return to base after the crew had failed to find a suspect,
who had escaped on foot. Therefore, the stories bear tremendous relevance to the present situation, contextualizing a failure as the kind of
thing that inevitably happens—not because of the incapacity of the crew,
but because of the inherent difficulty of the task. The relevance is contex-
tual, rather than explicit, and hence is all the more effective, since it
excuses failure without mentioning it.

The most complex type of negotiation occurs when there is uncertainty
about whether values are shared, and about what values should be held
in an ambiguous situation. The following example is a narrative about a
ground pursuit of a provocatively lawless motorcyclist, which involves
negotiating what constitutes unacceptable behavior on the part of a motorcyclist, and what constitutes a legitimate response on the part of the
police:

6. FO: I have a solution for those guys [re: prior narrative about "this guy [who] was a local doper and all that good stuff."]

   (Both gesture as if shooting a gun).

   P: Heh-heh.

   FO: Or if they want a chase when you get the opportunity just tap 'em with a push bumper at ninety miles an hour //P: Yeah// let 'em go for the ride.

   P: Yep, a little road rash.

   FO: A lot of road rash.

   FO: I'll never forget this one we had in Midville. We had this guy on uh um it was a Kawasaki, one of those nine hundreds or whatever it was. //P: Yeah// We got in a pursuit of this guy and he went off the freeway; it was one of those kind of there's about four motorcycles speedin' and he's the one that split off to the side street and really gunned it and took off so we decided to chase him instead of takin' the other three. //P: Yeah// The pursuit's on, I'm a, it's, we're workin' graveyard and my partner's drivin' and we take the guy on the straight aways but he, he was killin' us on the curves //P: Yeah// Well, he got on this, the uh, an expressway and we finally got up to him and every time we'd get close enough to read the license plate this guy is smart enough he'd hit his brakes and make us back off //P: Yeah// So we're so busy ya'know we couldn't ever get his license number and every, we did this about 4 or 5 times and finally got off on another city street and hittin' curves and all that stuff, and we're just kind of got a straight away and we're startin' to catch up with him and I, I mean, we'd been chasin' this guy ten, fifteen minutes, and I said to my partner I said next time he, he hits his brakes just nail the son of a bitch //P: Heh-heh// O.K. son of a gun if he didn't hit his brakes and my partner not listening to me he hit the brakes but we chased the guy and the brakes had gotten hot and were fading //P: Yeah, yeah// he hit his brakes and we didn't lock up we just kinda rolled into him //P: Yeah// and tapped him just enough bike went this way and he I mean he just dropped right on the ground //P: Yeah// but the bike went on up the road and I looked over at my partner and I said "You really did it" (laughter) He said "No" (laughter) but uh you shoulda' seen the look on the guy's face when we nailed him in the bush finally //P: Yeah// all it did was bend the rear fender //P: Yeah// of the bike and uh I think we flattened his rear tire or something.

P: Yeah, it doesn't take much to knock a guy over on a bike.

FO: No.

FO: Then, of course, the dummy wanted to get up and run, ya'know kinda draggin' one leg, limpin' a little //P: Yeah, yeah// he's got road rash on the knee. So ah the wrestlin' match is on so we all felt better at the end.

P: Yeah.

There is a moral ambiguity and a moral debate in this narrative: whether it is right to knock a motorcyclist over with a car, depending on how provocative his behavior has been. The narrative itself is ambiguous about whether in fact the officers in the car intentionally or accidentally knocked the cyclist over. Let us look at the moral points made on both sides.

**Point 1. The action was right:** This is established in a number of ways. The story is told in the context of a previous narrative about a local doper, suggesting that cyclists are likely also to be dopers. The flight officer suggests that when a cyclist is going 90 miles per hour, it is correct to **"just tap 'em with a push bumper."** The pilot agrees, evaluating this with the humorous and mitigating phrase **"a little road rash,"** a term common among cyclists. The cyclist is described as provocative: he split from his group, he really gunned it, and he was smart enough to hit his brakes every time the police came close enough to read his license plates. Because of this provocation, the speaker suggested to his partner, who was driving: **"next time he, he hits his brakes, just nail the son of a bitch."** The pilot indicates his agreement with laughter.

**Point 2. The action was unintentional, an analysis suggesting that it was wrong and must be excused in this way.** Several points are made to establish this. Although the speaker suggested that his partner hit the cyclist, his partner is described as not having listened to him when he hit the brakes, and as having struck the motorcycle by accident, not because of the speaker's suggestion. The accident came because the brakes were fading and didn't lock, and therefore it was not the officer's fault that the car rolled into the cyclist. This is stated explicitly in the story, and proved, so to speak, by the exchange of dialogue between the speaker and his partner:

**You really did it. He said "No."**

The pilot's response agrees to the analysis of the action as an accident:

**Yeah, it doesn't take much to knock a guy over on a bike.**

The cyclist is described as first attempting to run away and then trying to fight. This underscores that his behavior was indeed unacceptable, and that he himself knew it. Therefore, the police officers' uneasiness about their action was unwarranted:

**So ah the wrestlin' match is on so we all felt better at the end.**

This narrative is interesting because it uses a single incident to allow the two interlocutors to discuss the central ambiguity of their situation as police officers. They are sworn to stay within the law as they attempt to enforce the law, and yet this is often impossible. Many ethnographic studies have investigated how police bend and sometimes break the law as their only way to enforce it (Meehan 1986; Rubinstein 1973).

The ambiguity inherent in the necessary lawlessness of officers of the law can further be seen in other kinds of narratives that they tell about their life before they became police officers. (Unfortunately, these tales were told during break periods, while the officers were waiting for emergency calls, and were not recorded, since they had no relation to original purpose of the study; consequently, I must rely here on notes and my memory of the types of stories told.) Many stories describe how wild the narrators were as boys, and the kinds of reckless driving and provocation of police they indulged in. Further, the stories suggest that their narrators loved to tell them, almost as if they were in competition with the lawbreakers they now chase.

This narrative perfectly expresses this ambiguity. The fact that the narrative leaves ambiguous the central question of whether or not they intentionally knocked the cyclist over reflects the larger ambiguity of how far the law can and must be broken in order to enforce the law. This narrative thus functions as an extremely effective negotiation of group values in a situation where such values are and will remain ambiguous. We thus see how narrative, both in its expressiveness and in its possibility for ambiguity, can function as a major social resource for creating the self, both in its separateness and in its relation to others.

## Narrative and Reflexivity

Finally, we turn to the property of reflexivity, the ability to relate to oneself externally, as an object or as an other. This property of the self has been noted by researchers in many fields, including psychology, sociology, philosophy, and literary theory. We may now ask why we should want to be able to relate to the self as an other? This question has been asked in many ways, in many fields, and has received many answers. Here, we will sketch those that pertain particularly to narrative. Because of its social function, narrative is crucially involved with the social evaluation of persons and actions; it is always involved in the question of whether an action (and hence an actor) is expected or unexpected, proper or incorrect. Such judgments are not only—indeed, not primarily—external. Each speaker needs to be able to reflect, to judge, perhaps to enjoy the self, and this must be done from a removed standpoint. All questions of "How am I doing?" whether in relation to one's own standards or in relation to the standards of others (if such a distinction can even be made), require the ability to make evaluations, and the evaluations cannot be done by the immediate liver of the life; the task requires a watcher and narrator who is related but not identical.

Further, although narrative allows speakers to present themselves as being one actor among others, there is in fact a radical difference between the experience of the self and the experience of others. First, at a conscious level, everyone believes that he or she has privileged access to his or her own plans, motivations, and intentions, whereas these can only be inferred for others. At a much deeper level, there is a more radical difference—a difference in kind between the experience of the self and the experience of others. In addition to, or perhaps prior to, the self we present in narration, we have a nonlinguistic or nonpresentable experience of consciousness as slippery, shifting from one sense modality to another, ungraspable when we try to touch it, unseeable when we try to swing around fast enough to see it. We experience flashes, textures, smells, pressures, and ghosts of emotion that cannot be languaged. This kind of experience is extremely unlike what we seem to see others experiencing, since that experience is already packaged. Our own internal experience, if we permit ourselves to notice this, is of a self without armor—perhaps without boundaries as definite as we would like—walking around in a world of others who appear to have proper boundaries and effective armor. Hence we may perceive ourselves to be in an alarmingly vulnerable position that must be remedied. And the remedy is to narrate, to create a self as other, replicating our experience of the actual others we seem to experience.

This discontinuity between inner experience and the presented self has been discussed as a central issue by Lacan and his followers. Because of the well-known (and principled) impenetrability of Lacan's style, I here cite a review of his thought (Benstock 1988), rather than a primary source:

> As Jacques Lacan has noted, the "mirror stage" of psychic development that initiates the child into the social community and brings it under the law of the Symbolic (the law of language as constituted through society) serves up a false image of the child's unified "self." This unity is imposed from the outside (in the mirror reflection) and is, in Ellie Ragland-Sullivan's words, "asymmetrical, fictional, and artificial." As Ragland-Sullivan continues, the "mirror stage must, therefore, be understood as a metaphor for the vision of the harmony of a subject essentially in discord" (26–27). The "discord" that gives the lie to a unified, identifiable, coterminous self has been built up out of the images, sounds, and sensory responses available to the child during the first six months or so of its life; it is called the unconscious or that which derives from an experience of "self" as fragmented, partial, segmented, and different. The developing child drives toward fusion and homogeneity in the construction of a "self" (the *moi* of Lacan's terminology) against the effects of division and dissolution. The unconscious is thus not the lower depths of the conscious (as in Olney's description of it) but rather an inner seam, a space between "inside" and "outside"—it is the space of difference, the gap that the drive toward the unity of self can never entirely close. (p. 12)

Developmentally, the emergence of the reflexive self—the self that can see itself as one among others—is an extremely important stage in the development of the child. (For a discussion, see Stern [1989].)

This need for the possibility of reflexivity of the self is to some extent supported by any act of speaking, but it is perhaps most effectively established by narrative. Reflexivity in narrative is created by the separation of the narrator from the protagonist of the narrative. It permits the narrator to observe, reflect, and correct the self that is being created. The act of narrating itself requires self-regard and editing, since, a distance in time and standpoint necessarily separates the actions being narrated from the act of narration. Even in apparently simultaneous narratives, such as sports broadcasts or descriptions of off-stage actions in classical plays that obey the Aristotelian unities, some necessary gap separates the time of action from the time of narration. This is all the more true when the actions narrated are one's own.

Perhaps the most important function of reflexivity is to establish the moral value of the self. People do not want just any objectifiable self; they want a good self, and a self that is perceived as good by others. In a sense, this property follows naturally from the previously discussed property of the self as relational. As soon as the self is seen as existing in relation to others, that relation must be some particular relation. Immediately, the issue of norms, values, and judgments becomes possible, since various relations can be distinguished and, once distinguished, compared and judged.

Within developmental psychology, researchers have shown considerable interest in the development of moral reasoning in children (Kohlberg 1981; Gilligan 1982). Various stages of understanding of moral reasoning have been posited; more recently, scholars have extensively discussed whether the stages of moral reasoning that have been posited as the norm are not stages in the development of a male style of moral reasoning, rather than a description of styles of moral reasoning characteristic of human development as a whole. In any case, this research crucially involves children's abilities to understand stories about moral dilemmas and their abilities to discuss and construct such stories.

Narrative is thus an extremely powerful tool for creating, negotiating, and displaying the moral standing of the self. This is centrally established by the evaluation component of narrative and by the social negotiation of evaluation. As we discussed in Chapter 3, all complete narratives contain various linguistic means for expressing evaluation—that is, for indicating the meanings of events and the view that the addressees should take toward characters. Further, while one might narrate anything within a great range of possible moral values and possible transgressions, the most basic moral proposition, which is contained in some form by all first-person narratives, is "I am a good person." The values and behaviors that constitute being a good person vary enormously, of course, from person to person, from group to group, and from culture to culture, and they are in fact to some extent negotiated, as we have seen, within the process of narration. But although narratives may be told for many reasons and with many points, part of the hidden point of any narrative is to show that the narrator knows what the norms are and agrees with them.

Reflexivity is made possible by narrative most particularly because of the nature of the evaluation possible in first-person narratives. The act of narration itself creates a split between the narrator and the protagonist. It allows the narrator to stand apart from and comment on the actions of the protagonist. Even if the two have the same name and are connected in time, as is the case in first-person narrative, the reflexivity created by the act of narration means that the speaker is always moral, even if the protagonist of the narrative is not. Thus, if a person tells a narrative that indicates that he or she acted badly, the fact that the narrator knows and indicates that the action was not right reveals under-

standing of and allegiance to the norms shared by the speaker and addressees, even if the protagonist did not know them, or was not able to
live up to them at the time. In response to such narratives, a negative
judgment can be brought against the protagonist, but not against the
speaker. A negative judgment of the speaker can be made only in a
narration in which no agreement is reached between the interlocutors, so
that the speaker tells a story presenting an action that the speaker evalu-
ates as good but that the addressees feel is not. Because of narrative's
inherent property of reflexivity and distancing, confession may be good
for the soul, but it is also excellent for the self-image.

Let us consider several narratives from the life story data in which
speakers criticize the actions of protagonists. Example 7 is a narrative
by a manager of technical research projects, in answer to a question
about whether she is satisfied with the course of her career:

7. Well, I think I'm reaching that point in my life where I'm willing
   to, you know, think about (pause) well, sort of think about,
   instead of just drifting with the opportunity. Like this last project, I really (pause) I really got stuck in it. OK. I really had
   wanted to (pause) look around outside XYZ for a job and to see
   what things were available and what I really thought I wanted to
   do. (pause) And then, this (project) came along and I had a lot
   of experience in it and I told the person who was running it that
   I, you know, would join it and help him run it. And then he
   left, so I sort of got stuck with it. And it's been very interesting,
   but I still think that I should have done you know, uh (pause) I
   never intended it last for three years. Which is the same as with
   the speech work. I had never, you know, thought that that was
   going to last for five or six years. (pause) So there's nine years
   of life that I uh (pause)

The speaker characterizes the trajectory of her professional career as
"drifting with the opportunity," and indeed had told several previous
narratives in just these terms. She then says that she had wanted to stop
such drifting, to think clearly about what opportunities were available
to her and what she actually wanted to do. (She had previously explained
that her heart was really in research rather than in management.) But
the ill-conducted protagonist of this narrative continues drifting; she
agrees, without doing such a life review, to work on a project that
ends up taking much longer than she expects it to; and by force of
circumstances, rather than by her own choice, she finds herself managing
the whole thing. The protagonist is presented as a drifter, albeit a drifter

who drifts into some excellent positions; but the narrator, at least, presents the social knowledge that one should be more in control of one's life choices and should make choices consciously rather than by drifting.

Example 8 presents another instance of a speaker telling of similar mistaken actions of the protagonist — a failure to make decisions about his profession. Example 8 takes the form of a narrative followed by an explanation, which is given in answer to a question about whether he felt he had made decisions about his career (as a housing administrator, soon to enter business school):

8.    SPEAKER: No. No, I've fallen into, a lot of st- (pause) um I certainly don't feel I've made decisions about what my profession is. I've very clearly made some decisions about the jobs I've taken. Uh teaching was, the the <u>bank</u>, first of all was no decision at all. I mean sure I said yes to it but I, I was, I was kind of flat out, and I didn't have a whole lot of choice (unclear) speaking. Um

INTERVIEWER: How'd you get that job?

SPEAKER: I wanted to go into movies. And uh I had a job lined up when I graduated from college and it fell through and I was in debt, probably all of four or five hundred bucks but that seemed like a lot of money at the time. I was without a job and uh my girlfriend at the time was the granddaughter of the, was the niece of the chairman of the board of a bank. And the job was there I and took it. I probably shouldn't have. It was probably a mistake to do that. But I did it and (unclear) //Int: Why?// and well I went to New York and I was drafted. I was drafted out of that job and uh so that was the end of it. It lasted ten months. And I moonlighted at the American Place Theater. But um that, so I didn't really make much of a decision there.

I think, that's, that's one way of looking at it. I made a, I made a decision. It was the decision that I didn't like at the time so that's why I, I, I, I have the sense that I was forced into it but there are all kinds of, there are all kinds of psychological things that make you do things at various moments in your life. And uh I think that was a, that point in my life was a particularly weak point, I was, I was at a very vulnerable and, and weakened position and uh not ready to take my destiny into my own hands and roll it up into a ball and say "I'm, you know, I'm taking off." Which is what I should have done. I should have stuck out my thumb, come out here [California] ten years ago. And, which I, which I eventually did but it took me four years to do it.

The narrator has many criticisms to make about the protagonist, both overt and covert. He makes the point that the protagonist did not make a proper decision, that he did not "take my destiny into my own hands and roll it up into a ball and say 'I'm, you know, I'm taking off.'" The irony of this phrase provides additional distance between narrator and protagonist, as does the irony of the narrator's recognizing, as the protagonist does not, that a $500 debt is not a major debt. In addition to showing that he knows better than the protagonist, the narrator also provides some excuse for him, by indicating that he was in a vulnerable position. (We will consider this justification in greater detail in Chapter 6.) Both the narrative and the explanation are well-crafted to show that the narrator is a much more knowledgeable and capable person than the protagonist and probably would not make the same mistakes again. It is exactly the reflexive property of narrative that permits him to establish this evaluation.

# 5

## Coherence Principles: Causality and Continuity

*[handwritten note: Causality:
a) narrative order
b) lexical devices
c) social practice
(negotiated)]*

Chapter 4 demonstrated that temporal order of main clauses—that is, narrative order—represents one of the most fundamental principles for creating English texts. Narrative order is the basis for the two major coherence principles of life stories: causality and continuity. As discussed in Chapter 4, we tend to read causality into the narrative sequence of clauses. There are, of course, other lexical devices for establishing causality—for example, formal markers such as **because, since, therefore,** and **the reason that**. Indeed, English makes it very easy for speakers to set up and for hearers to draw causal inferences. But the morphological/syntactic structure of narrative order is the most basic and pervasive of these resources. We move now from these lexical and syntactic resources, which permit the inference of causality, to the social practice of establishing that the events of one's life have been motivated by adequate causality. We will first examine the issue of adequate causality for a single professional choice. We will then discuss the management of a sequence of more than one profession, a pattern that involves the adequacy of both the causality of the choice of each profession and the continuity between the choices.

We may define adequate causality as a chain of causality that is acceptable by addressees as a good reason for some particular event or sequence of events. In the case of the particular data of this study, establishing adequate causality for a choice of profession means establishing that good reasons exist for the speaker's choice of profession, or showing that, even if the reasons do not look good (or indeed are not good enough) somehow, they still can be seen as acceptable, given special

Causal grounds: (God's will? or,
a) chance. b) common sense c) create. bag?)
128        *Life Stories*
- third or the/determin. is random.

circumstances or special understandings. In particular, correct and sufficient causality requires the narrator to establish that the protagonist
exercised correct and sufficient agency.

The establishment of adequate causality for a given professional
choice or for a sequence of events is both a social and an individual
achievement. There are cultural and subcultural beliefs about the nature
of proper lives, proper sequences of events, and proper reasons for professional choice. As we shall see, the strongest form of adequate reason
for the choice of a profession is character: for example: **I was good at it,
I like that sort of thing.** Similarly we have beliefs about what would
constitute inadequate or frivolous reasons for choosing a career: **I was
in love with a girl who was enrolled in pre-med, so I decided to become
a doctor.** Such reasons are adequate or inadequate depending on how
well they accord with a store of common-sense beliefs about the world
that the speaker and hearer can be assumed to share. The nature of
common-sense beliefs about professional choice will be discussed more
fully in Chapter 7.

In addition to this store of common-sense beliefs, a strong element of
individual creativity contributes to the creation of adequate causality.
The individual speaker's adroitness or ineptness in framing his or her
narrative can also determine whether a given sequence is acceptable to
its addressees. We will investigate this individual aspect of the creation
of adequate causality more fully later in this chapter.

Part of the speaker's task in creating adequate causality is to establish
a chain of causality that is neither too thick nor too thin; that is, the
speaker must give enough causality, but not too much. Too thin an
account suggests that one's life has proceeded at random, without direction. Too thick an account suggests that the speaker implicitly accepts a
deterministic or fatalistic theory of causation. Neither of these extremes
is generally acceptable, and therefore each is subject to correction. Often, the correction is made by the speaker, by following a deterministic
account with an accidental one or vice versa. We may view this process
as a sort of philosophic wobble around a socially determined equilibrium
point, which carefully avoids taking any position to its logical extreme.
If the speaker does not maintain this equilibrium through self-correction,
he or she may be subject to correction by hearers. The data of this
study is not suitable for the collection of examples of other-correction.
However, as discussed in Chapter 1, I have observed examples of it in
spontaneous conversation, with respect to both too accidental and too
deterministic narratives. The addressee may correct accidental stories by
adding further facts about the speaker's history that the hearer happens

to know. The addressee may correct deterministic stories by issuing a direct challenge to the speaker's belief system, such as by asking whether he or she really believes in fate.

This description of the equilibrium point for adequate causality is almost certainly not universal, nor even applicable to all English speakers. For example, observations suggest that for working-class speakers, analyses in terms of fate or destiny are much more common than they are for middle-class speakers. Labov (1972a, 1966) mentions class differences in the extent to which fate or destiny is used in narratives. One may also wonder whether upper-class speakers find it necessary to account for birth into a particular family by appeal means of fate or luck, or whether they assume that birth into a particular family assures an individual of having the family character traits that validate the family's prominence. Maintaining the proper balance of causality seems particular important as an issue for middle-class speakers, who have had some degree of opportunity for professional or class movement and for whom, therefore, fate or determinism on one hand and randomness on the other represent undesirable ways to understand one's professional position, since either would detract from the individual's personal achievement. This area merits a great deal of further research: whether indeed there are such class differences, how these differences relate to particular class positions and class histories, how narratives in cross-class interactions are formulated, and so on.

## Creating Adequate Causality

We will first discuss the creation of adequate causality and then consider the management of inadequate causality. The two forms of adequate causality found in these accounts are character traits and multiplicity of reasons. Let us look at character traits first.

### Character as Adequate Causality

One of the most powerful types of adequate account for choice of profession is character. Speakers usually take character traits as a primitive, using them as obvious causes for career decisions, with no further explanation of how those character traits came about. Thus we find statements like example 1a, which is given by a professor of English literature as the first account of how she arrived at her profession:

1a. **I seemed to be very good in** reading and analyzing books and writing so I became an English major

1b. and from then on since **I knew that I would go as far in whatever I chose as I could possibly go**, getting Ph.D. became a necessity.

This example refers the major choice of the study of literature to two character traits, one explicitly expressed and the other implied but not named. The first is ability, and it is given as a very first account, in example 1a. The second, in example 1b, is determination or ambition. The syntactic form of example 1b shows that the speaker takes her determination as a background assumption to understanding her actions; it is given in the complement sentence of the verb **know**, which in forms like this one presupposes that the speaker believes that the clause following it is true. For example, consider the implications of examples 2 and 3:

2. John thinks he's a genius.
3. John knows he's a genius.

It is clear that the speaker of example 3 believes that it is true that John is a genius (excluding irony). It is not clear what the speaker of example 2 believes; the verb **think** does not presuppose either the truth or falsity of its complement sentence. Thus, in example 1, the speaker presupposes as true that she would of course go as far as she possibly could.

Character traits can be used as an organizing principle for a whole family of accounts. Consider the following sequence, spoken by a production editor:

4. SPEAKER: I've been doing it for years. I started out proofreading and ended up an editorial assistant and it just growed.

INTERVIEWER: And how'd you, how'd you get into the whole field?

SPEAKER: Um I started out freelancing in um, with people that my father knew while I was in college. No, actually, my first proofreading was in summer school, between high school and college.

INTERVIEWER: And how'd you get into it as a full time job?

SPEAKER: It was the thing to do. When I decided not to go into graduate school.

INTERVIEWER: Mm hmm. Why?

SPEAKER: Um, **I always knew I could correct grammar fairly easily and mark things up and then from the first job I got it seemed interesting enough to stay in.**

. . .

But it's just, it was a natural evolution. **I always was nitpicky, I was always good at grammar, um I like to correct things rather than create them. And I'm interested enough in reading and I like to spend the time reading, that at least now that I'm on journals that are even vaguely interesting, it c- it can be a lot of fun.**

. . .

Yeah, It's almost unbroken flow. Also, I mean, being with Bob [her former husband] and correcting, you know, working on *Write-On* magazine with the writers [a magazine that her former husband edited] **I really enjoyed that.**

This speaker's entire narrative demonstrates the adequate causality of her career choice. Her account is structured around the claim that her present profession is the result of a natural evolution, based on her character traits: her nitpickiness, her preference for correction rather than creation, her liking for reading, her ability at grammar. However, this account is not the only one she could have given. Normally, we cannot say anything about alternative accounts that might have been possible, but in this case we can see that the speaker's account contains the materials for a different structuring principle—namely, opportunity based on family connections. She mentions these opportunities: her father knew publishers (because he was a freelance writer); her husband was a writer and editor. But although she mentions these opportunities, she does not use them as the basis for her explanation; they are merely additional facts in an account based on character.

This choice of character over opportunity as a coherence structure is extremely interesting. It seems likely that an explanation rooted within the self and the self's agency, as character traits must be, is preferable to one rooted outside, since an externally based account invites attribution to either accident or determinism.

The opposite principle—citation of lack of opportunity as an account for one's career — is notably absent from the narratives of these middle-class professional speakers. As we have seen, speakers may indicate the presence of certain opportunities, even though they do not use these to structure their accounts. But none mentions restricted opportunities as a reason for professional choice. The only account that comes close to doing this does so in the context of a discussion of the difference between the opportunities open to the speaker (a computer programmer) versus her father's lack of opportunities:

5. And the whole process of finding what it is that gives you your strokes, OK? is not an easy one. Well I don't know, really. I look at somebody like my father who was a CPA because he almost didn't have a choice, you know, coming from the Depression, etc. and what was available and how much schooling he could afford etc. etc. He said, "I didn't think about it, you know, that was open to me and that's what I did." And he loved it. He just loved it. I don't know how, some people seem to be <u>that</u> kind of lucky. He said "I never th-" I can remember talking to him about this whole problem, he said "I never thought about being happy, I thought about eating." You know, um, having that kind of pressure absent from my, I don't know what the key is.

The belief that one is not subject to external limits of opportunity imposed by gender, social class, race, or ethnicity appears to be common to middle-class Americans of the postwar generation. The speakers in the preceding examples are not unusual in their presupposition that professional choice is dictated by personal abilities and degree of psychological health, which either permit one or prevent one from taking advantage of opportunities. This view of a world without politics and without social class has been characterized as typically American and typical of the postwar generation (Lasch 1979; Schur 1976; Sennett 1977).

One final observation may be made on the use of character traits as adequate causality: they appear not to be given as a reason for career choices that the speaker characterizes as unsuccessful. Thus, **I was good at it** is an adequate reason for a successful career choice — that is, for a career that the speaker still follows. But I have not found **I was bad at it** given as a reason in these data for abandoning a career choice. The reasons for unsuccessful choices are either shown to be external — that is, due to circumstances that forced the choice on the speaker — or specifically evaluated as undesirable because of the speaker's character traits. But the speaker's incapacity is never given as a reason. An example of both strategies is given in example 6, which is an explanation by a technical editor of his previous career in physics, a career choice he has already evaluated as unsuccessful:

6. Cause I, I dunno, I thought, at that time my uh motives were mainly uh to be good, you know, to get, to be secure. First of all to get a job, a decent job. At that point it looked like physics would be a good way to do it. And second of all to satisfy my father who thought that uh being in anything like English or history was ridiculous. So uh I, physics was even better than engineering, cause engineering was even more arithmetic, you know, physics at least had some philosophical background to it. So it's kind of a compromise in that direction. **But even so, I didn't like it very much.**

The speaker attributes his choice of physics to three external motives — motives not directly related to character traits that would tend to make a choice of career successful. These are to be good, to be secure, and to satisfy his father. The subsequent direct evaluation that the choice was wrong is given in terms of internal states: **But even so, I didn't like it very much.**

We find a similar pattern in the account given by the computer programmer of her previous career as a social worker:

7. I was working as a social worker in a general hospital. And was bored and frustrated etc. Uh and took a course in the evening at R University and it was a course in Fortran programming.

. . .

I really enjoyed the course, I enjoyed working uh and I spoke to the people at R, mainly my professor about uh getting into the field and so he gave me advice and he encouraged me to continue

Her discussion includes one apparent counterexample, in which she explains a failed professional choice in terms of personal characteristics:

8. And I said I was, I was interested in people and I wanted to work with people, whatever that all means. Uh. So when I was doing social work, and I did that for five years, I need results. I'm a result person. OK. I need to, I like to manipulate symbols, I like those kind of machinations in your head. And I also like to see what I've done. OK? If I, **I cannot go extended periods**

**without that, I don't have the tolerance for it** and it was, I came
to that realization while doing social work, that I had to find
something that was, that gave me that kind of concrete kind of
[unclear]. And that's what started me looking.

We might read the boldfaced portion of this account as the speaker's
confession of a personal weakness, a lack of patience or imagination.
But there is no evidence that she herself reads it that way. Rather, in her
previous narratives, she seems to equate this character trait with effi-
ciency and good management. Thus, in a previous narrative, she criti-
cizes a previous employer for having no sense of results:

9.  I was very naive about XYZ when I went there. It <u>has</u>, it has a
    good reputation, that people say, you know from years ago,
    but uh they do all kinds of interesting work uh, when I got
    there, I <u>really</u> I didn't feel personally failed, I felt that I, I had
    contributed a great deal but I had felt very foolish about doing
    it t, because there was no, there was just uh, it was kind of like
    a welfare-ism thing, they were doling out this money and there's
    no thought to getting a product done. You know, they have a
    commitment but that doesn't, they don't feel personally that
    they have a commitment to accomplish anything. And they
    don't, or not very recently, you know, grants go until they run
    out, grants don't go until you produce something for somebody.
    Uh and I, I just found that extremely frustrating, extremely frus-
    trating. It was like throwing money down the sewer, I couldn't
    understand why the government was doing it.

Evidently, according to this speaker's set of values, the need for concrete
results that caused her to fail at social work is actually a positive (and
indeed necessary) characteristic for any person or business that wants to
be successful.
   To reiterate, the pattern we have seen is that positive character traits
are used to explain a positive career choice, while negative character
traits are not used to explain an unsuccessful choice. The only major
exception to this pattern occurs when a speaker reports himself or herself
to be severed from previous selves, so that past character traits such as
tastes are taken as irrelevant to the present person. This is similar to the
widely repeated finding of attribution theory, in social psychology, that
subjects tend to attribute their own behavior to their own character traits
or dispositions, rather than to situational effects (Kelley 1967).

## *Richness of Account*

As we have seen, identifying character traits as a reason for career choice is one way in which speakers can establish adequate causality. A second form of adequate causality is richness of account. An account may be rich because it covers a long period of time; that is, the reason for choice of profession may be located far back in the speaker's past. An explanation based on character traits is one form of an explanation rooted in the past, but there are other forms as well, including overlap of account. Different but noncontradictory accounts provide an extremely strong coherence for an explanation; they say in effect "There were many goods reasons for this choice."

Let us begin with an account structured in terms of time, given by a musician:

10. Well music was always, I was always <u>doing</u> music and uh I never really stopped and classified myself as a musician until around uh, after a couple of years of college when I realized that I still hadn't declared a major and the reason I hadn't was cause I didn't really have, I kept changing you know ideas about what I was majoring in. **But music was something that I had always done** and it was great, a thread, you know, cause it, I had always played in bands since I was about 13 years old and had always made music and I just, and I was in a band at the time and just stopped and said "Wait a minute. I'm not going to be an anthropologist, I'm not going to teach uh you know, philosophy, and I'm not going to do any of these other things, you know, because this is what I'm already doing."

In this narrative, the speaker differentiates between doing music and classifying himself as a musician. For him, doing music goes very far back; in a later narrative he takes it back to the age of four, when he asked for guitar lessons.

Temporal depth is a very strong form of causality. One tenet of our common-sense view of the self is that an activity, an aptitude, or an ambition that goes back to early childhood must be seen as intrinsic to the self. A profession based on such aptitude or ambition therefore cannot be challenged as having inadequate causality. This presupposition is used in stories that must account for discontinuities of career choice. One such strategy is to relate the new career to early abilities or interests, so that the discontinuity with respect to the unsuccessful career is only an apparent discontinuity in the greater life story.

*Life Stories*

Another form of adequate causality is multiple noncontradictory accounts. As an illustration, we will use a complex series of accounts given
by a professor who holds a degree in seventeenth-century literature and
now works in the area of medical ethics, which she characterizes as
being at the intersection of science and the humanities. She begins these
accounts with a very interesting remark: **I'll start with the second one
first.** As we shall see, the sequence she mentions has to do with the
principle of narrative ordering. The second reason is stated first, presumably because it is more salient, although it is later in time than the reason
that follows it. Here is her narrative:

11. Well I'll start with the second one first. That was almost by
    (pause) of being in a certain place at a certain time. That was
    by dint of being a certain type of graduate student with certain
    interests that people around me knew I had. Um, at school, at
    Ivy University, where there was a program in, uh, that was
    trying to bring together the academic disciplines and medical
    educators um and so I got into that program and I kind of got
    into it for a number of years and then, then things developed.
    But the orig- the reason for that original interest in what prob-
    ably are ca- what are called the two cultures issue um I think I,
    when I was an undergraduate I, well I guess I should start
    when I, way back when I, when (pause) My family is very, my
    parents were very literary, my father was a writer and my
    mother was, was for a time a librarian and I was always much
    better at uh verbal sk- my verbal skills were always much better
    than my mathematical skills. And so I, for a number of reasons
    I think I just didn't study too much science as an under- as a
    high school student. I um, then when I got to college I really
    developed a strong interest in it and for a while I wanted to go
    into medicine, but I realized that I didn't have a lot of forces
    working for me that would be helpful. I didn't have a, an, an
    early interest in science and in scientific ways of approaching
    problems that many of the people around me who were prepar-
    ing for scientific careers had without even having to think
    about it, having sort of absorbed it through their environment.
    And so I had really an amateur interest at that time. But none-
    theless I did take these science courses and I, then I graduated
    not really knowing what I was going to do, without any strong
    career goals and I went into VISTA for a year and then decided

that I needed to sort of play from my strengths. So I went to graduate school in literature.

And um, but still, even though I didn't expect it, those interests surfaced. And when I, when it came time to do my dissertation, the thing I wanted to do it in was on a scientist in the seventeenth century who had um related more than anyone else his scientific ideas to his theological ideas. So I think uh, I think that explains it probably.

This example employs an extremely complex strategy establishing rich multiple causality for the speaker's professional choice. The speaker begins by attributing her professional position partly to accident and partly to character traits. She then goes far back in time, possibly even to before her own birth, to explain how she became that kind of person, relating her interests to the jobs her parents held. Notice that she relates her interest in literature, which is formally her field, to her family; her interest in science dates only as far back as college. She then uses the late date of the beginning of her interest in science to explain why she did not go into some scientific field. Both her central choice of literature and her interest in science are well grounded in the past.

Thus far, we have seen an account that uses both temporal depth and character traits to establish adequate causality. The speaker then goes on to enrich the account further. After discussing how she decided on her dissertation topic, she adds another narrative, with no prompting from the interviewer:

12. But the thing that always amazes me about this is that I really wonder what sorts of forces are, are at work in the way we sort of turn out, um because I have very vivid memories of listening to a, when I was an undergraduate, Marjorie Holt, Hope Nicolson was brought to X where I was an undergraduate to speak, and it was a lecture on English gardens. Well um I was really not interested in English gardens and I didn't understand very much of what she said but I remember that a professor of mine whom I really admired and liked a great deal was <u>enthralled</u> that they, that they had been able to stage this <u>coup</u> of getting her to speak. And when I got to Y, and I had in no way applied to Y because she was, or <u>had</u> been there, and in fact I've never met the woman, but many of my interests, people, whenever I talk to people about my interests

Note: causality comes from just "detail," even from the weight of "unresolved" or pointless stories.

they must sort of immediately say "Oh that's Marjorie Hope Nicolson stuff." Um, so I don't know, you know. Maybe that's some sort of retroflective order creation that I'm doing, but I, I uh, I don't know.

This is a particular interesting case of enrichment. The narrative recounts that the speaker had an early encounter with someone who had similarly diverse interests. She adds the narrative, even though she does not make its explanatory force explicit; that is, by telling the narrative, she implies that this experience had some effect on her, but that she does not know what it was. If we looked at this narrative in isolation, without considering its role in the context of a larger life story, we would probably view it as a weak narrative with an unclear (or perhaps nonexistent) point. But even so unresolved a narrative as this serves to enrich the speaker's account of her professional choice with further coherences, and so is tellable. (In the next section, we will see a similar use of stories with very weak points to serve as secondary material to enrich an account.)

The speaker then enriches her account further with an explanation of her character traits, and the reasons why she has such traits:

13. Another um idea that, well, in my more uh, I often wonder why I have this need to uh make, to to write, to kind of split myself off into two directions or to try and take on many, to take on what might seem to be warring, I see what I do as, as reconciling things, and why do I need to reconcile things? I came from a family that was very conflict prone. And I was the peacemaker in the family. And I don't like conflict. And I um, or rather I, I am really very upset by it. And when it, when it, when it upsets me I immediately want to uh, to find some middle ground. So you know temperamentally I, I seem to be, I like what I do.

In this explanation, the speaker presupposes that her desire to reconcile things is one reason for her interest in topics that fall at the intersection of science and literature. She goes on to explain this character trait in terms of her family history. This is a strategy of complex enrichment that even gives reasons for the reasons. This account is a rare exception to the general principle that character traits tend to be taken as primitive. We may account for this unusual treatment of character by the fact that the speaker is no longer operating within a common-sense framework but rather within the special explanatory system of Freudian psychology, in which character may and indeed must be explained by reference to early childhood experience. Chapter 6 discusses this more fully.

Let us consider another multiple noncontradictory account, given by a professor of engineering:

14. For example, one as- one part of the profession is doing scientific work and I think I arrived at that much earlier than I did becoming a university professor. //Interviewer: Mm Hmm// Um (pause) When I was about eleven or so, there was a, a c- a day, well it was a teenage camp program that I went to which had um trips to different inter- spots of interest. And there was a trip to S University on which we went to see the engineering school. And there was some discussion with the dean of engineering and two things happened. First he gave a talk about electron- about molecular structure, and I asked a que- he was talking about the influence of uh well, the way in which the nucleus basically exerted a poly- a strong force upon the electrons. And I asked whether the electrons exerted much influence on the nucleus. And he said "Hey why don't you come back here when you (laughs) graduate high school?" I had to, he, in the talk he mentioned that ceramic engineers made a lot of money and I thought that was very interesting. And so I developed an, partly I was interested in getting as a sort of secure job, that would pay well, and ceramic engineering, which I knew nothing about nevertheless was just said to be such and it seemed like a very interesting environment. When I was in high school, I got into being a radio amateur and then I got interested in electronics and I thought that um electrical engineering had something to do with that, had something to do with communications, and I really didn't have much idea of what it was but I uh I certainly enjoyed being a ham radio operator (unclear) myself sufficient electronics to tinker with equipment and chose to go to an engineering school. That's sort of like Act One. [Continues with discussion of choice of college, and the influence of the particular college on later career moves.]

In this example, the speaker provides a variety of accounts: early interests and early encounters that, combined with his choice of college, account for his current professional position. While none of the reasons given are decisive, together they add up to a sufficient account.

Multiple noncontradictory accounts provide adequate causality because they show that a choice was not random or insufficiently motivated. Although none of the individual reasons may in itself be adequate, the sum of all of them is sufficient.

## Management of Inadequate Causality

Thus far we have considered cases in which the construction of coherence appears to have caused little difficulty for speakers—cases in which the sequence of career moves is a socially recognizable one, or one for which the speakers are able to provide an account that establishes the existence of adequate causality. We now turn to the more difficult cases, in which socially recognizable (or individually perceived) inadequate causality must be managed.

Two major types of relations exist between events that appear to be treated as involving inadequate causality: accident and discontinuity. In general, the categories of accident and discontinuity are quite similar, but they differ in scope: a particular career move or choice may be referred to as accidental; while a sequence of moves, viewed as a sequence, may be treated as discontinuous. Both types involve a deficient degree of intention and/or agency by the protagonist. In both types of cases, speakers who recount segments of their lives either as accidentally motivated or as discontinuous have a special job of management. Somehow, they must show either that, although it might seem that their lives have been accidental or discontinuous, this is not really the case or that there are reasons why this apparently problematic state of affairs is not a problem for them, that the ability to profit from circumstances beyond one's agency is a virtue rather than a failure of proper agency.

Once again, the analysis of this study is not concerned with the issue of whether the accounts offered in these narratives are correct—that is, whether some happening was truly accidental and whether some sequence was truly discontinuous. Accident/causality and continuity/discontinuity are interpretive categories that we use in creating understandings of our perception or our memory. For the purposes of this study, which seeks to demonstrate how such understandings are created, it is not helpful to inquire whether these analyses are correct, since its theoretical background of assumptions is not one against which correctness may be judged. For other types of study, of course, the correctness of the speaker's analysis may be the crucial question. For example, from a psychological viewpoint, one may be concerned with whether some narrative tends toward neurosis or toward psychological health. But for the present study, we must rely on the speakers alone; if they label some sequence of events as accidental, we must assume that they mean something by this analysis and must try to determine what they do mean.

## *Accident*

Let us begin with accident. We will count as accounts of accident all narratives, explanations, and so on that explicitly characterize some event or sequence of events as **accident, random,** or the like. In other words, these involve events that the speakers themselves characterize as insufficiently caused in some way. We will begin with an extended analysis of a narrative and explanation offered by the professor of medieval literature. She has already explained her choice of literature as a field; example 15 is a response to a question about her choice of medieval literature as her specific field:

15. **That was more or less an accident.** Uh, I started out in Renaissance studies, but I didn't like any of the people I was working with, and at first I thought I would just leave Y and go to another university, uh but a medievalist at Y university asked me to stay or at least reconsider whether I should leave or not, and um pointed out to me that I had done very well in the medieval course that I took with him and that I seemed to like it, and he was right. I did. And he suggested that I switch fields and stay at Y and that's how I got into medieval literature.

This appears to be a perfectly comprehensible narrative. Unlike example 12, it does not seem weak or lacking in a point. But we must ask how we are to understand the evaluation of this sequence of events as **more or less an accident.**

What is an accidental event? The prototypical case of an accidental event seems to be an event that is not intentionally caused by any of the participants — for example, an automobile crash or a meteor striking someone. Even these need not be understood as entirely accidental, since we may be able to assign causes to some accidents of this prototypical type. For example, we may be able to say that an automobile accident happened because a driver was drunk or because a car had a mechanical failure. Indeed, in the case of airplane accidents, a complex social mechanism is mandated by law to investigate the facts and determine the causes of the accident, which may include a main cause or causes and possible secondary contributing causes. In every case, these causes may involve actions by the participants, but they do not include the intention to bring about the state of affairs described as the accident.

In light of this discussion of the normal use of the term **accident**, we may now ask in what sense the events described in example 15 can properly be characterized as accidental. The narrator is in graduate school; she has studied literature; she has taken a course in medieval literature. These all appear to be proper preconditions for a choice of medieval literature as a field of study, and they imply that the narrator probably had some intention in that direction or a neighboring one. Yet since she herself characterizes the choice as accidental, we can not reject her characterization, but rather must try to make sense of it.

In her account, the deciding factor is the influence of a professor of medieval literature who suggested the choice to her. In a later retelling of the same narrative, she describes him as **this one man whom I admired enormously, whose scholarship I admired and whose teaching methods I admired um and and who I personally admired.** Personal influence and the importance of personal relations are an important theme in this narrative, as well as in the rest of her account. For example, she gives as her reason for considering leaving the university at which she was enrolled: **I didn't like any of the people I was working with, and at first I thought I would just leave Y and go to another university.** An alternative characterization, using the same facts but not framed in terms of personal relations, might be **The people I had to work with weren't any good.**

We are now in a position to ask what it could mean that personal influence by an admired professor is presented as an accident. As we have seen, the prototypical cases of accident are those involving primarily physical events that occur without the agency or intention of the participants. The present case does not match this prototype. But if we broaden our understanding of **accident** to include **an event whose causality is insufficient or in some way problematic,** we can handle this case — as well as other narratives in the data that include an analysis of some sequence of events as accidental. We may say that the insufficiency of the causality lies in the speaker's relative lack of agency: her professor's beliefs and actions, rather than her own, are presented as determining her actions.

Let us consider in more detail the speaker's formulation of agency. In the case of the professor of medieval literature, we may say that she analyzes her choice of profession as an accident because she does not view it as having sufficient causality of a culturally standard type; that is, she does not relate it to her own determination, to a long-standing interest, or to a special aptitude. She could have done so; for example, in an earlier narrative, she mentions that she studied Latin throughout high school and college, which surely could have furnished the material for an account framed in terms of a long-standing interest. But instead, she gives as the cause an apparently casual or chance remark by someone she liked and admired. Within the general system of values of our culture and the particular values of the academic profession, this is an insufficient cause. It is consistent with the speaker's apparent value system, however, which is concerned with the quality of human relations: she mentions issues of whether she likes the people there and whether she has good friends, as well as the more conventional relational issue of whether she likes and respects an authority. The speaker's way of solving this conflict between her own values and the more generally held values of her group is to label the cause that she herself considers most important as being **more or less an accident**. This solution permits her both to give the cause as she herself sees it and to indicate her knowledge of and obeisance to the more general set of values in her professional world regarding acceptable reasons for the choice of profession.

In this narrative, the speaker has reached some accommodation between her own perception of the cause of her choice and more generally accepted academic beliefs about proper reason for professional choice. However, her account is framed in a way that suggests she still sees some problems with it, as suggested by the hedge **more or less** an accident. It is psychologically and socially difficult to admit that some important choice in your life has been accidentally or insufficiently motivated. The speaker here handles this difficulty by immediately following her narrative with an explanation proving that the accident really made no difference:

16. Sometimes I don't think that it makes any difference. Uh I don't think I could've ever specialized in a very late field and been happy. I mean, I think if I had been in the nineteenth or twentieth centuries I would've gotten bored and probably turned in desperation to literary theory, which is what a lot of people do. Um, now that seems to me like a horrible sin, but it might have happened.

     As for the difference between medieval or Renaissance or seventeenth century, I don't think it makes much difference. Um I'm very happy being a medievalist and I now couldn't imagine switching, but if I had liked the people in the Renaissance and had stayed in it I would never have imagined switching either. So, um, you know, I mean it was a right choice

because it led to a job and it led to good friends and it led to a
good career and a lot of satisfaction, but uh in other circumstances I think staying in the Renaissance would have led me
to the same place.

One way to deal with this explanation, as we saw in Chapter 3, is to
analyze its structure as a proof of equivalence, establishing that the choice
between medieval and Renaissance literature makes no difference, since
either choice would have led to the same results. The first part of the
explanation specifies that only medieval or Renaissance or seventeenth-
century literature were possible choices; all later fields would have been
mistakes and need not be considered. Consequently, the first part of the
explanation establishes that the choices dealt with in the second part are
the correct ones, since no other possibilities need be considered. The
second part then establishes the equivalence of the two relevant fields in
the areas that are most important to the speaker: a job, good friends, a
good career, satisfaction. (It is worth noting that at least one of these,
good friends, seems to reflect the same personal values that led the
speaker initially to assign the cause of her choice of career to personal
influence.)

The preceding discussion relates to the formal structure of the explanation alone. Another way to view this explanation is to consider the relation of the explanation to the narrative in example 15, which precedes it.
Viewed in this context, the explanation establishes as acceptable the fact
that the choice of profession was **more or less an accident.** The strategy
for establishing this is quite complex. The speaker shows that the restriction of possible fields to medieval or Renaissance literature was well
motivated for her. The choice between the two of them can be seen as
accidental, but the two are so nearly equivalent that it is not disturbing
to see the choice in this way. In other words, the explanation establishes
that only an unimportant part of the decision was accidental.

We may characterize this strategy more generally as being a demonstration by the speaker that there were alternate routes to the same goal,
so that, although the choice of a particular route may have been poorly
motivated or accidental, the goal itself was not accidental at all. A number of examples of this strategy appear in the data. The speaker (an
optometrist) in example 17, for example, had begun his account of how
he chose this profession by indicating that he felt family pressure to
become a professional of some kind: **I was an aspiring dentist uh mainly
because, uh, (pause) My mother denies it but the pressure was, the whole
object was, you know to be a professional man.** He followed this with
an explanation showing that being a professional man was indeed a good

choice. The explanation demonstrates that it was correct and obvious that he should learn a profession; he reserves his actual first narrative for a description of how he arrived at his particular profession of optometry. (Note the similarity between this and the previous case, in which the speaker establishes it as obvious and unquestioned that she should be involved in the academic study of literature, while reserving her explanation for the choice of a particular field of literature.) Here is the optometrist's narrative:

17. Um I was an aspiring dentist and uh I was in a field called general curriculum at State where you could take from different, right? And they told me they wouldn't sign my study list unless I was taking Spanish. I had already taken Spanish three times (laughs) and I finally got a C in it, languages not being my forte, so I turned around and already now I had been at State six years, five years, something like that. So I had known my way around and so forth and I said "I'll take it next summer," they said "We won't sign," so I said "OK I'll be back." So I went down to the School of Public Health where I was working and I said "Hey do you want my body?" And in those days they wanted anybody they could grab ahold of. And they said, "Yeah" I said "Will you waive my language requirement?" and they said "Sure." So I told General Curriculum to go screw themselves and I went into the School of Public Health.

    And as I was going through I got interested in statistics and uh one of my stat professors uh turned around and uh I was looking for work and he said "I know of a job up in the School of Optometry, for a fellow by the name of T, HT." I said "God that name sounds familiar," and I knew his sister in M (unclear) so there I was working in the School of Optometry and um one friend of mine, a guy I had known in Public Health quit Public Health and went into the School of Optometry. And what's really very interesting is back in 19- I guess it was about 1954 or 55, uh a fellow tried to talk me into going into optometry and I said no, I was going to be a dentist. (inaudible) So I ended up then and it wasn't very much before I got to knew [sic] people there, uh the next thing I know I had all the prerequisites and I was in the School of Optometry. And there I was. So that's how I got into optometry.

This narrative is not as clearly an "accident" as the narrative given in example 15; the speaker himself gives no such evaluation of the chain of events that led to his becoming an optometrist. If we rely on our own knowledge of cultural values, however, we must judge this as a relatively accidental account of a choice of profession. The speaker was in a course of study that required study of a foreign language, which he felt unable to complete. He therefore transferred into a second, related program because administrators there were willing to waive this requirement. While in this program, he took a job in a third program suggested by a professor of his, and then eventually enrolled in that third program. Such a sequence may not be labeled as accidental, but it is clearly not the result of longstanding personal preference or long-range decision making on the part of the speaker. The impression the speaker gives is of drifting from one field to the next — an impression strengthened by the fact, mentioned in the orientation section of the narrative, that he had already been a student for five and a half years at the beginning of this sequence.

If we accept the analysis that this narrative presents an inadequate causal chain, we can begin to make sense of a number of otherwise obtrusive elements in it. Consider, for example, the following segment of the narrative, which appears to contribute little or nothing to the sequence of events:

17a.   And what's really very interesting is back in 19- I guess it was
       about 1954 or 55, uh a fellow tried to talk me into going into
       optometry and I said no, I was going to be a dentist.

At first glance this seems far from interesting; indeed it appears to be a pointless elaboration by a poor storyteller. But it becomes quite interesting when considered as an aspect of management of a sequence of insufficiently motivated events. This is another instance of the strategy used by the previous speaker to construct a chain of events that only appears to be accidental. The strategy is to show that although a particular route to a goal may seem to be accidental, there were in fact many routes to that same goal, and hence the accidental nature of the particular route taken does not mean that the speaker's life is truly accidental and without pattern. On the other hand, these speakers do not use the strategy of multiple routes to structure their primary narrative. Such a structure would say in effect: there were many many routes to my goal; indeed, all roads seemed to lead there. An analysis of this sort would fail philosophically through the opposite fault: not too accidental, but too determined.

A number of other seeming coincidences are included in the optometrist's narrative. One is that his statistics professor's recommendation of an employer in the School of Optometry was only one possible route to that employer, since the speaker also knew the man's sister. Similarly, he tells us that a friend of his had quit public health to go into optometry, which shows yet another route by which he could have been influenced to take the course he did in fact take. Although he does not give an overt evaluation of this point, the speaker offers enough instances of multiple alternate routes to show that he did not really act accidentally.

Readers who are interested in narratives that include multiple possible routes to the same goal are invited to consider how they met their spouses, and to ask their friends and acquaintances for similar stories. This topic provides a particularly appropriate arena for such a structure. People commonly have spouse-meeting stories of the following structure: "We met at So-and-So's party, but we could have met because she was in the chemistry section where I was a TA, and also my sister became a member of the same sorority she was in." One notable phenomenon is that couples who have such stories love them: they tell them with great pleasure and enthusiasm.

I believe that one reason why such stories have the structure of multiple routes (and also why they afford their tellers so much pleasure) is that our culture in general prescribes no correct or obvious way to meet a spouse and, for any given person, suggests no correct or obvious spouse. Certainly there are some constraints: not just anyone is a possible spouse. But the pool of potential spouses is very great, and at the same time, the ideology of romantic love urges that it is possible, desirable, and perhaps even necessary to find the unique right one. The combination of these two factors sets up a narrative paradox: unlike the situation with regard to choice of profession, we cannot establish that we have met exactly the proper spouse in precisely the proper way. (This analysis is supported by the observation that stories of the multiple ways in which one might have met one's spouse seem much more common in stories of first marriages than in reports of second or subsequent marriages, which resist application of the full ideology of romantic love.)

Let us now consider several more examples showing how speakers manage choices that they themselves analyze as being accidental. In example 18, the computer programmer analyzes her choice of a degree program in computer science as being accidental, and then she manages this account by a strategy of self-distancing:

18.        SPEAKER: I was working as a social worker in a general
                hospital. And was bored and frustrated etc. Uh
                and took a course in the evening at R Univer-

sity and it was a course in Fortran programming. That's how I got into this profession.

INTERVIEWER: Uh huh.

SPEAKER: That kind of started me off. I just continued.
Do you want a more detailed answer than that?
OK

       [           [

INTERVIEWER:         And then    Yeah sure

SPEAKER: Um I really enjoyed the course, I enjoyed working uh and I spoke to the people at R, mainly
my professor about uh getting into the field
and so he gave me advice and he encouraged
me to continue, which I did do and I don- it
must have been about six months or a year
later, I don't remember which, uh I went over
to the N School, the dean of the N School, and
said "You know, can I take courses here?" and
I spent about an hour and a half with him
(laughs) and by I (fin-) out of the office I was
enrolled in a master's program [Int laughs] and
uh he told me I had to go back and take all of
my math courses. So I had to get an undergraduate math major. And so I did that concur-
rently with going for my master's degree. So
that's how it all happened actually. **Kind of by
accident.**

INTERVIEWER: How had you decided to take that first course?

SPEAKER: Uh, you know, that's interesting. Because I'm
not sure I remember exactly. I have a cousin
who lives in V who is a programmer and was
doing very well. And I don't, I don't think it
was any more, I think it's because she was making a lot of money that I decided that I ought
to look into this thing and see why she was
making so much money. I can't remember at
this time any other reason why I did that.

The speaker has used a strategy of self-distancing, splitting the narrator and the protagonist of the narrative so that the narrator does not
have any privileged access to the thoughts and motivations of the protag-

onist. Thus, if there was a lack of agency, it can be blamed on the protagonist, not the narrator. (We will see further examples of this strategy of self-distancing in the section on discontinuity in this chapter.)

Once again, we may wonder what is wrong with the agency of this narrative; one might think that a belief that there are well-paid jobs in a certain field is a good and sufficient reason for entering it. And certainly the speaker has provided the materials necessary to construct a narrative about a well-informed and well-motivated person who trained for a career because she had evidence that it would be rewarding. The problem, as the speaker constructs it, seems to be that it was not her agency but rather the dean's that led her to a master's degree, since she had only wished to take a few courses. In a later version of this narrative, she emphasizes the overriding agency of the dean:

19. I spoke to Dr. K a long time. He decided, oh yeah, I had really gone over there, wasn't asking to go to graduate school. I was asking to take a course in the evening. And I figured I could qualify because I had graduated from R and it wouldn't, what big deal would it be for him to let me take a course. I, **by the time I was out of there, he had me enrolled in this whole program**, and he says, "Oh you have to do it this way." **And it must have appealed to me**, because I went ahead and did it.

This version of the narrative brings out both the speaker's self-distancing from the protagonist of the narrative and her stress on the agency of the dean.

At this point, we may begin to wonder whether, in the creation of a life story, any sequence of events is ever analyzed as being purely accidental. The preceding discussion of accident might suggest that accident is too extreme an analysis, and that no speaker will ever give a bare, unrevised account of a career decision as being purely accidental. However, this is an overstatement of the case. The data contain one instance in which an event is labeled as accidental, and no subsequent remedial work alters that analysis. In this case, however, the event is one small accident that does not form the basis of a career. The narrative is told by the musician:

20. **You know, a lot, and a lot of stuff has happened in a totally accidental way (pause) to me**, like um, the whole publishing thing. I um (pause) got an idea at one point to do a banjo instruction book about a, a kind of a certain development that had happened in the banjo, but it had changed for about the

last ten or twelve years at the time I wrote the book, had changed what banjo players were doing, and nobody had written anything about it yet. Although it had been going on for over a decade, so I started to write that book and, um, well, I winded up and published <u>that</u> myself and uh, as a result got, when I moved down here, got into a, a lot of other publishing stuff, totally unrelated to that. I mean, somebody called me up asking me to do a jazz guitar book, a transcription of Wes Montgomery music, on the basis that I had published this banjo book, this bluegrass banjo book (laughs) and wh- which I couldn't see, you know, I could't see that, how that followed all that. **But it was, it was just a fortunate accident really**, because when I got into doing a lot of other, projects like that, that, that were a lot of fun and also made a good living for me.

Why is it possible for the speaker to call this an accident, without any of the kinds of the remedial work we have discussed previously? The answer is simple: it is one small accident in an otherwise very well-motivated life. We have already seen, in example 10, that this speaker has been able to provide strong adequate causality for the major decision of being a musician: he has been doing it since he was four, and he has always done it. Given this fundamental strong motivation for the major decision, the speaker has no problem in seeing one relatively unimportant event as an accident.

In the course of doing the interview, I became curious about this narrative, however, so I followed it with the question **How was it an accident?** The answer, example 21, amounts to a claim that it was a chain of events that could not have been predicted and that no one could have planned; that is, the accident was a chain of events that lacked proper agency:

21. Oh well, it was just a funny sequence of events. I went to this one publisher to try to get <u>him</u> to publish my banjo book and he said "OK" he would do it, and, they picked it up for a <u>while</u>, and, um, a new company that had just started out, uh, called them to find out who could do this jazz guitar book that they wanted done and he recommended <u>me</u>. Well to <u>me</u> that was an accident, because the guy didn't even know that I played guitar. He had just <u>met</u> me, and he <u>liked</u> me, so he just recommended me. And, uh, and any other banjo player that <u>I</u> know that, that would have gotten recommended for that proj-

ect, would have (pause) wouldn't have been able to do it, because it's totally different, you know, most bluegrass banjo players mainly, that's what they do. (laughs) That's <u>all</u> they do. You know, they might play guitar, bluegrass guitar, as well, or some other instrument, but jazz guitar is another world, you know, and there's very little communication between the two worlds, although that's <u>started</u> to change a little bit. (pause) **So it was just a, it was an accident in the sense that uh, you know, I could <u>do</u> it**.

The accident lies in the fact that, contrary to what one would predict from knowledge of the musical world, the speaker could fulfill an unexpected request. We may note that it is impossible to tell from the account as it is given why the speaker was asked to work on a transcription of jazz guitar music; the publishing company's motives are left opaque.

The important point about this narrative and the subsequent explanation is that the accident was a minor one — not one that involved a major career decision or career change. It appears that only accidents at major decision points require some form of remedial analysis; minor events may well be presented as being accidental.

## Continuity and Discontinuity

Thus far, we have considered the management of causality as the major task in creating a coherent life story. We now turn to a different but related coherence principle: continuity and the management of discontinuity. We may view inadequate causality as a form of local discontinuity between cause and effect. But there are other types of discontinuity as well. The most important type for these life stories is discontinuity at a higher level — that is, discontinuity between professions, which arises when a speaker has changed professions and must in some way handle a discontinuity between these professions or between phases of a single profession. Identification of such discontinuities is a matter of social knowledge. Thus, if someone begins working as a proofreader, then switches to a job as a copy editor, and moves to a job as a production editor, people within that professional world would see the succession of jobs as a continuous sequence. But someone who moves from a position as a banker to one as a candlemaker is seen as having a large and recognizable career discontinuity. One very clear principle that emerges from the data is that, like accident, discontinuity must be given some sort of explicit treatment. A discontinuity in a narrative cannot simply be left without any further accounting; a speaker who presents a discontinuous sequence must present some evaluation of explanation of the discontinuity.

A number of strategies are used for managing discontinuity. We will here consider the strategies that occur in the data of this study. However, such a list cannot include all possible strategies, since managing discontinuity appears to allow for great individual creativity.

## The Strategy of Apparent Break

One strategy for handling professional discontinuity is to treat the break as only apparent. A later profession might seem very different from an earlier one, but the speaker shows that they have characteristics in common that allow us to see their sequence as continuous. For example, a speaker might tell us: **I used to be a banker and now I'm a candlemaker, but really what I liked about banking is just what I like about candlemaking.**

Strategies of this type are extremely interesting and sometimes amusing, since the coherences the speaker creates are necessarily nonstandard and home-made. Given an unexpected sequence of professions, the speaker is faced with the task of showing that the sequence can still be seen as continuous.

Let us look at an example from the housing administrator's narrative. This passage is taken from the very end of his discussion. He has already explained that he has worked at a series of jobs that appear related and coherent to him, although they might not appear coherent to the average job interviewer. He has also mentioned that he had an early interest in going into the theater as a profession. Now he makes the following statement:

22. What happened in those seven years was that what I think is a natural liking for administrative work took over. And that I found my way through that, and that was a fairly natural good process. Um that rep- that that was there intuitively before. **I saw myself as a producer in the movie industry. So, and I had been a producer in college. I produced three shows. So there was, in that sense it was not a break.**

The speaker is attempting to reconcile his early work in theater and his desire to do it professionally with his history of work in housing administration. He does this by showing that, while he was interested in theater, he had always approached it as an administrator, and therefore this early interest can be seen as continuous with his present career.

This analysis of continuity is certainly idiosyncratic; in fact, whenever I have presented it as an example, it makes audiences laugh. But it is important not to view this as an example of someone fooling himself into believing that his life is more coherent than it really is. To the extent that the connection holds for him, these portions of his life are coherent. Moreover, the speaker knows that this analysis of continuity will not be acceptable to everyone; he indicates this by immediately offering the following qualification:

> 23. So there was, in that sense it was not a break. But in the sense that working in, in, in a poverty community for non-profit agencies and governments is a long way from, I don't know, working for United Artists producing a movie, to that extent it's a long distance.

We need not try to decide which of these accounts he himself really believes. The important point for this analysis is that he is able to create this continuity between theater work and administration in his narrative.

Another example of the strategy of apparent break is given in example 24, an account given by the technical editor. This is an attempt to make physics, his original choice, continuous with geology, the field he is just entering. At first glance, this would not seem too difficult to do, since they are both sciences. In previous stories, however, he has strongly rejected physics as unattractive and unpleasant, so something more personal than the analysis of science as a superordinate class is required to join the two. Here is the technical editor's account:

> 24. Uh, also I think I must have some uh real liking for that, that kind of stuff on some level, even the physics and stuff, you know, cause when I was a kid, even, I was really **hot** for astronomy, I went crazy, I read all the books and it, but again it was a romantic kind of thing, you know, and the, and the, the, the, the, specifics of it, the reading about it and learning all the numbers and everything followed from the romantic part. **Which is what I really like about the geology too.** It's just this feeling of "That's really fascinating" you know, it's really kind of magical and I really want to, I want to get a hold on it somehow, you know, even if it means doing numbers and stuff.

The coherence that this speaker identifies is an emotional one rather than an intrinsic connection between the two subjects: it is not that the two are similar in content; it is that his attitude of romantic fascination toward them is the same.

Examples 22, 23, and 24 are quite different, and any further example of this strategy would undoubtedly present additional novel connections between professions that are usually viewed as being very different. The important similarity lies in the structure of the strategy: reconciling discontinuity between professions by showing that a break is only apparent, since a connection can be drawn to join the two.

### *Strategy of Temporary Discontinuity*

2)

Another strategy for handling a professional discontinuity is to show that the discontinuity is not fundamentally real, since it represents only a temporary break in interests or activities. For example, a second career may be shown to be the result of an early interest that was abandoned for a while and then resumed. This represents much less of a discontinuity than would the development of an entirely new interest. Example 25 has this structure:

25. And so I, for a number of reasons I think I just didn't study too much science as an under- as a high school student. I um, then when I got to college I really developed a strong interest in it and for a while I wanted to go into medicine, but I realized that I didn't have a lot of forces working for me that would be helpful. I didn't have a, an, an early interest in science and in scientific ways of approaching problems that many of the people around me who were preparing for scientific careers had without even having to think about it, having sort of absorbed it through their environment. And so I had really an amateur interest at that time. But nonetheless I did take these science courses and I, then I graduated not really knowing what I was going to do, without any strong career goals and I went into VISTA for a year and then decided that I needed to sort of play from my strengths. So I went to graduate school in literature. And um, but still, even though I didn't expect it, those interests surfaced. And when I, when it came time to do my dissertation, the thing I wanted to do it in was on a scientist in the seventeenth century who had um related more than anyone else his scientific ideas to his theological ideas. So I think uh, I think that explains it probably.

The speaker here is explaining the apparent discontinuity of her training in literature with her interest in science and her choice of a scientist as the subject of her dissertation. She shows that in college she developed an interest in science, but that she abandoned it temporarily because she did not have the background to do well at it. Her current interest in science can thus be seen as a return to her original interest, rather than as an utterly new departure from her work in English literature.

A similar example of the strategy of merely apparent discontinuity is given in example 26 by the computer programmer. In explaining the discontinuity between her former career as a social worker and her present career as a computer programmer, she connects her career in programming to an earlier interest in mathematics that she did not pursue when she was in school:

26. I had never, I don't, never pursued math when I was in high school or when was in college and I really don't know why, OK, I g- I never really followed through with the things I enjoyed OK? When I look back on high school I guess what I took, I always liked (unclear) I always liked geometry, and I liked algebra. I never thought I was, I just never pursued it. When I was in college, it was the last thing that I wanted to do. And yet that was really, I loved physics, and I said I was, I was interested in people and wanted to work with people, whatever that all means.

This strategy of establishing a discontinuity as temporary by referring to earlier interests is clearly related to the strategy of establishing adequate causality via character traits of ability or interest. As we have already seen, character traits of this type are taken as explanatory primitives: they need not themselves be explained, and they may be used as the basis for extremely strong explanations. Similarly, early interests may be used to form a strong claim that some later career choice was well motivated.

## Strategy of Discontinuity as Sequence

A somewhat different strategy for managing discontinuity is to show that, although two professions A and B are discontinuous, they are significantly related because in some way A led to B. Even if A is very different from B or is something that the speaker now rejects, the fact that it can be seen as leading to B or developing into B makes the sequence coherent. For example: **The skills I learned as a banker are helpful to me now in my candle shop**.

An example of this sort is given by the technical editor, who was about to begin graduate study in geology at the time he gave this narrative. In example 27, he answers a specific question about the relation of geology to his former profession of physics:

27. INTERVIEWER: Do you feel it's um, it's related to the uh physics and engineering stuff you were doing, or do you feel it's a sharp break?

SPEAKER: Oh no, it's definitely related. I think that, having that degree has made a tremendous, has given me a tremendous advantage in the, in the courses I have taken here, I think, it's, it's much easier for me than it is for a lot of the people. I know how to think in those terms. I'm not afraid of uh, uh, analytical, an analytical approach to things, I don't panic immediately, you know, at the sight of logic or something.

The speaker's argument is that, although he has rejected physics as subject, it gave him the background necessary to do well in geology, and so was usefully related. The relation he mentions is not an intrinsic relation between the content of geology and that of physics, but rather a relation in the style of thought required for each of them, so that having studied physics makes it easier for him to understand geology.

### Strategy of Self-distancing

Thus far, we have considered strategies for handling discontinuity that attempt to show that an apparent break is not really as great as it might seem. The next two strategies we will consider are somewhat different; they admit that two professions or two choices are indeed discontinuous, but they go on to show that the discontinuity is acceptable because of the speaker's attitude toward it. The first of these is the strategy of self-distancing. The speaker says, in effect, "For me, there is no discontinuity, since I am a different person from the person who was involved in the initial profession." Example 28 is an example of this strategy, given by a professor of sociology:

28. I think that the probability of my ending up in academia was largely a product of the fact that my father was an academic and his father was a scientist and the values I was raised in were very much academic intellectual values. So I think there's a sense in which uh it would have been extraordinarily difficult for me to have ended up in another kind of life, although I entertained that at various points. **Um I thought, as one, as adolescents without talent are prone to do, of the performing arts in various ways.** Uh I was in theater for a while in high school and college and I was an actress through college **and had fantasies about making that a life which were of course unrealistic.**

The speaker's problem is to reconcile her early interest and work in the performing arts with her eventual career in sociology. We have already seen, in example 22, a similar problematic career sequence; there the speaker solved the problem by creating a continuity between his early interest in theater and his current career in administration. The speaker of example 28 uses a different strategy. She handles the discontinuity between theater and acting on the one hand and an academic career in sociology on the other by indicating that she now knows that her early interest was a mistake. She uses a great number of evaluation devices to distance herself from the person who wanted to be an actress. She puts herself in the class of adolescents without talent, identifies the desire to make a life of the performing arts as a fantasy, and assures us that such fantasies were, of course, unrealistic. The current speaker knows that the interests and ambitions of the teenager who happened to bear her name were impossible and unrealistic. By distancing herself in this way, she has disavowed responsibility for the actions and desires of that person, and therefore does not have to reconcile an interest in acting with an interest in sociology. In a first-person narrative, some degree of distancing necessarily exists between the narrator and the protagonist, as discussed in Chapter 4. But in this example, the necessary separation is taken much further, so that it becomes an explicit strategy for managing discontinuity.

## Strategy of Discontinuity as Meta-continuity

The next strategy for managing discontinuity is logically the most complex of those we have encountered. In this strategy, the speaker takes a series of professions or actions that clearly appear to be discontinuous and uses them to affirm his/her desire for multiplicity, change, or the like. In effect, the speaker using this strategy affirms: "Discontinuity is my continuity."

Example 29 illustrates this strategy. The housing administrator has just described the sequence of different jobs he has held.

29. The only thing that maybe doesn't feel right is that I, that I'm at a, I'm at a point where I'm past, I'm past the point where I can experiment easily and yet I'd kind of still like like to continue to do it. **I think I could be a dilettante all my life as long as I could, could do it with some intensity.** You know, each <u>section</u> with some intensity.

This is a very clear statement of the speaker's belief that the sequence of different jobs he has held is valuable just because the jobs differ. After this statement, he goes on to say that, in general, employers do not understand his professional choices and do not see them as consistent. But by his use of the word dilettante, which normally is rather pejorative, the speaker indicates that he is attempting to revalue this concept and create his own evaluation of a discontinuous professional history.

A similar instance of this strategy is found in example 30. The speaker here was trained as a psychologist; she is currently the manager of a computer systems design team. In this example, she is providing an evaluation of the range of jobs she has held, some of which she liked better than her present position as a manager:

30. In fact I, I think that (pause) I like getting a broad view (pause) you know, of the world and what's going on in different areas. You know, I, I think I get itchy when I stay in one (pause) you know, working on one thing for too long.

Like the previous speaker, this one also provides her own evaluation of a discontinuous career path as being desirable just because it is discontinuous.

### Discontinuity Without Account: One Thing Leads to Another

Rather than adopting one of the previous strategies for managing discontinuity, some narratives discuss discontinuity itself, without finding an immediate way to manage it acceptably. However, this failure itself is criticized, thus indicating that the speaker recognizes it as problematic—

as a less than desirable way of presenting a life story. This strategy is similar to the one used in managing accident; they differ in that discontinuity requires a sequence to be managed, while accident may involve a single event.

For instance, in example 31, a computer programmer presents a narrative about his choice of profession that goes from an unsuccessful and unsatisfying college career in physics, to a choice to attend graduate school to avoid the draft, to entering a doctoral program (which he did not complete) rather than the master's program he had preferred because of available funding. After leaving school, he found a series of jobs related to the part of the work that had interested him in graduate school.

31.    SPEAKER: You know, so it, it's always seems, it's just uh, I've never, you know, like I said, set out to put, you know, set my life in a particular direction. Th- then have it, uh, I jus- more taking advantage of what's there at a particular time.

INTERVIEWER: Is that a problem for you?

SPEAKER: Sometimes I think it is. I don't uh, you know (pause) I feel and I have been accused of just floating along.

INTERVIEWER: Why?

SPEAKER: In fact, um, people that I've been close to have found this to be a problem. And I've heard it from (pause) a number of people that I don't seem to have any commitment. Ma- I don't, uh, I'm just drifting through life and getting, getting what I can out of it, you know, and uh, like that. And, I have a feeling sometime that (coughs) Well, I should be, you know, setting, I should be defining my goals, uh, things like that, but I just (coughs) I don't know. It, sometimes I think that, you know, that I'm not doing it right, or something along those lines.

INTERVIEWER: Have you always found it this way?

SPEAKER: Yeah. I've always found it this way. (pause) And, you know, uh, I don't find it to be a bad life in general (laughs) You know (pause)

INTERVIEWER: Do you think other people live less accidentally?

SPEAKER: Well they sure talk like they do. (Both laugh) You know. Really, I think. I mean, people <u>talk</u> to me about this like it's a major character flaw of mine. You know. That I'm not taking responsibility and making decisions. You know. And not taking things seriously. You know and thinking about what I want my life to mean. //Int: Um hmm// You know. What my, what my goals are. And I <u>don't</u>. And it's, I'm kind of, uh, split on my feelings, i- you know, in, in one, sometimes I feel well they just have a different, I don't know "I really don't understand what you're talking about. My life isn't so bad." I - really you know (Both laugh) Other times I kind of think of it, yeah, well, I see kind of what they mean. I'm not (pause) I have a, there's a kind of weasely aspect to this whole thing. Kind of opportunistic, uh, you know what I mean, it's just (pause) kind of uh, a rat scurrying around and picking what he can, you know, and gettin', getting the hell out of there, um (Both laugh)

This speaker reflects on his life as lacking sufficient continuity — specifically, the continuity that would arise from the culturally given notions of proper agency, of having specified desires, goals, and so on, and of shaping one's life in accord with these. In a series of striking animal metaphors, the speaker indicates that his narrative can be seen as the story of a weasel or rat: **scurrying around and picking what he can, you know, and gettin', getting the hell out of there.** At the same time, he indicates that this feeling is his response to the norms of proper continuity based on agency that he knows are current in our culture, and to criticisms by others of his failure to meet these norms.

Interestingly, this speaker's narrative provides the materials for a very different analysis of the same sequence if a high value is placed on the ability to be **opportunistic,** to take advantage of whatever comes along. However, this is apparently not a type of character that the speaker feels he can claim for himself or that would be acceptable in his social world.

A similar analysis and criticism of discontinuity can be seen in example 32, which is given by the speaker of example 30:

32. Well, I think I'm reaching that point in my life where I'm
    willing to, you know, think about (pause) well, sort of think
    about, instead of just drifting with the opportunity. Like this
    last project, I really (pause) I really got stuck in it. OK. I really
    had wanted to (pause) look around outside XYZ for a job and
    to see what things were available and what I really thought I
    wanted to do. (pause) And then, this (project) came along and
    I had a lot of experience in it and I told the person who was
    running it that I, you know, would join it and help him run it.
    And then he left, so I sort of got <u>stuck</u> with it. And it's been
    very interesting, but I still think that I should have done you
    know, a (pause) I never intended it last for three years. Which
    is the same as with the speech work. I had never, you know,
    thought that that was going to last for five or six years. (pause)
    So there's nine years of life that I uh (pause)

As we discussed in Chapter 4, the speaker characterizes herself as "drifting with the opportunity," which she believes is inappropriate. The problem is not her actual job history, which has involved a number of excellent jobs, but her lack of agency in arriving at that particular sequence
of jobs.

   The speaker of example 33, also a computer programmer, presents his
present profession as a matter of having moved from one thing to another, but unlike the previous two speakers, he gives this a positive
interpretation as an example of **Irish luck:**

33. As I always say, it's Irish luck. Uh (pause) I fall into things.
    But of course I'm very ready (pause) to fall (pause) into things.
    Uh (pause) I've been very fortunate. I, I, at, just <u>before</u> (pause)
    I, this thing, I w- uh, <u>before</u> I'd, w- started that interview with
    XYZ [his current employer] (pause) uh (pause) I had about,
    oh, I guess about six months before, I had gone and looked at
    a chartered accountant's job! And, they had these big elaborate
    <u>tests</u> you could take, and I went in and <u>took</u> the tests. It took
    (pause) all of a day (pause) and they marked them and came
    back and said "Not," and I said "Why?" And they said, uh,
    "You're not suitable. You're too energetic for a chartered ac-
    countant." (laughs) Well. That was a godsend. I might be a
    chartered accountant or (pause) vice president, or something
    like that, or president, for that matter, or something today.

162                              *Life Stories*

This narrative is followed by another in which another unforeseen and unplanned-for series of events, arising because he was at that point unemployed, leads the speaker to his current and much-loved job as a programmer. This analysis of Irish luck is in striking contrast to the previous speaker's analysis of his ratlike opportunism. Starting from very similar perceptions of their motivations and relatively low degree of agency, the two speakers come to almost opposite evaluations of what these mean, how they are to be understood and valued, and what they say about how the speaker is leading his life. What leads two people to such different ways of understanding and valuing their own lives? We may note that, although the speaker in example 33 takes credit primarily as an individual for his own readiness to take advantage of whatever comes along, he also explains the formation of his individual character within a family context as being part of his entire family's values, stemming from their pioneering life in Canada, in which any able-bodied person was expected to turn his or her hand to whatever task came along: farming, fishing, lumbering, coal mining, and so on. He indicates that this background is unusual: **I was born in the seventeenth century and I'm currently living in the twenty first and I've covered everything in between.** His interpretive strategy of taking advantage of Irish luck is perhaps more available to him because of his family background; indeed, it depends on a self-understanding not only as an individual but as a member of a distinctive group.

## Conclusions

We have now surveyed the last of the strategies for managing discontinuity that are found in these data. However, the list of strategies examined here is by no means exhaustive. Many other strategies are possible, since, unlike the factors that constitute adequate causality, these methods for handling inadequate causality or sequence are at least partially idiosyncratic, depending on the creativity of the individual to formulate a convincing coherence or meta-coherence that the hearer can accept. In any event, we have established that the narration of the life story calls for such strategies, and that they can be investigated as an important part of the process of constructing the life story.

– Note: These are all professionals, not
grad. school-trained.
Thus, by low-agcy is not the norm.

– what place does agcy (strategy?) have in
China etc?

# 6

# Coherence Systems

*[handwritten marginal note, partly illegible]* Note: Ky quesh had overlooks: why does no men. recurrent to an expert system → to supplant own rel of belits?

In Chapter 5, we discussed the establishment of adequate causality, and the management of inadequate causality and accident. Moving up from this local level of the construction of causality, we will next examine the level of the **coherence system,** a more global cultural device for structuring experience into socially sharable narrative. A coherence system is a discursive practice that represents a system of beliefs and relations between beliefs; it provides the environment in which one statement may or may not be taken as a cause of another statement. More specifically, a coherence system of the type discussed here is a system of beliefs that occupies a position midway between **common sense**—the beliefs and relations between beliefs that any person in the culture may be assumed to know (if not to share) and that anyone may use—and **expert systems,** which are beliefs and relations between beliefs held, understood, and properly used by experts in a particular domain.[1] A coherence system is a system of beliefs derived from some expert system, but used by someone with no corresponding expertise or credentials. The term **coherence system** represents an intermediate-level system that, to my knowledge, has not been previously noted or studied. As we shall see, the differences in social standing among the users of various kinds of systems imply a difference in the kinds of social practices in which these systems may participate.

To clarify the definition of a coherence system, let us turn to two (constructed) example pairs, which we first encountered in Chapter 1.

---

1. The term "expert system" as used in artificial intelligence refers to an attempt to produce a computer representation of some body of knowledge (Clancey 1992). As I use the term here, it refers to a system of knowledge, beliefs, values, and actions situated in human social practice.

Example 1 gives a reason that relies on common-sense beliefs to account for professional choice:

1a. How did you come to be an accountant?

1b. Well, I guess I have a precise mind, and I enjoy getting all the little details right.

In contrast, to understand example 2b as a relevant answer to 2a, the hearer must know (if not share) the popular Freudian coherence system, which attributes the real causes of events to experiences in early childhood:

2a. How did you come to be an accountant?

2b. Well, my mother started toilet-training me when I was six months old.

In later sections of this chapter, we will see that the coherence systems present in the life story data are popular versions of expert systems. However, not all coherence system are expert systems. We may view the ordinary system of common sense as the most pervasive (and the most unnoticed) coherence system in our culture.

Common sense is a system of beliefs that is assumed to be shared by everyone in a given culture and that requires no special circumstances or standing for its use. Thus, a speaker who said **I quit banking because I didn't like it** would be invoking a coherence principle from the common-sense coherence system. In contrast, a speaker who said **I quit banking because my father was a banker, and I've always had a love-hate thing with my father** would be constructing an explanation that relies on the semi-expert coherence system of psychology.

We now turn to an exploration of the semi-expert coherence systems most fully represented in the life story data. We will discuss the system of common sense as it relates to profession and choice of profession in Chapter 7.

## Definition and Function of Coherence Systems

We begin with a fuller definition of the notion of coherence system. As the examples already given should suggest, a coherence system is a system that claims to provide a means for understanding, evaluating, and constructing accounts of experience. Thanks to that understanding, such a system may also provide, either explicitly or implicitly, a guide for future behavior. As we shall see, the coherence systems present in the data, at least, are popular versions of expert theories.

This definition of coherence systems includes local or restricted coherence systems, like theories of the right kind of food to eat to maintain optimal health or the best way to win at roulette. There are, of course, many of these. However, the interesting examples of coherence systems are those that have some reasonable claim to completeness—those that purport to explain most or all realms of experience, not merely local areas of life. The most obvious examples in wide current use are Freudian psychology (or more generally, psychoanalytic theory), Marxism, and most religious systems. An understanding of much of experience as the product of a world-wide conspiracy of the Bavarian illuminati or of the unrecognized influence of higher-plane entities would equally qualify as coherence systems, albeit less widely held ones.

This definition of coherence systems is not equivalent to any concept in general use. It is related to the term **belief system** or **cultural system** as used, for example, in Geertz (1973), but it differs in recognizing that the coherence system is specifically a semi-expert system, related but not equivalent to either belief systems shared by an entire culture or belief systems that are properly held only by some class of experts.

## Coherence Systems in These Data

The theories I have found in these data are versions of Freudian psychology, behaviorism, and astrology, as well as some indications of feminism and Catholic confessional accounting. All of these theories have their associated expert—for example, a practicing psychoanalyst, an academic psychologist, an astrologer, or a priest. In this chapter, I shall explicate the first three, since they are most fully represented in the data.

This list of coherence systems raises a number of questions. Is the list exhaustive? How many more coherence systems would be discovered by doing more interviews, or by doing interviews on another topic? How many such coherence systems can be present in a culture at a given time? It would take a different and rather extensive research program to answer these questions. However, I suspect that this list is not at all exhaustive; other interviews and particularly interviews on other topics would undoubtedly produce further examples. On the other hand, the number of coherence systems cannot be very great. There is a necessary limit on the number of coherence systems that can be present in a given culture at a given time, since one's addressee must at least recognize if not share any coherence system one chooses to use.

Certain absences in the list of coherence systems evident in these data are particularly striking. For example, economically based or class-based systems are absent: no one cites economic opportunities or class limitations as factors in professional choice; the speakers all appear to assume that professional choice is dictated by personal ability and by degree of psychological adjustment, which either permits or prevents one's seeing and taking advantage of opportunities. This view of a world without politics and without social class appears to be particularly American. (For a further discussion of this, see Lasch [1979], Schur [1976], and Sennett [1977]; see also Chapter 7.)[2]

Another striking absence is the lack of invocation of race or ethnicity to explain available opportunity. Since all the speakers are white, it is perhaps understandable that race is not present as a coherence system that can be used to illuminate the factors shaping their professional lives. But the sample does include people from a variety of ethnic groups and religious backgrounds, only one of whom mentions this as a factor influencing his personal psychology. This is in strong contrast to a previous generation of speakers, including the parents and grandparents of a number of these speakers, for whom ethnic origin – and more specifically, generation of immigration – was crucial in understanding anyone's life story.

## Coherence Systems in These Data

Of the coherence systems discoverable in these data, the most common appears to be that of Freudian psychology, so I shall begin with it, give it the fullest discussion, and use it as a detailed example of the relation between expert and popular versions of a coherence system.

### *Popular Freudian Psychology*

To get the flavor of this coherence system, consider the following example, which concludes a story about how the speaker took a banking job that he did not like and that did not last very long.

---

2. The data discussed were gathered from 1977 through 1979. I have noted that, in periods when economic conditions worsened, stories of professional choice began to include at least a mention of economic circumstances, although they still did not mention social class.

3. So I didn't really make much of a decision there. I think that's one way of looking at it. I made a decision. It was the decision that I didn't like at the time, so that's why I have the sense that I was forced into it, but there are all kinds of psychological things that make you do things at various moments in your life.

From a common-sense point of view, this seems to be a rather weak justification of a bad decision: common sense suggests that one should be in control of one's action; or that, if one is not, one should only be forced into making bad decisions by irresistibly strong external forces. But further analysis suggests that this text implies a coherence system that offers a way of making sense of the phenomenon of doing things that one does not like or approve of.

The speaker himself gives a clue to the system he is invoking by his use of the phrase "psychological things." This system is a psychological model—more specifically, a popular version of Freudian psychology. Three components of this popular version show up in the present data:

1. The splitting of the self into component parts that are in disagreement
2. The notion that real causes are to be found in childhood and childhood experiences
3. The notion of levels of personality, some of which are deeper than others

Let us begin with the split of the self into component parts that are in disagreement. The speaker of example 3 feels that he was **forced** into a decision, and attributes this to **psychological things that make you do things.** The fragmentation of experience and the identification of the speaker with the fragment not in control form a strong component of popular Freudian psychology. A related notion at work in this example is the idea that one can act for reasons one is unaware of or does not understand. Thus, we hear statements like **I was in Paris at the time and I thought I was happy, but really I wasn't.** A more extended example of this phenomenon is shown in example 4:

4. I married someone who was older than I was, who was a bit of a self-centered tyrant, and for that I got, uh, to whom I was not very, even sexually attracted, and was very temperamentally different than I am, and uh although I was in a certain way attracted to him sexually I was not, really.

Here again we have an example of someone telling about acting because of feelings that she had or thought she had that were in fact not real.

Both assumptions about the nature of action are based on a complex form of distancing. The first is the distance the speaker maintains from the protagonist of the story—a necessary part of any form of narration. However, in stories that contain the additional element of a Freudian coherence system, speakers can place themselves in the position of being an expert commenting on their own lives, thereby achieving an additional layer of distance.

Another form of distancing, buried more deeply within the story, is the distancing between component parts of the person. The part that feels or believes it feels is not the part that causes action. As the speaker of example 3 indicates, this permits a curious paradox in which one is simultaneously active and passive, forced into action by oneself.

A second, perhaps more familiar tenet of popular Freudian psychology is the notion that real causes are to be found in childhood and childhood experiences. We can see a version of this belief in example 5, where it is combined with the metaphor of splitting oneself into component parts. The speaker, who is also the speaker of example 4, is explaining her combination of literary and scientific interests. She has already told a number of stories about how she arrived at these interests, which have to do with the opportunities that were available to her in the course of her education. She then steps back, as it were, from this historical presentation to give what the language interestingly allows us to call a deeper reason:

5. Another um idea that, well, in my more uh I often wonder why I have this need to uh make, to, to write, to kind of split myself off in two directions or to try and take on many, to take on what might seem to be warring, I see what I do as, as reconciling things, and why do I need to reconcile things? I came from a family that was very conflict prone. And I was the peacemaker in the family. And I don't like conflict. And I um, or rather, I, I am really very upset by it.

The assumption of this explanation, which permits the speaker to offer it as an explanation, is that one's childhood emotions and actions are crucially relevant in providing an explanation of any further developments. I am not claiming here that only Freudian psychology recognizes childhood experience as important. Rather, I am pointing out that Freudian psychology gives it primacy, which means that any adequate explanation within this system is very likely to be based on it.

A further theme of the coherence system of popular Freudian psychology—and one related to the splitting of the individual into component parts of the personality—is the metaphor of levels, the notion that some parts are deeper or more hidden than others. We see an oblique reference to this notion in example 6:

6. And I think that the source of one's power professionally comes from some deep s- deep thing. And if you don't tap that, you're sunk.

The idea here seems to be that the components of the personality are ordered vertically, with the higher ones' being more accessible to consciousness and the lower ones' being out of the reach of ordinary self-inspection. A further aspect of this metaphor is that the deep components have a certain amount of autonomy and can, in unseen ways, motivate actions that may or may not accord with the desires and plans of the more conscious surface components.

The foregoing discussion has presented a sketch of a semi-expert theory of the mind, which contrasts both with a common-sense theory of the mind and with the professional Freudian model. D'Andrade (1987) provides an explication of the common-sense or cultural theory of the mind that clearly differs from the Freudian model in both its expert and semi-popular forms. The most interesting locus of difference lies in causality: the cultural model treats conscious mental states as having central causal powers, while the Freudian model treats unconscious mental states as being the causal center.

The popular Freudian coherence system also differs from a professional or expert Freudian model in a number of ways, as we will later discuss in detail. In brief, like all cultural models, the popular Freudian system represents a considerable simplification of the original model, reducing both the number of themes and concepts it uses and the complexity of the connections between these.

## Behaviorist Psychology

The popular Freudian psychological coherence system is, as we have seen, quite familiar and pervasive in our culture. By way of contrast, let us consider behaviorist psychology, a quite rare system that is represented in these data by a single speaker. More specifically, one speaker presents her life in behaviorist terms, taking the role not of the conditioner but of the subject of conditioning—that is, the role not of Skinner but of one of Skinner's pigeons.

Her account of her life includes three themes that support an analysis of her coherence system as behaviorism:

1. The need for reinforcement, and reinforcement as the cause of action
2. The separation of the self from emotion
3. Nonagency—the self described in such a way as never to be an active agent in causing events

Reinforcement, the most obvious component of the behaviorist coherence system, is the factor that this speaker uses explicitly in explaining her history. After college, she worked as a social worker, and then she went back to school to get a master's degree in computer science; at the time of her narration, she worked as a computer programmer. The two major foci in her account of her career history are the change from social work to programming and the fact that she has held a number of programming jobs at different companies. She feels that both of these facts require some explanation, and she accounts for both of them as arising from her need for reinforcement:

7. I like concrete results. I, I need to, to be able to see what I've done. I need that kind of reinforcement. If you get me out of that mode, I'm just, I have little tolerance for it. I, I need the strokes of seeing what I'm doing as I'm doing it.
8. So when I was doing social work, and I did that for five years, I need results. I'm a result person. OK. I need to, I like to manipulate symbols, I like those kind of machinations in your head. And I also like to see what I've done. OK? If I, I cannot go extended periods without that, I don't have the tolerance for it and it was, I came to that realization while doing social work, that I had to find something that was, that gave me that kind of concrete kind of (unclear).
9. I guess my chief feeling about XYZ Co. [where she formerly worked as a programmer] was that it was very, there was no point in working. Because it didn't matter whether you did or whether you didn't. There were no strokes for working, there were no punishments for not working.

This notion of reinforcement as the motive for behavior is identical to Skinner's views, with the additional specification of the speaker's personal need for a reinforcement schedule with a very short time delay. Although "reinforcement" and "strokes" have become part of the common vocabulary, such an account of one's life is not coherent within the common-sense coherence system, but only within the expert system of behaviorism.

Another similarity to Skinner's thought lies in this speaker's treatment of her emotions and mental states. In her stories about her professional history, she frequently mentions that she must have had certain emotions, but she does not claim them directly. Consider example 10:

10. And it began to be very demoralizing to me. Uh so I left and whatever I, and I had at that time decided that I really wanted to get to, I guess somehow I had decided I wanted to get serious again about working.

The correction from **I had at that time decided** to **I guess somehow I had decided** is a perfect example. Most psychologists would regard this as a small but pathological form of distancing oneself from one's emotions. From a behaviorist point of view, however, the belief in autonomous mental states that act as determinants of behavior is an error — indeed, the fundamental error in understanding human psychology. Still, it is an error that nontechnical language almost forces one into. The speaker here denies any actual belief in or sensation of decision as an autonomous mental entity, while simultaneously indicating some loyalty to the ordinary forms of discourse and understanding, which require them.

Closely related to the nonexistence of mental states is the third theme: nonagency. This term is chosen to convey that the speaker does not use personal agency in the way that most speakers do. Normally, speakers describe their experiences in such a way that they are active agents in their stories: **I did so and so; I decided such and such; I solved the problem facing me.** This speaker does not construct her narratives in this way: the active agents are either abstract motivations or other persons, not herself. The following story is an example of both kinds of agency. At the time being described, the speaker was working as a social worker, which she did not like, and was investigating the possibility of becoming a computer programmer, by speaking to a professor of computer science:

11. I spoke to Dr. K a long time. He decided, oh yeah, I had really gone over there, wasn't asking to go to graduate school. I was asking to take a course in the evening. And I figured I could qualify because I had graduated from R and it wouldn't, what big deal would it be for him to let me take a course. I, by the time I was out of there, he had me enrolled in this whole

program, and he says, "Oh you have to do it this way." And it must have appealed to me, because I went ahead and did it.

In this story, the agent is not the speaker but Dr. K, whose somewhat surprising actions move events along. The speaker had intended to take a single course; but as a result of Dr. K's actions, she finds herself simultaneously enrolled in a master's program and in a BS program in mathematics. Even in the smaller-level details of sentential construction, we find that she is not the agent. For example, notice the nonagency of the phrase **By the time I was out of there**, as compared with the more expected **By the time I left there.**

The theme of nonagency is extremely strong — so much so that later, when it is directly challenged, it is still maintained. As part of the interview procedure, after I had obtained the speakers' own accounts of their professional history, I attempted to reframe the questions, using coherence systems different from those the speakers had used. I did this in order to test the extent to which the speakers were willing to adapt their coherence systems to my apparent beliefs, and the extent to which they would maintain them in the face of a proposed alternative conceptualization. Example 12 represents the computer programmer's response to such a challenge. I had asked her about choice points in her life, a formulation that implies the status of choices as relevant entities. Although the speaker does not explicitly deny the existence of choice points or the possibility of choice, the story she tells, while apparently using this vocabulary, is completely consistent with her previous system of nonagency:

12.        SPEAKER: I chose to flunk out of a master's program in psychology. Uh huh. That was a choice point.

    INTERVIEWER: What do you mean, you chose to flunk out?

        SPEAKER: I got one too many C's.

    INTERVIEWER: Why?

        SPEAKER: Because I just didn't know that I w- I wasn't interested. I just couldn't bring, I had this big struggle with myself as to why I was doing what I was doing and I decided well I, I just have to do this because I'm supposed to do this, and it just didn't, it was, well there wasn't any rewards in it for me. And uh it's an interesting choice because I could have picked myself up and left, which I didn't do, I just sat there and waited for it to all come crashing down on me until <u>Oh jolly!</u> So, but that, but definitely a choice that I made somewhere in that, in that interim.

To speak of choosing to flunk out of a program by doing nothing until one is thrown out is clearly to subvert the ordinary meaning of choice. For a speaker operating within a psychoanalytic belief system, such a formulation might represent a recognition of personal responsibility for the unconscious motivation for events that in the common-sense system would be taken as falling beyond one's conscious control, and hence not one's responsibility. In this case, however, the speaker appears to be tacitly rejecting my formulation of life as motivated by choices that occur at choice points. It would be extremely difficult, both conceptually and as a matter of etiquette for her to make explicit and then reject my presupposition that choices exist and are relevant to one's life course; rather, she implicitly redefines the term "choice" until it can be used in a narrative that does not conflict with her own system.

Comparing this speaker's coherence system to the system expressed in the popular writings of Skinner (1979, 1948), we see that the two are in agreement. The one striking difference is that Skinner's model provides a place for the agent — the force that arranges the contingencies of reinforcement. In the laboratory, of course, this is the experimenter. In the ideal community, it is a planner or a board of planners, who experiment with various social and physical arrangements in order to produce happy and good people. In the ordinary state of affairs, the environment rather haphazardly supplies positive and negative reinforcement, which (in Skinner's view) would be better supplied by a more conscious agent.

The computer programmer's coherence system closely resembles Skinner's general views of how human psychology works, but it differs markedly from his descriptions of his own life. In his autobiographical works, *The Particulars of My Life* and *The Shaping of a Behaviorist*, Skinner does not explain his behavior in terms of reinforcement at all. Since he does not use mental states as an explanatory system either, these autobiographies read very oddly, as an unevaluated chronological sequence of narratives. For example, the following two paragraphs from Skinner (1979) are preceded and followed by paragraphs on two entirely different subjects:

During my first year as a Junior Fellow I met Nedda, who had come to Harvard for graduate study. She was younger than I by four or five years, but we liked each other immediately and after a date or two we made love.

She had an apartment where we spent a good deal of time. She cooked delicious meals, and I took her to the Boston Symphony and the theatre (we saw O'Neill's *Days Without End*). I fell very much in love with her, but I did not see much of her friends or have much in common with them. After two or three months it was clear that I was not really a part of her intellectual or social life. One evening I took her out to dinner and she told me that we should break it off. She had been more or less engaged to a young man who was chronically ill, and she was going back to him.

It was a reasonable decision, but it hit me very hard. As we walked back to her apartment from the subway, I found myself moving very slowly. It was not a pose; I simply could not move faster. For a week I was in almost physical pain, and one day I bent a wire in the shape of an N, heated it in a Bunsen burner and branded my left arm. The brand remained clear for years. My mother saw it once when I was changing my shirt and said, "Where'd you get the N?" I said, "It was an accident. I burned myself," and she wisely let it go at that. (p. 137)

Although Skinner avoids postulating mental states as reasons for actions, he also suggests that certain people may not be subject to the same kinds of deliberate conditioning. In *Walden Two* (Skinner 1948), Frazier, the character who has designed the utopia on psychological principles, is quite explicitly outside the full range of conditioning effects of the environment. In the following passage, he explains his separateness to a visitor who has just admitted that he dislikes him:

You think I'm conceited, aggressive, tactless, selfish. . . . You can't see in me any of the personal warmth or the straightforward natural strength which are responsible for the success of Walden Two. . . . In a word of all the people you've seen in the past four days, you're sure that I'm **one**, at least, who couldn't possibly be a genuine member of any community. . . . But God **damn** it, can't you see? **I'm — not — a — product of — Walden — Two.** How much can you ask of a man? Give me credit for what I've done or not, as you please, but don't look for perfection. Isn't it enough that I've made other men likeable and happy and productive? Why expect me to resemble them? Must I possess the virtues I've proved to be best suited to a well-ordered society? Must I exhibit the interests and skills and untrammeled spirit which I've learned how to engender in others? (p. 207)

The passage shows the unwillingness of the behaviorist to see himself as occupying the same position vis-a-vis conditioning as his subjects. Skinner's autobiography does not claim that he acted autonomously, but the absence of any account of the factors conditioning him strongly suggests a different status for his actions than for those of his subjects.

And so Skinner is a less thoroughgoing behaviorist than the speaker we have been investigating, who clearly admits that she is subject to conditioning.

In the examples we have seen in this section, and in the entire life story given by this speaker, there is no sense that reinforcement is provided by a particular agent. She speaks of the reinforcement process as something sought by the person to be reinforced, but in a rather passive way—something like Skinner's notion of shaping a behavior:

13. And the whole process of finding what it is that gives you your strokes, OK? is not an easy one.
14. So that's what you're asking about, the process of finding out what is positively reinforcing to you OK? is not an easy thing to do and I don't know how people hit upon

This is related to Skinner's notion of the environment as agent, except that the speaker here has not formed any notion of the environment as an entity that acts upon her.

A number of questions remain. One involves the rarity of this coherence system. Since only one speaker out of the thirteen in the sample, uses this behaviorist coherence system, is it justifiable to posit it as a coherence system present in the culture, or should it rather be considered a personal idiosyncrasy of this particular speaker? The system is unique in the data of this study; and I believe that, even in a considerably larger sample, it would be quite rare. However, although this coherence system sounds somewhat odd, its relation to a known expert system is recognizable. Furthermore, it is comprehensible; we may be surprised by the sorts of things the speaker cites as reasons, but we can understand why they count as reasons. This is in strong contrast to truly idiosyncratic coherence systems, whose connections are incomprehensible.

We may also ask how this speaker came to use such a rare system. Behaviorist psychology has had much less effect on popular culture than has Freudian psychology. Notions of behavior modification as a therapeutic technique are somewhat known to a general audience, but they have a very different character than do psychotherapeutic notions, because, as they are generally understood, they do not involve the core of the self. Either they are to be applied to others who are bad people and not like us—prisoners, the insane, and so on—or they are to be applied to some trait like nail-biting or fear of elevators that we do not see as being intrinsic to the self. Often, in popular articles about the use of behavior modification to remove undesirable traits in the self, the image used is of clearing away alien obstructions so that the true self can shine out.

Another trace of behaviorist views, I believe, can be found in the common computer-based metaphor of people being programmed to do things: "Oh she's just programmed to smile and offer you coffee, tea, or bouillon." As this metaphor is used, however, it tends to be applied to others, not to oneself. (This observation is quite compatible with the findings of attribution theory (Kelley 1967).) It is much easier to see others' behavior as motivated by external causes than to see one's own in the same way. (In this context, it is interesting that the behaviorist speaker is a computer programmer, although she does not use the metaphor of people being programmed.) To understand this speaker's use of the behaviorist system, we would need a detailed study of the effects of behaviorism on popular culture (which, like most of the other historical studies this investigation requires, does not yet exist), as well as a full biographical study of the speaker. Since such psychological and biographical information lies beyond the scope of this study, how the speaker came to use such a system must remain a tantalizing question.

### Astrology

Another coherence system present in these data is astrology. In the examples that follow, this system is used only jokingly and, indeed, in the relaxed later part of an interview as it modulated into a flirtation. This is not surprising. Since astrology is a less intellectually respectable coherence system than the others we have examined, it is less likely to turn up at all in an interview situation. Therefore, only traces of the system are present, and it is impossible to list all the themes that constitute the system.

One important social function of astrology is to explain people's character and character differences as caused by specific configurations of planets at their birth. It is used, both in the examples that follow and in casual uses I have heard, as a basis for understanding why an incomprehensible or obnoxious character trait cannot be changed or why two otherwise reasonable people cannot get along with one another. Unlike many psychological explanations of character types, astrological types are not presented as pathological; therefore, there is no demand or expectation that a person of a particular type could or should change that type by becoming (for example) better adjusted or more mature.

The following instances of use of an astrological coherence system are taken from an interview with a single speaker:

15.  SPEAKER: Yeah. The one thing that I don't miss from the East Coast are the arguments.

INTERVIEWER: (Laughs) Yeah.

SPEAKER: OK. (Laughs) Talking, yeah, uh but the arguments, and almost the creation. It's sort of like, my mother does that too. She's really beautiful. She called me up one night and she said "How are things?" And I said "Fine, you know, kind of beautiful, right in the middle." Which is where I like things, being a Libra. And she says, "Oh, I can't stand them when they're that way." She says, "I gotta have some excitement in my life." She says, "I noodge your father a little bit to get." So she creates an argument just to get a little stimulation. Yeah. I, that's not for me. That's for my m- who's a Scorpio, my mother is a Scorpio, so.

16.  SPEAKER: What's your sign?

INTERVIEWER: Uh, Capricorn.

SPEAKER: Perfect. Methodical. They like it to go right. Intelligent. Yeah.

INTERVIEWER: I'm not methodical.

SPEAKER: You're not? Your mind works that way.

INTERVIEWER: Hm. (Laughs) You should see my drawers.

SPEAKER: The hell with the drawers. (Laughs) Your mind works very methodical. I have a very close friend that's a Capricorn. And he uh, you know, he, everything is, he does it right the first time. He can't do a half-assed job. It'd bug the shit out of him. He figures, you know, and I agree with him, too, that the easiest way is the right way.

INTERVIEWER: Capricorn has always struck me as one of the more boring signs.

SPEAKER: Hmmmm. Not to me. Well, I dig minds, OK. So minds have uh, uh, they turn me on. I dig when I I'm talking to people, somebody intelligent.

In an ethnography of modern British witches and occultists, Luhr-mann (1989) suggests as another function of astrology that it offers an apparently objective and technical way to talk about oneself:

> I used to call this "astro-speak": people would settle down over tea and bis-cuits and discuss why their twelfth house moon made them tidy or obsessed with work. Britain is a private culture which frowns on intimate discussion. Within an astrological vocabulary, the magician could talk openly about personal feelings under the guise of intellectual exploration. (p. 245)

Certainly this function of astrology within this mode of discourse is found in the United States as well. Perhaps it is not present in the data of this study only because the interview situation already provides the speaker with authoritative empowerment for self-display.

These examples represent a popular form or use of astrology as a coherence system. In its more serious use, it presents an explanation and reconciliation of character types. Its use as a flirtation device functions both by rekeying the talk on a less serious level than that of interview and by providing a socially legitimate basis for talking about the other person's character.

Like the other coherence systems discussed in this study, astrology has in addition to its popular form an expert version. And like other experts, astrologers may provide not only an account of character but advice on how to live.

## Other Coherence Systems in These Data

Freudian psychology, behaviorism, and astrology are the three coherence systems most strongly represented in these data. In addition, two oth-ers — feminism and Catholic confessional practice — are represented to some degree, although each is used less pervasively in the speaker's entire narrative.

The feminist system is used in example 17 by a technical manager. She does not frame the story of her entire professional career in terms of her being a woman in a predominantly male field. However, she does make what amount to side remarks to me, as the interviewer, indicating what we both know about what happens to women:

17. INTERVIEWER: How did you get into your profession?

      SPEAKER: Oh that was interesting. Because I was working at the S Corporation. They were look- they were doing some work in social psychology which was the area I was interested in. And their lab closed up. And so, um, I could have come over when XYZ started and worked at XYZ, but I thought I'd like to do something with computers that was, let's see, that was around 55, something like 1955, so I went for an interview at ABC and **I was hired by a man who was told to only hire men with math degrees (Interviewer laughs) because he didn't like being told what to do** (Interviewer laughs) so that's how I got started. And I, you know, worked for him and it worked out. (pause)

INTERVIEWER: What was that job?

SPEAKER: That was, uh, sort of like a programmer trainee. On the Univac One computer.

INTERVIEWER: Um hum. And then what happened?

SPEAKER: And then he uh left ABC and went to QXR and asked me to join, you know, to join a small group that he was let's see starting at QXR. And so I went over there (short pause) and I worked there from (short pause) oh, probably close to two years, until I got married and I was traveling for PQR. And my husband was traveling for MNO. And so, I think two weeks after our honeymoon I was supposed to pick him up at the airport and instead I was flying up to Sunnyvale when he was (laughs) flying down from San Francisco. And I left a page saying well you can get the keys to the car at such and such a desk (short pause) and that's when we decided that maybe both of us traveling wasn't a very good idea **so you know who gave up the traveling.** (Interviewer laughs) So I switched jobs.

In this example, the speaker relies on mutual knowledge of conventional sex roles — a reliance justified by the interviewer's laughter, which signifies an understanding of the way the story is framed. In a later discussion of her success, this speaker explicitly refers to a feminist work

on women in management, as well as to her own experience in nontradi-
tionally female activities like football:

18.      SPEAKER: In fact, it's interesting, I was just talking to
                  Laura the other day if, maybe if, (pause) if
                  since Well, I was reading this book about
                  women in management that was saying that the
                  one thing that women have a hard time under-
                  standing is that management is just one big
                  game and that football is one of its best models
                  (Both laugh) Therefore women are at a disad-
                  vantage because they've never played football.
                  Right?

INTERVIEWER: Yes.

     SPEAKER: OK. I happened to have been a woman who
              played football when I was a kid. That

INTERVIEWER: Well, no wonder you were so successful.
             (Laughs)

This speaker does not use the feminist coherence system fully enough
to allow for an elaborate analysis. However, such a system clearly does
exist and is available for use, at least in discussions among women. (At a
conference on cybernetics, I once heard a female speaker describe her
mode of work as that of a "spinster," a term revalued and redefined in
the feminist work of Daly (1978) as connoting a free woman who spins
her own being. While several women in the audience perked up immediately, a man of about 60 seated behind me whispered rather kindly to
his wife: "What a shame. She's such a pretty girl.")

Let us now turn to Catholic confessional practice. The speaker, a
professor of sociology, gives a very organized discussion of her life, in
terms of three areas: sexual relations, relations with friends, and work.
When I comment on how good her bookkeeping is, she herself relates
this form of organization to the Catholic confessional practice she
learned as a child but no longer practices:

19.      SPEAKER: So I guess two out of three ain't bad, but, there
                  should be a fourth area and there isn't and
                  maybe that's a failure, in terms of setting up a,
                  a spiritual esthetic life outside my work. I have
                  none. My life is three parts It's, it's, it's sex,
                  friends and work and that's all. Um and I do
                  occasionally feel sure that parts of, of develop-

ment of self have not been tapped. Nothing
happens there. Whatsoever. There is nothing.
At best I, I do art in my work. (pause) And
try, but I'm very very underdeveloped and su-
perficial in the spiritual areas, artistic or es-
thetic.

INTERVIEWER: Do you feel that you should be developed or
is, do you feel the lack of it?

SPEAKER: No I feel that I should.

. . .

Maybe if I ever give up on men as a theme,
maybe I'll be able to develop that area instead.
I guess that's uh one outstanding one, one
warm successful one, one terribly terrible one,
and often very painful area and one nonexistent one. (Laughs) Well um.

INTERVIEWER: You have your bookkeeping so well arranged.

SPEAKER: Yeah isn't that disgusting. Taxonomy of life, it
does sound a bit bookkeeping, doesn't it.

INTERVIEWER: Do you usually think of it that way?

SPEAKER: Yeah. I do. I give myself grades.

INTERVIEWER: Really?

SPEAKER: Well not A's and B's but I, I re- have re-
eval- periods of reevaluation, where I, and I
do tend to separate domains of function, yeah,
I really do.

After a discussion of counting one's lovers and of trying to decide
how many lovers is too many, the speaker explicitly relates this kind of
accounting to Catholic practice:

20.      SPEAKER: I w- I have gotten to the point where I, it's
much harder to count than it once was, there
used to be a very easy chronology, I could, well
remember, I was raised Catholic, so a lot of
this counting you know structure was built into
me very early. I mean, uh, you would have
to go through the examination of conscience.
Right, how many times did I disobey my
mother, how many lies did I tell, "Bless me

father, it has been two weeks since my last confession, um I was disobedient four times, I told
three lies, I um had impure thoughts once, well
twice." (Both laugh) And then I would get into
how long do you entertain a thought before it
becomes entertaining it on purpose. Oooh! I
mean all of the evaluation of whe- And now
I'm doing it with carbohydrates and calories.
You know, and then the carbohydrates and
calories are the input and then the weight is the
output and you know balancing one against the
other. Rosary beads, liturgical kind of repeti-
tive things to make it work. I have a <u>sacramen-</u>
<u>tal</u> approach to eating.

INTERVIEWER: Clearly.

SPEAKER: Um then, it's, it's almost scary the see the degree to which those, those structures are prede-
termining, although the content is just changed
radically. And clearly I do that with the lovers
too, I mean adding them up, categorizing
them, adding within categories, uh what do
you do with the ones that you had oral sex with
when you were still a virgin? You know, stuff
like that.

This speaker is aware of and explicit about the effect of Catholic
practice on her habits of categorization. We may view her use of it as a
coherence system, rather than as the full expert system for several reasons: she is no longer involved in the actual practice of confession with a
confessor; and she has extended the system to matters such as weight
loss and gain, which the expert system does not consider.

## Synchronic Relation Between Popular and Expert Coherence Systems

Thus far, this study has indicated the existence of a number of popular
coherence systems and has claimed a relation between these and corresponding expert systems. We must now examine the nature of this relation. The discussion first covers the synchronic relation between a
popular coherence system and its corresponding expert system; then it

*[handwritten margin notes: Popular the: 1) concept borrowed. 2) System not used as a system. * 3) Expert system do not support but support ... widespread belief / self.]*

considers the historical development of popular coherence systems from expert systems.

The discussion uses popular Freudian psychology as a model, since this coherence system is the one most fully represented in the data and for which the most historical evidence is available. I do not claim to have given a full picture of the Freudian coherence system as it is represented in popular thought. Rather, I am attempting to demonstrate the existence of popular coherence systems and to untangle some of the relations between popular and expert systems.

Let us begin by considering the current relation between popular and expert Freudian systems. The first point is that the popular version uses a very small number of the concepts present in expert Freudian psychology. Most notably lacking are any references to theories of sexual development and sexual functioning. These are, in fact, the concepts that first come to mind in any consideration of the influence of Freud on popular culture. However, the topic of the interview—professional history—does not encourage discussion of sexuality, although a number of speakers mention it anyway, as we have seen. Many other Freudian concepts are absent as well: the Oedipus complex; the tripartite structure of ego, superego, and id; the stages of psychosexual development; and so on. This comparative lack of detail and complexity in the popular coherence systems appears to be characteristic of all relations between popular and expert coherence systems. A professional astrologer looking at the popular use of astrology as a coherence system would perceive a similar impoverishment of the system in including only birth or sun sign while failing to consider rising sign, moon, and other important aspects of the chart.

A second point is that isolated concepts have been borrowed, but not the entire system as a system. The concepts of popular Freudian psychology do not require the dense interconnections of Freud's argumentation. Similarly, the difference between a popular use of astrology and a serious professional use can be seen in the expert's drawing up of an astrological chart, to allow investigation of patterns, rather than relying on isolated interpretations of individual signs. For both of these coherence systems, therefore, it is more difficult for speakers to debate an interpretation meaningfully within the system than it would be for legitimate practitioners of the expert system, since the coherence system does not present a system sufficiently rich to support multiple interpretations.

Finally (and perhaps most important), the concepts of the expert coherence system are those that do not strongly contradict other popular theories of the mind and the reasons for human behavior. Thus, Freudian psychology, as it filters into popular thought, is an expert coherence system that supplements more widespread theories, rather than supplanting them. We will return to this point later.

Let us now turn to the historical process by which an expert coherence system can develop, give rise to popular coherence systems, and finally become part of common sense again, using Freudian psychology as a model. This process raises many fascinating issues in intellectual history, but unfortunately it has been studied little if at all. Quite a lot of information is available about the history and technical background of the various psychological theories themselves, but little information has been gathered about popular theories of the mind that were extant at the time of the formation of the major psychological theories, or about the ways in which these theories fed back into popular thought. For example, Ellenberger (1970) discusses the social history of the development and spread of Freud's thought; Sulloway (1979) discusses the relation of Freud's theories to the expert theories of biology of his time; Bakan (1958) discusses Freud's debt to the Jewish mystical tradition of linguistic interpretation; and Hale (1971) traces a history of the acceptance and modification of Freud's thought in American professional psychological circles. All of these works, though, concentrate on Freud's relation to other expert systems and on his acceptance or rejection by other experts. No systematic history focuses on the effect of Freud's thought on the general public.

Figure 1 gives a sketch of the historical relation among a common-sense theory, an expert theory, and a semi-expert coherence system. The first part of the process consists of the move from common-sense theory to expert theory. For the Freudian example, the starting point is approxi-

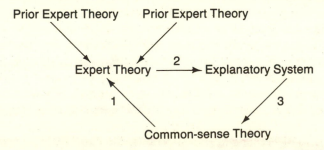

FIGURE 1. Synchronic relation among popular, semi-expert, and expert systems.

mately the year 1895, just as Freud was beginning his work. To trace changes, of course, we need to know the nature of popular models of the mind before Freud. In other words, if an interviewer had asked the same question about professional choice a hundred years ago, what common-sense assumptions would speakers have used in giving their reasons? What semi-expert systems would have been available to them (Mesmerism, animal magnetism, phrenology, social Darwinism, and so on)? This is a question for detailed research in the diaries, letters, and popular fiction of the time. Current scholarship actually affords us very little information about the common sense of the day and about the popular coherence systems with which Freud's theories competed and to which they assimilated.

In this intellectual environment, whatever it was, Freud began to develop his expert system. He was affected by the current common-sense view of the mind in two ways: much of what he said opposed this common-sense view; but at the same time, his theories were constrained by the common sense of the time, since too radical a theory of mind could not have been recognized as a theory of mind at all. Freud was also affected by other expert theories extant at the time—both theories of psychology different from his own and scientific theories in fields such as hydraulics and Darwinian evolution (Sulloway 1979).

We now turn to the second leg of the diagram, the move from expert system to semi-expert coherence system, and consider the process by which this diffusion of ideas takes place. As Freud developed his ideas, and continuing after his death, these ideas began to enter the popular culture, where they became a semi-expert coherence system. As we noted earlier, not all his ideas became part of this coherence system; only a limited subset of these was chosen. While we do not know in detail how the selection took place, the common sense of the period undoubtedly affected the selection. Thus, certain ideas like the "Freudian slip" that were less radical entered most solidly into the common-sense-beholden semi-expert system; the most radical did not.

We may now inquire into the process by which this coherence system was developed. Here again the research is almost nonexistent. However, we do know that the diffusion of Freud's ideas proceeded on a number of intellectual levels. Professional psychoanalysts writing in technical and medical journals worked to convince practicing psychologists and neurologists to adopt the new ideas. Both professional and lay analysts worked to introduce Freudian ideas to intellectuals. One of the most effective routes for the introduction of these ideas was through literary works, both popular and artistic. We can get a feeling of the novelty of

Freudian notions as they were first introduced to the general public by observing how they were expressed in the writing of the 1920s and 1930s, when intellectuals began restating and disseminating them. The following passage is from a detective story first published in 1935 (Blake 1935, p. 106). Michael, who is suspected of having committed a murder, is having an affair with Hero, who is married to Percy, Michael's boss:

"I think we ought to tell Percy."

"Get in our word before it all comes out in the general washing of dirty linen. Your psychological motives are highly questionable."

Hero flushed and stiffened a little. "You have rather a mean mind sometimes. I hate this talk about psychological motives. What's the point in rooting out all the bad reasons that one does a good thing for?"

"I didn't say 'bad reasons.'"

"Oh don't be silly. You know that whenever you say 'psychological motives' you mean to imply the worst. Presumably there are psychological motives behind our loving each other, but you don't talk about them. No doubt you'll start to when you get tired of it."

In the absence of a history of the diffusion of Freud's ideas in popular culture, it is impossible to be certain, but the popular fiction of the last seven decades suggests that this sort of explicit awareness of that man in Vienna—who has such nasty ideas but who, as everybody knows, has brought about such remarkable cures—was much more common during the first part of the century than it is today. By now, Freud's ideas have been developed into a popular coherence system that is so successful and ubiquitous as to be almost unnoticeable. But passages like the preceding one, which is by no means unusual for its time, show that the system was once seen as quite novel and indeed radical.

By the 1940s and 1950s, Freudian ideas were so thoroughly a part of the professional psychological scene that they were routinely disseminated in articles on child rearing and family dynamics in women's magazines. Even advice columnists such as Dear Abby drew on the expertise of psychoanalysts to assist them with certain types of questions.

Finally, we turn to the final leg of the diagram, the move from coherence system to common sense. As a given coherence system becomes better known and more widely held, it moves closer in status to common sense, and may eventually come to form a part of common sense. As an example, we may take the notion of the **Freudian slip**, which seems to be a part of the general, common-sense body of accepted notions and does not require the support of the Freudian coherence system to be comprehensible.

### The Dissemination of Other Expert Systems

The previous section presented a model for the historical development of a coherence system, using Freudian psychology as an example of such a system. The model should apply to the other coherence systems, too, although even less documentation is available for those discussed in this work.

Behaviorist psychology has had much less effect on popular culture than Freudian psychology, possibly because it is more alien to popular notions of causality and agency. Notions of behavior modification as a therapeutic technique are somewhat known. However, they have a very different character from that of Freudian notions, since in their popular form they do not involve the core of the self.

Materials for a popular history of astrology are similarly scanty. We do know that popular interest in astrology is not new: astrological metaphors are common in Shakespeare; eighteenth- and nineteenth-century farmers' almanacs routinely included astrological informations as a guide for planting times. However, little information has been adduced about the historical relation between popular astrology and other forms of occult belief (alchemy, magic, omen reading, and the like). To answer this question, one would have to determine when newspapers began to carry astrology columns, when horoscopes began to be mass-marketed, and so on.

For all these coherence systems, the necessary research in the history of popular culture remains to be done. This section has attempted to indicate a model for such a history and to suggest the value it would have in advancing our understanding both of coherence systems and of common sense.

## Coherence Systems as Social Practice

We may now ask how these coherence systems function for their users — that is, what social practices they facilitate. I believe that this question crucially involves issues of possible stance and distance that a speaker may take toward a life story. As Chapter 4 demonstrates, the act of telling a narrative permits the speaker a reflexive stance — the ability to report and evaluated his or her own actions as though they were those of another. This split between narrator and protagonist permits a psychological distance of varying size, which the speaker can exploit for a variety of purposes. There are also, of course, linguistic distancing strategies at the level of sentence construction. For example, I ask someone involved in a divorce how she feels, and she replies: **How can one feel when one's husband leaves one.** Clearly, both the universalizing strategy of the response and the speaker's use of the rare impersonal pronoun, which in American English is part of an extremely formal register, indicate that the speaker is putting as much distance as possible between herself and her linguistic production (and of course, her interlocutor). But special coherence systems permit an even greater distancing at the level of construction of the narrative. Because of their historical relation to expert systems, the coherence systems under investigation here permit their users to establish a significant distance between themselves and the protagonists of their (first-person) narratives, based on the stance of the narrator.

One important aspect of stance toward a narrative — one's own or another's — has to do with possible evaluations of it. Any member of the culture may judge a narrative on the basis of truth, plausibility, or the like. In addition, however, there exist certain classes of credentialed experts who have been trained in the terms and argument forms of an expert system that claims to give a principled basis for deciding whether the speaker's account could possibly be valid, given the organization of the account, its coherence, and its choice of topics. Such a system may be a political theory, a psychological theory, or a religious theory. For example, for a Marxist analyst, none of the accounts of career choice given by these speakers could possibly be valid, since they are not based on (and indeed make no mention of) social class or economic circumstances. Within the Marxist explanatory system, real explanation lies in the domain of economics; all other forms of explanation thus represent surface phenomena or false consciousness. Similarly, a psychologist or psychoanalyst, relying on an array of psychoanalytic techniques and argument forms or on the armamentarium of diagnostic psychology including personality tests and projective tests, can claim to have the necessary resources to determine whether a speaker's explanation is a correct product of genuine insight or merely one of the many strategies the mind uses to hide from itself. Given the social practice of expertise, the recognized implements of expertise have primacy; they confirm or invalidate the correctness of the speaker's own life narration in ways that may have serious medical and legal consequences. (See Frank [1981] for a discussion of the basis of such validation.)

But experts do not have a monopoly on theories that purport to explain the real reasons for people's behavior. Any adult has access to a wide variety of theories that can be used to make sense of the events of life. These theories may be explicit systems that require such practices as formal allegiance to the system and its beliefs; attendance at events; contributions of money; and changes in sexual, dietary, or drinking practices. Or they may be extremely inexplicit systems — beliefs implicit in the culture that require no formal recognition or allegiance and that, without careful analysis by a hearer or reader, pass unnoticed as theories, appearing instead to be just one further example of the normal way of speaking.

When we examine the ways in which coherence systems are used, we find that, because they are all popularized versions of expert theories, they permit the speaker an extra level of distance, allowing the speaker to take a stance as his or her own expert, to step back from the account to give a deeper (or apparently more objective or truer) set of reasons than can be conveyed in a common-sense narrative. To clarify the nature of the distance created by the use of a coherence system, recall from Chapter 4 that all first-person narration contains an implicit distance between the narrator and the protagonist. This distance permits us to tell a story about some bad or ill-judged or embarrassing action we took, since, even though the protagonist acted improperly, the narrator knows better and can therefore tell the story in a way that indicates present allegiance to the norm that was in the past broken. However, using an expert coherence system introduces an additional form of distance, beyond that of narrator and protagonist. In a narrative that is told without the use of a special coherence system, although the narrator may know better than the protagonist, they are still the same order of being, operating by the same rules and with the same type of knowledge. In contrast, the expert differs from the protagonist in possessing superior knowledge of why the protagonist acts in a certain way and how the protagonist should act — knowledge that is inaccessible to the protagonist during the action.

Coherence systems such as the ones described in this chapter provide people with a vocabulary for creating a self. It is also possible to directly adopt an already existing-self. This may be done at the level of archetypes, as by (without conscious formulation) seeing one's life structured in terms of the story of Cinderella or the lone cowboy. Considerable discussion has recently taken place on the consequences of the choice of these archetypes — some of it deep, some of it ridiculous. Or the adoption of an already existing self may be more detailed, as when one takes as one's identity the whole persona of some already developed fictional character (Martin 1988). Martin, a psychoanalyst and professor of literature, explores the ways in which his patients and others use fictions to create their identities; he notes cases such as the identification that Mark

Chapman, the killer of John Lennon, had with the character Holden Caulfield in the novel *Catcher in the Rye*, and the identification that John Hinckley, the attempted assassin of Ronald Reagan, had with Travis Bickle, the main character in the film *Taxi Driver*. Martin argues that all persons construct roles for themselves to play, but he adds that most people's constructions include a belief in the existence of other people, who are similarly attempting to construct truthful and useful versions of existence. However, some people are drawn to preexisting roles: they feel inauthentic in a personally constructed reality; but the roles offered by movies, television, and novels appeal to them as being more intense, more convincing, and more real.

However, examples of this sort are not present in my data, and Martin's discussion suggests that they constitute a relatively rare pathology that may indicate the outer limits of self-distancing.

## Conclusion

This section discusses some questions that may arise about coherence systems, and it sketches possible directions for further research in this area.

This work has shown that one component of oral life stories is the coherence system, which furnishes a system other than that of common sense by which the actions narrated can be understood and justified. One might ask whether this analysis does not make too much of the available evidence. That is, we have seen speakers using phrases like **strokes** or **reinforcement** or **deeper reasons** or **Libra**; since these words and phrases are common in ordinary conversation, what justifies our using them to posit an entity as complex and hypothetical as the coherence system?

One argument for postulating the coherence system is that speakers do not use metaphors from several competing systems. That is, we do not find a single speaker using both Freudian and behaviorist metaphors. Orwell (1956), for example, has argued that the use of a mixed metaphor like **The crowd was like a sea of faces, turning upward like flowers to the sun** suggests that the connection between the metaphor and its literal sense is dying—that the speaker is in fact unaware of or not paying attention to the actual meaning of the metaphors that are being used:

> The sole aim of a metaphor is to call up visual images. When those images clash—as in "The Facist octopus has sung its swan song, the jackboot is thrown into the melting pot"—it can be taken as certain that the writer is not seeing a mental image of the objects he is naming. (p. 361)

Setting aside the issue of whether metaphor is intrinsically visual, it is certainly the case that mixed metaphors are common phenomena in speech; consequently, when we find the metaphors of a coherence system kept separate, it argues that they come from systems that are separate for their users. However, this question warrants further investigation. It would be worthwhile to determine whether metaphors from noncontradictory systems like Freudian psychology and astrology are mixed. (Such a mixture is not found in these data, but since only one speaker uses an astrological coherence system, the absence is not in itself significant.)

A second argument is that, in narratives exhibiting the effects of a particular coherence system, the details of construction at the sentence level and at the level of the entire narrative are consistent with the content of the coherence system claimed for the life story. This effect is particularly evident in the behaviorist life story examined earlier; however, it is present to some extent in all life stories that use a special coherence system.

These two arguments together suggest that, however common the metaphors of these coherence systems may be, their selective use does indicate the existence of a number of systems, rather than an unstructured collection of concepts that can be mixed promiscuously.

The postulation of coherence systems suggests a new research paradigm, within which a number of questions for further research are raised. For instance, how many coherence systems are present in a given culture, and what are they? This question could be answered by extensively studying a number of types of discourse on a number of different topics and by analyzing the most widely disseminated forms of popular culture. A second issue involves the relation between popular and expert forms of a coherence system. As we have already discussed, this could be investigated by using the usual techniques of social history. A third issue is more psychological: how serious are these coherence systems for their users, and how are they related to their behavior? This is a more difficult question, but it could perhaps be approached by using a mixture of psychological and participant observation techniques.

These questions, I believe, form an important research paradigm that has implications for linguistics, anthropology, and cultural history. The present research indicates the existence of a level of conceptual organization that must be understood in order to describe fully the structure of life stories. This is already an extremely important finding, since it allows us to understand one of the mechanisms by which people make sense of their own lives.

# 7

# Common Sense and Its History

In Chapter 6, we considered coherence systems—systems of beliefs and relations between beliefs that are used to structure life stories, explanations, and (presumably) other discourse types as well. The systems considered so far are all special systems that are synchronically related to and historically derived from professional coherence systems, which have a social framework that may include credentialed practitioners and specified occasions on which practitioners and clients meet to apply them. Special coherence systems are not used or even necessarily known by everyone in the culture, and they are not always used even by speakers who do know and use them.

Let us now consider the system of beliefs that serves to structure explanations when no special coherence system is used. It would be naive to assume that, in the absence of a coherence system, simple truth or factuality remains as the explanatory principle. Rather, the system used consists of assumptions and beliefs that everyone can be assumed to share—beliefs that are, within a given culture, so obviously true that it is difficult to see them as beliefs at all. These beliefs, or this belief system, we may call **common sense**, a term itself taken from the common-sense system.

## What is Common Sense?

Let us consider various approaches to the definition of common sense. From a sociological perspective, Garfinkel (1959, p. 59) describes common sense as follows:

the socially sanctioned grounds of inference and action that people use in their everyday affairs and which they assume that other members of the group use in the same way. Socially-sanctioned-facts-of-life-in-society-that-any-bona-fide-member-of-the-society-knows depict such matters as conduct of family life; market organization; distributions of honour, competence, responsibility, goodwill, income, and motives among persons; frequency, causes of, and remedies for trouble; and the presence of good and evil purposes behind the workings of things. Such socially sanctioned facts of social life consist of descriptions of the society from the point of view of the collectivity member's interests in the management of his practical affairs.

Irrespective of what a proposition proposes, it is a member of the common-sense corpus if its use as correct grounds of inference and action is, for a user, a condition of his bona-fide status as a collectivity member. Descriptions of social structures whose use is governed by the user's expectation that he will be socially supported for using them may be called, following his own way of referring to them, "reasonable" descriptions.

Labov (1966) uses common sense as a topic for linguistic interviews because it is of interest to speakers and because they are accustomed to discussing it. Indeed, it is striking how much people enjoy such discussions of what is and is not common sense, and who does or does not have common sense, suggesting that, contrary to its name, this faculty is not so common as to be unreportable. Labov argues that the usual meaning of the term **common sense** is very close to **good judgment**: practical knowledge that cannot be acquired from books. However, there are variations in how the term is applied. Some speakers use it to indicate the ability to solve difficult problems rationally; others, to indicate the ability to make moral judgments; others, to indicate what everyone knows. These differences can lead to disagreement over whether a given person actually has common sense.

Geertz (1983*a*) points specifically to the disguised normative nature of common sense:

> There are a number of reasons why treating common sense as a relatively organized body of considered thought, rather than just what anyone clothed and in his right mind knows, should lead on to some useful conclusions; but perhaps the most important is that it is an inherent characteristic of common-sense thought precisely to deny this and to affirm that its tenets are immediate deliverance of experience, not deliberated reflections upon it. Knowing that rain wets and that one ought to come in out of it, or that fire burns and one ought not to play with it (to stick to our own culture for the moment) are conflated into comprising one large realm of the given and undeniable, a catalog of in-the-grain-of-nature realities so

peremptory as to force themselves upon any mind sufficiently unclouded to receive them. Yet this is clearly not so. No one, or no one functioning very well, doubts that rain wets; but there may be some people around who question the proposition that one ought to come in out of it, holding that it is good for one's character to brave the elements — hatlessness is next to godliness. And the attractions of playing with fire often, with some people usually, override the full recognition of the pain that will result. Religion rests its case on revelation, science on method, ideology on moral passion; but common sense rests on the assertion that it is not a case at all, just life in a nutshell. The world is its authority.

The analysis of common sense, as opposed to the exercise of it, must then begin by redrawing this erased distinction between the mere matter-of-fact apprehension of reality — or whatever it is you want to call what we apprehend merely and matter-of-factly — and down-to-earth, colloquial wisdom, judgments or assessments of it. When we say someone shows common sense, we mean to suggest more often than not that he is just using his eyes and ears, but is, as we say, keeping them open, using them judiciously, intelligently, perceptively, reflectively, or trying to, and that he is capable of coping with everyday problems in an everyday way with some effectiveness. And when we say he lacks common sense we mean not that he is retarded, that he fails to grasp the fact that rain wets or fire burns, but that he bungles the everyday problems life throws up for him: he leaves his house on a cloudy day without an umbrella; his life is a series of scorchings he should have had the wit not merely to avoid but not to have stirred the flames for in the first place. The opposite of someone who is able to apprehend the sheer actualities of experience is, as I have suggested, a defective; the opposite of someone who is able to come to sensible conclusions on the basis of them is a fool. . . .

This analytical dissolution of the unspoken premise from which common sense draws its authority — that it presents reality neat — is not intended to undermine that authority but to relocate it. If common sense is as much an interpretation of the immediacies of experience, a gloss on them, as are myth, painting, epistemology, or whatever, then it is, like them historically constructed and, like them, subjected to historically defined standards of judgment. It can be questioned, disputed, affirmed, developed, formalized, contemplated, even taught, and it can vary dramatically from one people to the next. It is, in short, a cultural system, though not usually a very tightly integrated one, and it rests on the same basis that any other such system rests; the conviction by those whose possession it is of its value and validity. Here, as elsewhere, things are what you make of them. (pp. 75–76)

Thus, common sense by its very name claims to be universal, to be that which any reasonable person would believe or feel or do in a given circumstance. While it attempts to pass itself off as merely describing the way things are, the notion of common sense also represents a normative attempt to suggest the way things ought to be. Common sense is talked about as if it were natural, as if it were something that could not be any other way. When we look closer, however, we see that any common-sense state of affairs is an organization that represents a social achievement. We can see the moral nature of apparently factual states in such common expressions as **He's a real man, She's not a real woman, Be a mensch, That's inhuman behavior, He's got no common sense**.

Locutions of this type reveal the achieved quality of normality, through criticism of a nonnormal state or praise of the normal state. If common sense were, in fact, that which everyone does or knows, it would be incoherent to complain about someone's lacking common sense. Common sense is thus an issue of morality disguised as an issue of universal factuality. Recent investigations of this dual nature of common sense have attempted to show in a variety of domains such as sexual behavior, food choices, and the understanding of disease that what appears to be nature is, in fact, culture disguised. The act of disguise is a deliberate or near-deliberate attempt by those in power to use the discourse of normalization to make the achieved order of the world appear to be a fact of nature, because then their dominant position in this order is also a fact of nature, and hence cannot be changed. In other words, the best way to avoid change or revolution is to make change or revolution unthinkable (Aries, 1981; Barthes 1982, 1972; Foucault 1985, 1980*a*, 1980*b*, 1979).

The history of the term "common sense" indicates something of this disguise of culture. Let us consider the first two senses given by the Oxford English Dictionary for this term:

> 1. An "internal" sense which was regarded as the common bond or centre of the five senses, in which the various impressions received were reduced to the unity of a common consciousness. OBS. First citation 1543 (but with reference, via common wit to 1398): Traheron *Vigo's Chirug.* i. ii. 3 They [eyes] were ordeyned on nature in the former part [of the head] . . . that they might carye visible things to ye commune sens.

> 2. The endowment of natural intelligence possessed by rational beings; ordinary, normal or average understanding; the plain wisdom which is every man's inheritance. (This is "common sense" at a minimum, without which a man is foolish or insane.) First citation 1535: Jove *Apol.* Tyndale (Arb. 36) I am suer T(indale) is not so farre besydis his comon sencis as to saye the dead bodye hereth cristis voyce.

> b. More emphatically: Good sound practical sense; combined tact and readiness in dealing with the every-day affairs of life; general sagacity.

First citation 1726: Amherst *Terra Fil.* xx. 100 There is not said a shrewd
wag a more uncommon thing in the world than common sense.

As the first meaning of this entry shows, "common sense" was a technical term, originating in Aristotelian psychology, indicating a faculty
that mediates and communicates among the five physical senses. Common sense in this meaning was thus something that even animals pos-
sessed, and it was necessary for achieving even a low level of cognitive
functioning. The later development of the term to mean ordinary understanding, plain wisdom, or practical sense indicates an extension of the
term from a description of a natural fact that constitutes part of the
psychology of sentience—that is, common among the senses—to a description of a cultural fact that constitutes an understanding of the basis
of one's social and cultural world—that is, common among all people.

When common sense is assumed to be natural, there is a strong claim
to universality implicit in the term. However, this claim is not well
founded, and therefore common sense must be viewed and studied
as being located in time and space: twentieth-century American common sense, or seventeenth-century French common sense, or precolonial
Javanese common sense.

## How to Study Common Sense

Let us now consider the nature of common sense assumed by the data of
this study. Since common sense is a system that claims to be transparent—that is, to be no system—studying it is a great deal more difficult
than studying special coherence systems; by definitions, the expressions
of the common-sense system are not marked. One way to study common-
sense assumptions about occupational choice is to identify some of the
characteristic omissions from the life stories studied; in dealing with
common sense (the unmarked system), we can expect omissions to be
as revealing as or more revealing than inclusions. We considered such
omissions in some detail in Chapter 6.

In addition to investigating omissions, we may also look at "of
courses"—examples in which speakers overtly refer to what is obvious.
Consider the following example:

1. Well, uh, it doesn't seem as though there was ever a time, well
   there was, I was a math major when I was a freshman in college,
   but in my sophomore year I discovered that I wasn't going to be
   a great mathematician and uh I seemed to be very good in
   reading and analyzing books and writing so I became an English

major and from then on **since I knew that I would go as far in whatever I chose as I could possibly go, getting a Ph.D. became a necessity.** And once I had a Ph.D., getting a job as an English teacher **seemed the logical choice** and that's how I arrived at my profession.

This example shows a citation of character and ability as the natural determinant of career choice—that is, as a cause properly treated as a matter "of course."

We may also look at the presuppositions that underlie the assumption of adequate causality. As we saw in Chapter 5, one of the strongest forms of adequate causality is character: ability, aptitude, or liking for a given career. Causality by character shows us very clearly the presupposition of individualism: the individual's own strengths and aptitudes determine his or her professional position, with little or no reference to external or environmental causes.

Besides character, the other two strongest principles of adequate causality are temporal depth (a choice is well founded because it is based on early interests and aptitudes) and richness of account (a choice is well founded because the speaker can identify many reasons that led to that choice). Both of these are also versions of individualism, based on the notion that the individual is stable across time and across circumstances. Thus, current common sense assumes not only that the individual has control of personal circumstances, but also that the individual of today is fundamentally the same as the individual of the same name twenty years ago. If a speaker can show that a career choice was motivated by a very early interest or by a group of interests and aptitudes, this constitutes an adequate account because it is based on the characteristics of what a proper individual should be.

The techniques for handling inadequate causality also give indirect support to the common-sense system. We have seen that accident and discontinuity are problematic in a narrative and must receive special management. Accident is problematic because it suggests that the individual is not in control of his or her personal destiny. Discontinuity is problematic because it suggests that the individual is not stable across time, but has different desires (and perhaps even different aptitudes) at different times. This, too, is a challenge to the common-sense notion of the individual. We encountered one very interesting case of discontinuity of the individual in Chapter 5:

2. I think that the probability of my ending up in academia was largely a product of the fact that my father was an academic

and his father was a scientist and the *values* I was raised in were very much academic intellectual values. So I think there's a sense in which uh it would have been extraordinarily difficult for me to have ended up in another kind of life, although I entertained that at various points. **Um I thought, as one, as adolescents without talent are prone to do,** of the performing arts in various ways. Uh I was in theater for a while in high school and college and I was an actress through college **and had fantasies about making that a life which were of course unrealistic.**

In this narrative, the speaker manages the discontinuity between her attempts at a career as an actress and her eventual career as an academic by claiming a discontinuity of self — the unrealistic adolescent without talent trying something that the later, more realistic self recognizes as doomed to failure. It would appear that in this regard the speaker endorses a notion of a discontinuous self. But she also makes clear that her eventual career derives from the values she was raised with as a child. The discontinuity of self is thus shown to be only an apparent discontinuity, a momentary interruption — of a type common during the upheaval of adolescence — in the development of the basic character of the individual.

We have seen examples taken from the life story data that illustrate the principles of the common-sense coherence system. To examine this system in more explicit detail, we may also ask whether any codifications or presentations of the common-sense system exist within the culture. An encyclopedia of the obvious might at first appear unlikely. (The exception would be such an encyclopedia devised as a knowledge base for computer systems, and indeed such work is in progress in the field of artificial intelligence. As yet, however, the common sense required by computer systems is at the level of the properties of physical objects or simple stereotypical human actions, rather than complex social and psychological belief systems.) Nonetheless, although such obvious knowledge does not take the form of an encyclopedia, it does appear in the form of advice literature — information on how to live properly, healthily, or successfully. Bookstores are full of self-help books; books on popular psychology; books on how to improve your health, relationships, appearance, and finances; and so on. Because the interviews that furnish the data of this study are about professional choice, the advice literature most relevant to these data is the literature on success, which constitutes an enormously widespread and popular genre. For reasons we will examine later, this literature in America often has a religious tone, reflecting its origins in nineteenth-century Protestant thought.

Self-help literature on success is an ideal site for studying common sense, since it makes its assertions without proof and assumes that its statements describe the way things are. Since this genre of literature has no standards of proof, it cannot make entirely new claims; it can assert only notions that its readership already believes or that are interesting or seductive enough for its readership to consider in hopes that they might be true. As a result, this literature is extremely embarrassing, and hence nearly unnoticeable, to intellectuals. In researching this material, when I carry a pile of such books home, I want to announce to the world that my apparent desire to improve my life through positive thinking is, in fact, a meta-interest—a mere interest in the genre. Such embarrassment is an extremely important clue in any cultural investigation, since it accurately pinpoints the location of one's own unchallenged cultural assumptions.

Part of an intellectual's embarrassment at appearing to be interested in such literature is that it leads to the inference that something is wrong with the reader's life—that the reader is broke or unhappy or without a partner or trapped in some other undesirable (even shameful) state of affairs. But part of the embarrassment has to do with the nature of the genre itself, since an intellectual would probably be much less embarrassed at having people know that he or she was consulting a psychoanalyst, and yet this information might lead to all of the same inferences. The root problem for intellectuals is the noncritical stance of self-help materials—the extreme assertion of propositions about the world without proof—as well as the nature of the propositions themselves.

If self-help literature does present an account of certain elements of modern American common sense, what is the system it presents? In general, it can be described as positive thinking, which I consider the unnoticed religion of America. Positive thinking contains assumptions, beliefs, and practices that have been assimilated by every other religious and therapeutic system in America that has come into contact with it. Among the central elements of this system are the following:

1. Individualism
2. The formulation that thoughts are things
3. The understanding of ethics in terms of rights

Let us consider these in turn, beginning with individualism.

Individualism is perhaps the most pervasive aspect of positive thinking and hence of American common sense. The individualism of common

sense is, as Coles (1980, p. 137) defines it, ontological individualism —
the belief that the individual is the "only or main form of reality." This
belief in individualism includes the following tenets:

1. The individual is the locus of ethics and of actions.
2. Opportunities are open to someone because of that person's individual characteristics, not because of his or her group or class membership.
3. Fairness consists of a society's making opportunities be open to all.

Bellah et al. (1985) provide a fuller discussion of the role of individualism
in contemporary American society.

Individualism is reflected in the very existence of success literature,
since the presupposition of such literature is that you can, unaided (except by a book that enables you to help yourself), change your individual
circumstances, without changing your environmental conditions.

To review an example of individualism from the life story data, let us
examine again a narrative from Chapter 5 that gives an extremely strong
justification of career choice in terms of individual action:

3.  SPEAKER: I've been doing it for <u>years</u>. I started out proof-reading and ended up an editorial assistant and it just growed.

INTERVIEWER: And how'd you, how'd you get into the whole field?

SPEAKER: Um I started out freelancing in um, with people that my father knew while I was in college. No, actually, my first proofreading was in summer school, between high school and college.

INTERVIEWER: And how'd you get into it as a full time job?

SPEAKER: It was the thing to do. When I decided not to go into graduate school.

INTERVIEWER: Mm hmm. Why?

SPEAKER: Um, I always knew I could correct grammar fairly easily and mark things up and then from the first job I got it seemed interesting enough to stay in.

. . .

But it's just, it was a natural evolution. I always was nitpicky, I was always good at grammar,

um I like to correct things rather than create
them. And I'm interested enough in reading and
I like to spend the time reading, that at least
now that I'm on journals that are even vaguely
interesting, it c- it can be a lot of fun.

. . .

Yeah. It's almost unbroken flow. Also, I mean,
being with Bob [her former husband] and correcting, you know, working on *Write-On* magazine with the writers [a magazine that her former
husband edited] I really enjoyed that.

This speaker explains her career development in terms of her likes,
her aptitudes, and her character. Clearly, this narrative contains the
requisite material for an account framed in terms of the opportunities
available to the speaker because of her father's and her husband's connections in publishing. Instead, though, she presents her narrative as the
story of an individual and her choices — an approach entirely consistent
with the common-sense focus on the individual alone. As we have already seen, the life story narratives do not contain discussions of the
effects of class, race, or the economic climate of the time. Rather, they
are told in terms of individual character, ability, aptitude, cleverness,
and so on, which advance the strongest possible claim of adequate causality.

The second tenet of common sense about livelihood is that thought
is all-important in determining one's world. "Thoughts are things" is
a nineteenth-century formulation of this belief that is still used widely
in occultism, popular psychology, and self-help literature. It can be
found in the following verse by Ella Wheeler Wilcox (1902), an extremely
popular metaphysical poet of the late nineteenth and early twentieth
centuries:

> You never can tell what our thoughts will do
>   In bringing you hate and love,
> For thoughts are things, and their airy wings,
>   Are swift as a carrier dove.
> They follow the law of the universe —
>   Each thing must create its kind,
> And they speed o'er the track to bring you back
>   Whatever went forth from your mind.
>                                    (p. 25)

"Thoughts Are Things" is also found as a chapter title in the extremely popular and influential success manual, *Think and Grow Rich* (Hill 1985), originally published in 1937 and continuously in print to this day.

Let us consider a more recently written example of this notion, which appears in a discussion of how to have everything you want, from *How to Have More in a Have-Not World* (Cole-Whittaker 1983), a popular book on success in the domains of finance and spirituality:

> You can have exactly what you want, when you want it, all the time. There are people for whom this is true, and they become better off every day. . . . We live in a have-not world. The vast majority of the population of this earth, at least 95 percent, live as victims or potential victims of forces they believe are outside of themselves to move them, save them, or do it for them. . . . The more you *increase* the power the world has over you, the more you *decrease* the power you have over the world. In the Book of Genesis in the Bible there is a verse that says that God gave us dominion over the earth. It didn't give the earth power over us. (pp. 13–15)

Although Cole-Whittaker, like most writers of this genre, does not provide any evidence, documentation, or grounding for her assertions, she is unusual in providing the following far-ranging set of acknowledgments indicating her sources:

> Jesus of Nazareth is my savior and my guide to the Holy Spirit. The wisdom and teachings of Lao-Tzu and Buddha have also been a gift of God to me.
>
> Ernest Holmes brought me to the principle of life and taught me about who I am. The Course in Miracles is a constant source of love and truth for me.
>
> I acknowledge all those who came before me whose courage and vision as expressed through themselves and their work have brought us spiritually closer to our divine potential. I acknowledge the gnostics, metaphysicians, pentecostals, Martin Luther, Moses, quantum physics, Sigmund Freud, Ida Rolf, Rebirthing, nutrition, exercise, Oral Roberts, the Reverend Ike, Werner Erhard, L. Ron Hubbard, Robert Pante, Marshall Thurber, Bhagwan Rajneesh, Sondra Ray, Fritz Perls, William James, Abraham Maslow, Jamie Weinstein, Bel Evans, and Yoga. (p. 9)

The view that thoughts are things—a common, indeed commonplace theme in American success literature—represents a naive constructionism that holds that the world is formed by mind. Therefore, one can change one's world by changing one's mind; and one can change one's mind by changing one's will. Most writers who make this assumption offer techniques for changing one's mind, but they take the possibility of changing one's will as a given; rarely is any attention paid to the question of how this is to be done or whether it is possible. The few who do consider this question cite William James but do not indicate the difficulty of the process, which James discusses at length.

In the life story data, the speakers do not directly state a belief that thoughts are things. But the absence of discussion of economic or political influences on available opportunities means that the speakers have available to them only internal, psychological factors as possible causes for career choices. This is completely consistent with the belief that thoughts are things.

A corollary of the notion that thoughts are things is the tenet of abundance: scarcity of resources or opportunities is a mistaken mental construction, rather than a fact about the world. Thus, the proper response to a perception of limited opportunities is psychological change, rather than political action or a change of aspirations. This notion forms the basis of almost all self-help literature on how to succeed, and it can be traced back to very early examples of the genre. The basic idea is that objectively there is no material or cultural impediment to success, since abundant wealth exists for all who are brave enough or desirous enough to take advantage of it. Further, in terms of forming narratives, this idea implies that complaining about lack of resources or opportunities merely reveals the speaker's personal deficiencies.

Cole-Whittaker (1983) gives a full and typical statement of the proposition that thoughts are things:

### The Four Corners of Truth

#### Truth No. 1

*Abundance and wealth are natural.* There is abundant supply, always enough at the highest level, and a quality existence for everyone. Whatever you want and need you already have; it is available for you. You merely have to claim it. It's yours by right of your saying it is.

#### Truth No. 2

*There is always a way and a solution.* It is for everyone's highest good, with no one excluded and everyone included. Contained within every seed is everything it takes for the seed to fulfill itself, even to duplicate and produce more of itself automatically. Every idea or dream you have also has everything in it to produce itself. It requires your getting out of the way and being willing to let things work for you.

## Truth No. 3

*The only inevitable part of life is love.* You cannot stop God's plan for you; you can only resist it and delay it in your life. What is inevitable is living your vision, loving and being loved, and being secure and safe in God's love and wealth. There is no plan for your demise and downfall; you make that up.

## Truth No. 4

*You have what it takes. It all comes out of you as a channel or vehicle of God's power.* Whatever you want and need flows out from you. You have the ability to call forth into being what you say you will. You are a fountain of infinite supply and creativity, fed by an inner spring. The purpose of life is living, and living is experiencing yourself as being alive, whole, loving, and one with God. Actually, your experience of you is always valid and valuable, whatever that experience may be. To shut down on one experience because of another is not to be fully alive. It is in the full expression of the experience of living that life becomes ecstasy. (pp. 140–41)

This notion of abundance is reflected in the life story texts' lack of discussion of any effect of the economic or political situation prevailing at the time the speakers were becoming established in their professions. In a world without history or economics, character must be the most important determinant of professional choice. Although there have been some recent popular criticisms of this view (see, for example, Shames [1989]), they are still framed in terms of individualism: the need for the individual to develop better values than greed and to realize that resources may not be unlimited.

The third tenet of positive thinking involves the understanding of ethical issues in terms of rights, rather than in terms of duties and obligations. One formulation of this is that everyone has rights to psychological satisfaction and well-being. This belief is reflected in the life stories only in a negative way—in the absence of any discussion of duty or obligation to family or any larger unit. It is discussed at length here because it provides a valuable example of the way in which the common-sense system is the unmarked, default system.

Consider the following formulation of rights of interaction, taken from *The New Assertive Woman* (Bloom, Coburn, and Pearlman 1975):

1. The right to be treated with respect.
2. The right to have and express your own feelings and opinions.

3. The right to be listened to and taken seriously.
4. The right to set your own priorities.
5. The right to say "no" without feeling guilty.
6. The right to ask for what you want.
7. The right to get what you pay for.
8. The right to ask for information from professionals.
9. The right to make mistakes.
10. The right to choose not to assert myself. (p. 24)

This list is similar to bills of rights given in many contemporary works. They are presented with no grounding or warrant for such rights, although their rhetoric clearly is derived from the Declaration of Independence and the Bill of Rights of the Constitution. In contrast, however, these originating political documents make quite clear that the grounding of rights is in a political system that is pledged to uphold them. Thus, the Declaration of Independence begins with a religious grounding, by stating, "We hold these Truths to be self-evident, that all Men . . . are endowed by their Creator with certain unalienable Rights, that among these are Life, Liberty, and the Pursuit of Happiness." However, it concludes with an implicit political grounding as well, by stating, "And for the support of this Declaration, with a firm Reliance on the Protection of divine Providence, we mutually pledge to each other our Lives, our Fortunes, and our sacred Honor." In other words, the signers pledge to act to bring about a government in which these postulated rights will indeed be upheld as rights.

In contrast, contemporary works using the rhetorical figure of a bill of assertiveness rights give no indication of why one might have, for example, the right not to conform to others' expectations. No grounding, whether religious or political, is given; the right is assumed.

By calling this view of individual rights part of the common-sense system, I am asserting that it is a component of the unmarked system. This relation can be shown by demonstrating that it is assumed even in situations in which a special coherence system or ideology is also used. A very interesting example can be found in *Holy Boldness* (Cerling 1980)—a book on assertiveness training for evangelical Christians. Like most secular books on assertiveness, it provides a list of individual's rights, as follows:

1. You have the right to judge what is best for you and to be responsible for the consequences.
2. You have the right to act without defending or justifying your actions to others.

3. You have the right not to conform to others' expectations for you.
4. You have the right to be wrong—and to suffer the consequences.
5. You have the right to change your mind.
6. You have the right to your opinions, feelings and desires.
7. You have the right to be treated as fairly as others.

As in the preceding secular example, no grounding is given for this list of evangelical Christians' rights. This lack of grounding is particularly interesting in a religious work, whose orientation would easily permit the author to identify such rights as being part of God's design for man. However, neither this justification nor any other is cited. In a few cases, New Testament examples are given to show that Jesus or St. Paul acted assertively. But these are not used as warrants for the reader's having these rights; rather, they are used to allay the reader's fear that perhaps exercising such rights is inconsistent with Christian beliefs.

At this point, the reader may question my use of the term "common sense" to characterize the beliefs we have been examining. It is easy to object that the tenets discussed are complete nonsense and are clearly contrary to what we see before our faces every day. Such an objection raises an important point about the nature of common-sense beliefs. To be part of common sense, a belief need not be true nor be able to stand up to intense logical scrutiny. Rather, it must be plausible when not examined too closely, since common sense is composed precisely of beliefs that are axiomatic and, hence, unexamined. A similar phenomenon holds for proverbs, which can be seen as gnomic formulations of common sense. When examined, they often prove to be contradictory. For example, **Look before you leap,** but **He who hesitates is lost.** These contradictions do not invalidate the use of proverbs, exactly because the social practices in which proverbs function do not permit such analytic, decontextualized examination.

## History of Common Sense

We have inspected some of the tenets of modern American common sense—those that appear to be relevant to the study of stories about profession. Just as we inquired into the history of the special coherence systems, we may also ask about the history of common sense. Here, too, unfortunately, historical examinations of the relevant raw data (diaries, letters, journals, popular journalism, and so on of the late nineteenth and early twentieth centuries) have not been made. Studying the history of common sense is even more difficult than studying the history of expert systems, since it represents a systemization of beliefs about the world that are so obvious as to be unnoticeable as beliefs. It is possible to study the history of common sense with regard to a given topic: the common sense view of how to succeed professionally, how to manage one's sexuality, how to remain physically healthy, or the like. The nature of the appropriate subdivisions constitutes another topic of study, since what counts as an appropriate inquiry into common sense is itself dictated by common sense. However, once an appropriate topic is established, it is possible to find relevant materials for study in a given historical period. Advice literature, for instance, is a valuable source for data on common sense, both historically and synchronically. Literature of this type may include advice on how to succeed financially, how to move up in social class, and how to be happy. Such advice literature has been popular and extensive since the Renaissance, when social mobility became possible for a substantial portion of the middle classes. It furnishes a rich store of unexamined commonplaces on effective conduct. (A discussion of this literature in Elizabethan England is given in Wright [1958].)

For the purposes of our discussion, we will consider the history of common sense with regard to psychological well-being and business success, since the latter is the central topic of the interviews that make up the data of this study, and since the former is almost always invoked. We have already mentioned the main tenets of current common sense on this issue, which arise out of a radical utilitarian individualist stance: individualism, or the belief that the individual is the primary locus of ethics and actions; thoughts are things, or the belief that one's material world is entirely shaped by one's thoughts; and ethics as rights, or the belief that ethical questions can best be understood in terms of the rights of the individual.

These tenets can be found in self-help literature from as far back as 1840. (Again, self-help or self-improvement literature is common as early as the Renaissance, but the tenets of these earlier works are quite different from those of nineteenth- and twentieth-century self-help literature.) As Wylie (1954) comments:

> What makes the man? Is he shaped by conditions that surround him, or by forces inherent in himself? Through the long history of American thinking on the subject of success, no questions have been more central, and none have been answered more confidently. To the generation that sired Andrew Carnegie and John D. Rockefeller the relation of a favorable economic environment to personal fortune should have been obvious. And

sometimes it was. P. T. Barnum, for example, admitted that "In a new country, where we have more land than people, it is not at all difficult for persons in good health to make money." (P. T. Barnum, *The Art of Money Getting*, 1882, New York, p. 7) But most prophets of success refused to tell their tales in terms of the favorable ratio of men to resources, preferring instead to talk about how character could triumph over circumstance. "The things which are really essential for a successful life are not circumstances but qualities," one spokesman said. (Robert W. Cushman, *Elements of Success*, Washington 1848) "Not the things which surround a man but the things which are in him, not the adjuncts of his position but the attribute of his character." This had to be the emphasis, of course, for otherwise there could be no such social being as a self-made man.

The American success literature of the nineteenth century (as of the twentieth century) is thus one form of popular psychology literature, propagating the belief that one can change one's world by changing one's thoughts, and that one can change one's thoughts by an act of will. For an Old World contrast, consider one of the most popular English manuals on how to live: Samuel Smiles's *Self Help* (1859). While sharing the American belief that success is possible for anyone who attempts it, Smiles claims that the foundation of success is diligence, perseverance, and good moral character, rather than an abundance of resources in the world and a God who wishes the reader to succeed. Further, Smiles's book is addressed to healthy, ambitious males, whereas the American literature characteristically includes women, the ill, and the weak in its intended audience.

The primary basis of our system is early nineteenth-century American Protestant theology. At the beginning of the nineteenth century, developments in American Protestant thought moved it away from the emphasis on predestination present in Calvinist doctrine, which stated that only grace could assure one of salvation, to a stress on the possibility of achieving salvation through individual efforts. This more optimistic and action-oriented theology led to a ferment of religious and quasi-religious speculation and experimentation that is termed the Second Great Awakening. This provided the background for a vast array of religious, metaphysical, medical, and financial speculation and experimentation. Perhaps the first extension of the new theology came in the area of health. At the turn of the nineteenth century, faith healers of various sorts were extremely common. One of the most influential was Phineas Parkhurst Quimby (1802–1866), a New Hampshire healer with no formal training, who strongly influenced succeeding generations of healers, including

Mary Baker Eddy (the founder of Christian Science) and the founders of the schools of healing variously called mental healing, the mind cure school, the New Thought, the science of mind, positive thinking, the Higher Thought, Divine Science, and Practical Christianity. These, then, provided faith healing its original expert system. (See Dresser [1919], pp. 152–57, for a discussion of the origins and geographical distributions of the various terms, and Larson [1985] and Parker [1879] for a general discussion of the history of these movements.)

The interest in improving one's physical conditions by improving one's attitude and understanding expanded into a vast literature on material and financial success, as well — a literature that shares most of the same assumptions and techniques as the faith healing literature. As Meyer (1980) shows, the "mind cure school" was an ideology that emerged in opposition to the New England Protestant tradition. It was an organized movement, with leadership, churches, and so on, but it also reached many other people through its literature, because of its articulation of religious and material tensions within the larger culture.

At the turn of the nineteenth century Protestant thinking in the United States went through a radical change known as the Second Great Awakening, a period of intense revivalist activity based on "alleviated Calvinism" — a doctrinal change according to which sin, rather than being the result of inherent depravity, was the result of ignorance, lack of self-discipline, or faulty social institutions. Human nature was therefore potentially correctable, rather than being redeemable only by faith and divine election. This change in theological emphasis permitted the exploration of doctrines aimed at the immediate perfection of human beings (Fuller 1986).

Such experimentation included not only what we would now consider religious developments, but political, social, spiritualist, and medical experimentation as well. Christian Science is merely the best known of many contemporaneous religious and therapeutic systems; there were many others, most of which are now dead, but some of which continue to influence American culture today.

The mind cure school held that one is connected to God through one's unconscious mind, which is a great store of abundance and power. One's false ideas about one's poverty and powerlessness prevent one from using these available resources. Similarly, one falsely believes that one is ill and at the mercy of one's illness, and this mental construct actually causes the disease. Thus, illness can be cured by changing one's mental constructs. Poverty and powerlessness can likewise be remedied by coming to believe that one is in touch with the source of all richness and power. In this context we first encounter the tenets that all is mind and that there is inexhaustible abundance. Holmes (1919) offers examples of both propositions:

> All is law, and cause and effect obtain through all life. Mind is cause, and what we term matter, or the visible, is effect. As water will freeze into the form that it is poured, so mind will solidify only into the forms that our thought takes. Thought is form. The individual provides the form; he never creates or even manifests—that is, of himself; there is something that does all this for him. His sole activity is the use of this power. (pp. 28–29)

> The man who can control his thought can have and do what he wishes to have and to do; everything is his for the asking. Creation is always flowing by and we have as much of it as we can take and use; more would cause stagnation. We are relieved of all thought of clinging to anybody or anything. Cannot the Great Principle of Life create for us faster than we can spend or use? The Universe is inexhaustible; it is limitless; it knows no bounds and has no confines. We are not depending on a reed shaken by the wind, but on the *principle of life itself*, for all that we want, have, or ever shall have. It is not *some* power or a *great* power, we affirm again; it is ALL POWER. All that we have to do is to believe this and act as though it were so, never wavering, not even once, no matter what happens. As we do this, we shall find that things are steadily coming our way, and that they are coming without the awful effort that destroys the peace of the majority of the race. We know that there can be no failure in the Divine Mind, and this Mind is the Power on which we are depending. (pp. 22–23)

We find the same point about abundance made twenty-three years earlier by Trine (1896):

> We were born to be neither slaves nor beggars, but to dominion and to plenty. This is our rightful heritage, if we will but recognize it and lay claim to it. Many a man and many a woman is to-day longing for conditions better and higher than he or she is in, who might be using the same time now spent in vain, indefinite, spasmodic longings, in putting into operation forces which, accompanied by the right personal activity, would speedily bring the fullest realization of his or her fondest dreams. The great universe is filled with an abundance of all things, filled to overflowing. All there is, is in her, waiting only for the touch of the right forces to cast them forth. She is no respecter of persons outside of the fact that she always resounds to the demands of the man or the woman who knows and uses the forces and powers he or she is endowed with. And to the demands of such she always opens her treasure house, for the supply is always equal to the demand. All things are in the hands of him who knows they are there. (pp. 171–72)

The notion of abundance, like all the other tenets noted here, has its own history. Although it is not clear when abundance replaced scarcity as a model of the world's economic situation, we can certainly find evidence of a time when resources were viewed as zero-sum game, in which one person's gain was another's loss. Le Roy Ladurie (1987), in a startling discussion of beliefs about French rural witchcraft, finds this to be the dominant model:

> This thinking in terms of gains and losses that balance each other was once wide-spread in traditional societies. It implied that the distribution of wealth—more for some, less for others—took place, or seemed to take place, on the basis of a fixed amount of goods, which did not increase. "Growth," by contrast, was to be characteristic, for a whole period, of our industrial society, enabling everyone to increase his share without, as in the past, having to rob Peter in order to pay Paul. [This attitude] was not specific to the rural world: in the seventeenth century Colbert spoke similarly to Louis XIV, saying that "in order to increase the amount of money and the number of ships at the disposal of the Kingdom of France it is necessary to diminish by the same amount the quantity of both in the possession of neighboring states."

The mind cure school was an expert system, complete with its associated experts and its modes of practice by which the ill learned to restructure their beliefs and hence to change their worlds. Of the many forms that the mind cure school took, only Christian Science maintained a rigid organizational structure, with officially designated and trained experts. Most of the other founders of mind cure groups felt that the ideology of the potency of each person's unconscious mind was incompatible with a church organization or designated experts.

Some groups explicitly trained patients who wished to become curers. In other cases, founders attempted to maintain a monopoly on the curing practice and on institutional power, but were frustrated by schisms and secessions (Dresser 1919). Therefore, although this school represented an expert coherence system, it never became institutionalized to the degree that many churches achieved, or even to the degree of many schools of psychoanalysis. Rather, it attained a level of institutional prestige similar to the current status of amateur and professional astrologers. Professional astrologers are professional not by virtue of any certifying body or any specific institutional membership, but because they carry out certain practices that are more complex than those usually performed by amateurs, and because they may be paid for carrying out these practices.

As was noted earlier, a number of the tenets of the mind cure school have become a part of current twentieth-century common sense. However, when this school was first promulgated, it represented an expert coherence system, novel and opposed to the common sense of its time. The common sense of the time derived many of its tenets from the Calvinist theology that had prevailed in the United States from the time of the Puritans until the revolution of the Second Great Awakening. This period, in fact, represents a major fissure in the history of common sense; suddenly, in a matter of decades or less, there emerged the beginnings of a new form of common sense with regard to success — one that reversed or denied several of the major tenets of its predecessor.

This example suggests that the history of common sense does not exhibit regular continuity or a slow, imperceptible changing from one set of ideas to another. Foucault (1972) has argued for the discontinuity over time of what he terms "discursive formations" such as the discourse of medicine, grammar, or political economy. Even slow change in a common-sense system is a rare occurrence. A century or more may pass during which the surface form of common sense may change while the underlying structure remains the same. An excellent example of this is given by Green (1986), in a discussion of the relation between exercise and sexuality. The nineteenth-century view was that physical exercise is beneficial because it curbs excessive sexuality. The twentieth-century view is that exercise is beneficial because it increases sexuality. These may appear to be radically different views, but they represent transforms of the same underlying proposition: exercise is beneficial because it regulates sexuality to a wholesome and appropriate level, as defined by current cultural norms.

Another example, given by Zaleski (1987), involves narratives of near-death experiences, and journeys to the next world. Examining medieval otherworld journeys, nineteenth-century spiritualist accounts of the next world given by trance mediums, and twentieth-century accounts of near-death experiences, Zaleski found that the nineteenth- and twentieth-century accounts are fundamentally similar in content, although their vocabulary differs. Twentieth-century accounts tend not to resort to such metaphysical (or quasi-physical) terms as **ectoplasm, silver cord,** and **etheric double.** However, they closely resemble their nineteenth-century antecedents in describing the next world as an ecstatic, forgiving place of light, where one meets with loved ones who have already died. They differ strongly from the medieval otherworld journey narratives in giving no account of hell or punishment, or of a judgment of the narrator's deeds while alive. The notions of judgment and hell apparently have vanished so thoroughly from nineteenth- and twentieth-century thought that they no longer appear, even in visions.

Foucault (1985) gives another example of this type of rapid change—one that is catastrophic in the technical sense of catastrophe theory. Foucault examines attitudes toward the regulation of one's sexual behavior that were present in Greek thinkers of the fourth century B.C. and contrasts these with attitudes on the same topic held by thinkers of the early Christian era. He sees the Greek notion of sexual management as being concerned with issues of self-mastery and self-regulation, much like dietary management. In contrast, he sees the early Christian view as being occupied primarily with ideas of sin and the codification of sin:

> Now, it seems clear, from a first approach at least, that moral conceptions in Greek and Greco-Roman antiquity were much more oriented toward practices of the self and the question of *askesis* than toward codifications of conducts and the strict definition of what is permitted and what is forbidden. If exception is made of the *Republic* and the *Laws*, one finds very few references to the principle of a code that would define in detail the right conduct to maintain, few references to the need for an authority charged with seeing to its application, few references to the possibility of punishments that would sanction infractions. Although the necessity of respecting the law and the customs—the *nomoi*—was very often underscored, more important than the content of the law and its conditions of application was the attitude that caused one to respect them. The accent was placed on the relationship with the self that enabled a person to keep from being carried away by the appetites and pleasures, to maintain a mastery and superiority over them, to keep his senses in a state of tranquillity, to remain free from interior bondage to the passions, and to achieve a mode of being that could be defined by the full enjoyment of oneself, or the perfect supremacy of oneself over oneself. (pp. 30–31)

In this study, Foucault documents a system of common-sense notions about sexuality that radically differs from the system that succeeds it. Furthermore, the change from one to the other was not evolutionary, but abrupt and relatively sudden.

It appears that the history of common sense is organized into fairly long stable periods, punctuated by occasional catastrophic jumps, in which the common sense of a given period is entirely reversed or abandoned in favor of a new formulation. The change from the model of scarcity and powerlessness derived from Calvinism to the model of abundance and self-power propagated both by Arminian theology and the various mind cure schools is an important and striking example of such a historical fissure in common sense.

Although the rhetoric of current advice about mental control over success and health is somewhat different from that of the nineteenth-century mind cure schools, the techniques and the fundamental assumptions are the same. The major differences lie in the metaphors given to explain why the techniques work. For example, one important technique recommended by this school consists of using affirmations — short statements that express a desired state or result in the world. Thus, a recommended affirmation is "I am perfectly healthy." Such affirmations are to be repeated a number of times every day, to change the user's state of being. When use of these affirmations was first proposed, the explanation of their success was that the brain is like a daguerreotype plate, which can take impressions from the world around it. The current explanation for their success is that the brain is like a computer, which does what it is programmed to do. Most people are said to work with negative programs that hamper them, but it is possible to substitute healthy and effective programs. The following extended example of this metaphor is taken from a 1988 catalogue for the Gateways Institute, a commercial firm offering self-help tapes on topics such as business success, weight loss, relationships, and stress:

### You Are What You Think

Ever try to run a computer without a program? A computer is extremely fast and powerful, but unless it has a set of instructions called a program, it's practically useless.

Your subconscious mind is a lot like a computer program. It directs virtually everything in your life — your emotions, your habits, your relationships, your health, your financial condition, and more. Over 90% of your mental life is subconscious. It's on the job 24 hours a day. And from the time you were born up to the present, it has been accepting and storing a wealth of information, very much like a computer program.

What this so-called "programming" consists of is a vast storehouse of everything that's ever happened in your life, everything you've ever felt — failures and successes, happiness and unhappiness. We've all grown up with ideas about ourselves that are negative, inaccurate, self-limiting, or outdated. Over the years these self-defeating ideas persist and create even more self-limiting beliefs.

You've probably heard the expression "You are what you think." This doesn't simply refer to what you *know* you think. It also refers to what you *don't know* you think. For example, you may be unaware that deep inside your subconscious is the belief that you are unworthy, that you don't deserve financial success or lasting, loving relationships. And you wonder why you don't have the income you want, or your relationships are less than fulfilling. There's a good reason why this is so: it has to do with the fact that your subconscious exerts far more control over your life than you realize. It literally directs your reality.

### Take Charge of Your Subconscious Beliefs
### and Change Your Life

Many people wonder why the subconscious ever accepts negative, self-defeating beliefs in the first place. After all, don't we all want the best for ourselves? The answer to this question lies in the peculiar nature of the subconscious: it contains no reasoning power of its own. It's not at all like the conscious mind, which tends to be logical and objective. Quite the contrary, the subconscious accepts ideas implanted in it without question, and then influences your life accordingly. It's impersonal. Present it with negative goals, and it operates impersonally as a failure mechanism. Present it with success goals, and it will work just as hard as a success mechanism. Does this mean you are at the mercy of your subconscious "programming," that your patterns of behavior are "set"? Nonsense. You are not a machine. You can, however, think of your subconscious as a machine—a computer which you can control. Changing your life becomes a matter of changing your internal "programming" or the belief system in your inner mind. (p. 3)

Although the explanation and the metaphor of the mind here use a currently fashionable technology, the underlying theory of the mind (and the appropriate technique for dealing with it) remains fundamentally unchanged from its nineteenth-century formulation.

There have, indeed, been some changes in method, but none involving major changes in the theory. For example, there have been both technical and theoretical developments in the use of affirmations. The technical developments come from the widespread availability of cassette tape recorders, which permit the use of taped affirmations with appropriate background music. These have become extremely popular. A further development is the use of subliminal affirmations, with or without music, which can be used while sleeping. The main theoretical development, beginning at the turn of the twentieth century, is the recommendation that affirmations not contain negative statements. For example, an early affirmation might state "I am perfectly healthy. I have no pain." The revised theory recommends that this should be stated "I am perfectly healthy. I can do anything I want to do." This change in practice is currently being presented as a new development arising from research on the structure of the brain. It is said to work because affirmations work on the right brain, which, being intuitive and feeling-oriented rather than logical and linear, is unable to process negative statements. Therefore, when the user tries to work with an affirmation like "I have no pain," the right brain, being unable to process negative statements, hears this as "I have pain" and proceeds to create reality accordingly.

The common-sense system of our era continues to include positive thinking; therefore, any changes reflect technical developments, rather than radical restatements of the nature of what is obvious. There are no signs, at present, of a challenge to this extremely pervasive and influential system of beliefs. The major change in positive thinking from the nineteenth century to the twentieth century has been the change from an expert system to a common-sense system. The tenets of this system are now reflected in ordinary narratives, as we have seen. When they are made explicit in advice literature, they are not justified; the tone is pragmatic, not theoretical. They thus represent an unnoticeable set of truisms about the way things are.

When the tenets of this system are examined explicitly, it seems incredible that anyone could actually believe such things. We may, in fact, doubt whether anyone does. We cannot tell, of course, about the beliefs of the authors of self-help books. This literature is so popular, and the amount of money to be made by writing a successful self-help book is so great, that one cannot assume sincerity on the part of the authors. For very different reasons, it is impossible to tell whether the speakers in the life story narratives actually believe and structure their lives around such assumptions. We have already discussed the problem of assessing factuality in judging these texts. A similar problem applies in judging coherence systems — whether special coherence systems or the common-sense system — that are used to structure these stories. Asking the speakers directly about the presuppositions of the systems they use is not helpful, since we do not know whether their reported intuitions about such presuppositions are reliable — particularly since these presuppositions are structured to be covert.

My own belief is that such special coherence systems and most particularly the common-sense system, while not obligatory, are extremely persuasive, all the more so because their assumptions are implicit and hence hard to see. One does not have to believe in these systems, even if one uses them, but the existence of such a system in the language and the culture makes certain kinds of thoughts, beliefs, attitudes, and actions extremely easy to formulate and makes others almost impossible to think or convey.

Bellah et al. (1985) give an extremely interesting example demonstrating this. The argument of this example is that the individualism characteristic of American thought and discourse makes it difficult or impossible for speakers to formulate alternative conceptions such as obligation or commitment. Thus a discussion of why one remains married can be easily cast in terms of utility or pleasure: **It's a good marriage, It makes me happy.** But it is very difficult to cast the reason in terms of duty or obligation, because this vocabulary is not part of the current common-sense system. One of their subjects refers to life as "a big pinball machine" in which you have to "move and adjust yourself to situations" and "to realize that most things are not absolute." Although this speaker claims to be a psychologically oriented pragmatist, he also feels that he is married to the "special person" for him. He argues against this romantic formulation, noting that "you see a lot of people successfully married, and that many coincidences couldn't happen all the time." But he does feel that, even if there are "quite a few people with whom you could be equally happy in a different way, you've got to find somebody from that group." In describing why he wants a lasting marriage, he does not cite family upbringing, public commitment, or moral issues. Rather, his utilitarian argument is that he has found the best partner—that is, the partner who will bring him the most happiness. Even when asked about alternative kinds of reasons, he rapidly returns to the pragmatic argument: "I think there is an element, a small element of obligation. But I think mostly it's just, you know, this person is really good. It's worked so well up to now, and it continues to do that because you expect it to, and it does, by and large." It would be wrong to break up his marriage only because he would feel "a sense of failure at making the relationship work, because I know you have to work at it" and because it would be wrong for their children "not to be able to grow up in a family."

This example presents a situation in which a speaker appears to lack an intellectual and linguistic system that would allow him to state what he wants to state. The interviewer did attempt to elicit an explicit formulation of the possibility of a system of obligation, but failed to do so. This is reminiscent of the interviewer's attempt, reported in Chapter 6, to challenge a speaker's behaviorist coherence system. Even when the speaker explicitly attempts to formulate her story in terms of choices, as the interviewer requests, she recounts an incident in which she "chose" to fail out of college, which effectively subverts the notion of choice and the common-sense belief in individual responsibility for action of which it forms a part.

We may conclude that the prevalence of the common-sense system makes it very easy for people to speak (and presumably to think) in ways consonant with it. Although the common-sense system does not make it impossible to formulate alternative systems (as is indeed proved by the existence of the special coherence systems), it certainly makes it very difficult to entertain notions that contradict or directly criticize it. Its reflection in the life story data provides an important example of the ways in which the higher social level of beliefs and practices affects the detailed structure of narratives.

# 8

# Conclusion

Let us first review the argument of this work, and then discuss its importance, both for linguistics and for the other social sciences. This book has examined the oral life story, focusing on the social practice of creation, exchange, and negotiation of coherent life stories. We have observed how coherence is created, from the morphological level to the level of the discourse unit to the social and historical level of the coherence system. Coherence is thus created by interweaving many linguistic and social levels.

The practice of the creation of coherence and the life stories that result from it are important, both for understanding life stories themselves and for clarifying the wider role that life stories play as crossroads of personal and social meanings. Life stories express our sense of self — who we are, how we are related to others, and how we became that person. They are also one very important means by which we communicate our sense of self to others and negotiate it with others. Further, we use these stories to claim or negotiate group membership and to demonstrate that we are worthy members of these groups, properly following (or at least understanding) their moral standards. Finally, life stories involve large-scale systems of social understandings and of knowledge that are grounded in a long history of practice; indeed, these stories rely on presuppositions about what can be taken as expected, what the norms are, and what common or special belief systems are necessary to establish coherence.

The life story is an oral unit; written autobiographies have a very different character, due to their different conditions of composition and their different purposes. A life story is also a discontinuous unit, consisting of a set of stories that are retold in various forms over a long period of time and that are subject to revision and change as the speaker drops some old meanings and adds new meanings to portions of the life story. A life story is told over many occasions. Conventionally, it includes certain kinds of landmark events, including choice of profession, marriage, divorce, and religious or ideological conversion, as well as more idiosyncratic events that are particular to the speaker's life. Both in its content (the items it includes and excludes) and in its form (the structures that serve to make it coherent), it is the project of a member of a particular culture, in intercourse with other members of that culture. Other cultures may include different items and may use different forms. Indeed, the notion of a life story itself is not universal, but is the product of a particular culture.

In the life stories reported in this book, coherence is both a social demand and an internal, psychological demand. Although the life story as a linguistic unit is crucially involved in social interaction, it is also related to the internal, subjective sense of having a private life story that organizes a speaker's understanding of his or her past life, current situation, and imagined future.

Coherence in this sense is a property of texts; it derives from the relation that the parts of a text bear to one another and to the whole text, and that the text bears to other texts of its type. On this view, it is not possible or appropriate to judge texts on the basis of their relation to some postulated world of facts. Coherence, rather than factuality, is the appropriate criterion for judgment. A text can be seen as coherent if two sets of relations hold: the parts of the text must be seen as being in proper relation to one another, and to the text as a whole; and the text as a whole must be seen as constituting a recognizable and well-formed text of its type. Thus, a detective story is understood both because its internal structure is understandable—that is, the revelation of the identity of the murderer follows, rather than precedes the discovery of the corpse—and because it stands in a tradition of other texts recognizable as detective stories.

The coherence of a text is created at a number of levels. The first of these levels is imposed by the structure of narrative itself. The discourse form of narrative consists of a sequence of past-tense clauses, whose order is taken to reflect the actual order of the events reported. In addition, narratives contain various evaluation devices, which are the means by which the speaker conveys how the events are to be understood.

The second level of the creation of coherence is the level of coherence principles—a social level that strongly influences what can count as an adequate account. The coherence principles used in structuring the life story texts are primarily principles of appropriate causality and continuity. In telling a life story, the speaker must establish that the causal sequence of events is adequate. Adequate causality is defined as a chain of causality that the hearers can accept as constituting a good reason for some particular event or sequence of events. Establishing adequate causality for a choice of profession means either demonstrating that obvious good reasons exist for the speaker's choice of profession or showing that—even if the reasons do not seem at first glance to be acceptable—there are indeed sound reasons for accepting these reasons. The most powerful form of adequate causality for a choice of profession is character. Speakers and addressees appear to take character traits as primitives, referring to them as obvious and sufficient causes for career decisions. Thus, if a speaker claims "I like that sort of thing" or "I'm good at it," the accounts can be taken as offering an adequate and final reason for the choice of profession. Another strong form of adequate causality is richness of account, which a speaker establishes by giving many noncontradictory reasons, often rooted far back in time, for a choice of profession.

In dealing with the question of adequate causality, some accounts must handle the fact that the speaker (or possibly the addressee) perceives the causality or the ordering of events to be in some way insufficient or problematic. Situations of insufficient causality can be divided into accounts structured in terms of accident and accounts containing a socially recognized discontinuity. An example of an accidental account is the one in which the speaker explains that she became a scholar of medieval literature **more or less by accident**. When an event is thus presented as an accident, the speaker commonly follows the narration of the accident with a demonstration of why it was not really an accident, since multiple routes led to the same point. Discontinuities between careers, between career stages, or between actions and the reasons for actions are handled in more varied ways. An example of such a discontinuity is **I was a banker until I was 35, and then I dropped it and became a potter.** As members of our culture, we recognize that this is a conventionally discontinuous sequence of professions. One of the clearest patterns in the life story data is that this form of discontinuity must be managed in some way; some evaluation or explanation of the discontinuity must be given.

The third (and highest) level of the creation of coherence is the level of coherence systems. These are social systems of assumptions about the world that speakers use to make events and evaluations coherent. Many of these systems are semi-expert forms historically derived from systems originally the property of experts—for example, Freudian psychology, behaviorist psychology, astrology, and feminism. The coherence systems we examined include versions of Freudian psychology, behaviorist psychology, astrology, feminism, and Catholic confessional practice. All of these are products of a historical process by which formal theories and ideologies are popularized. As a result of this process, theories that have associated experts who alone are permitted to use them are transformed into theories that are available for use by anyone who knows about and chooses to apply them.

The most pervasive and invisible coherence system is common sense—the set of beliefs and relations between beliefs that speakers may assume are known and shared by all competent members of the culture. As a system, common sense is transparent within its culture: it consists of beliefs that purport not to be beliefs, but to be a natural reflection of the way things really are. Common-sense assumptions on the topic of professional choice in the life story data include the following:

1. Profession is a matter of personal choice; choices are limited only by personal ability and psychological adjustment, not by available economic opportunities or class background.
2. Personal desire, rather than obligations, family ties, or traditions, is the main and proper determinant of professional choice.
3. Character is an adequate explanation for professional choice.
4. Discontinuities between careers, career stages, or reasons and results must receive some sort of narrative management.

Like the special coherence systems, common sense has its own history. Current American common sense on the topic of professional success can be traced back to the early decades of the nineteenth century. It derives from religious currents of that time, which attempted to alleviate the rigorous theory of predestination of eighteenth-century Calvinism with a belief in the efficacy of individual will, the willingness of God to cooperate with the desires of the believer, and the infinite abundance of resources available to any individual who believed in such abundance. Starting as an expert theory in religious and faith-healing movements such as Christian Science and the Mind Cure or New Thought School, these beliefs became part of the general American common-sense system about the topics of profession and prosperity—a system that has persisted, with only minor changes in rhetoric, for nearly 150 years.

Our investigation of the life story has shown how coherence constitutes a social and psychological demand, one whose achievement involves a social practice that requires work at every linguistic level. This work is thus unique in investigating a single socially and psychologically important type of text (the life story) and providing a unified account of its structure, its social use, the larger belief systems that underlie it, and the historical development of those belief systems. Within linguistics, there is a history of work on discourse analysis: the attempt to describe elements of discourse as units within the linguistic hierarchy. Hitherto, however, there have been no descriptions of how such units function as part of the social practice of language; that is, linguistics has been able to describe the structure of narrative, but it has had no way of linking that structure to the ways in which speakers use narrative.

Researchers in a number of social sciences have recently shown an interest in what are called discourses, such as "the discourse of the family" (Kondo 1990), "the discourse of patriarchy," and "the discourse of resistance" (Scott 1985). This use of the term *discourse* is derived from Foucault, who speaks of such discourses as the discourse of medicine and the discourse of grammar. This term captures the intuition that, for example, doctors talk in a recognizable way when they are being doctors. Within linguistics, this level of analysis has been discussed either as the notion of register or as individual analyses of settings that appear to have unique discourse or interactional properties, such as classrooms or medical settings. However, Foucault's analysis adds two important dimensions. One is power relations: any discourse is partly constituted by the power relations between the participants, as well as by the relation of these local power relations to larger structures of power and control. While linguistics has given accounts of local power relations—for example, in studies of pronoun choices (Brown and Gilman 1960)—it has not linked these to accounts of larger-scale power relations. The second important addition is history. Foucault shows that such discourses have a history: they have beginnings; they have development; and these are linked to historical changes in power relations, ideas, technologies, and so on. This historical dimension has been conspicuously absent from discourse analysis within linguistics, which until now has been exclusively synchronic.

While Foucault's use of the term *discourse* could add important dimensions to linguistics, it is not currently usable, because of its ambiguity about whether a discourse is a linguistic object or a linguistic unit and about what constitutes it. If we were to talk about the discourse of resistance, we would certainly want to include examples of members of an oppressed group telling stories about successful or unsuccessful acts of resistance, grumbling to one another, or composing and singing satirical or political songs about their oppressors. We might want to include their use of such symbolic acts as wearing a button or clothing of a color that indicates a political position. But do we want to include as discourses acts such as secretly spitting in the soup before serving it? In his discussion of discourses and their history, Foucault has given accounts of discourses that are clearly linguistic. For example, his discussion of the history of sexuality as a concept focuses on the role of speech events such as the Catholic practice of confession and, later, psychoanalysis in construing "sexuality" as a unified category made up of certain physical acts, thoughts, fantasies, and dreams (Foucault 1980, 1985). However, in other kinds of events that Foucault terms *discourses*, such as public executions, the discourse consists not of deployments of linguistic units, but of actions such as decapitation (Foucault 1979). From the point of view of linguistics, terming such actions discourses is problematic.

I would argue that the notion of discourse is extremely important for linguistics to include, and that the task of linguistics is to make its meaning precise. In many of its present uses, the term seems to float in the air, with no feet under it; that is, the discourse of the family or the discourse of medicine is discussed, but the analyst never specifies exactly what kinds of linguistic units, used in what kinds of social situations, constitute the practice of this discourse. The methods of linguistics can be of crucial importance in specifying how particular linguistic units are used in particular speech situations to constitute the social practice of a particular discourse.

This book, then, has attempted to show that it is possible to link all these levels, beginning with the smallest linguistic level of morphological structure, continuing through the structures at the level of the discourse unit, and culminating at the cultural and historical level of the coherence system. Linguistic structure and social practice can be (and indeed, must be) linked in a single unified description. Such a unified description should serve not only as an account of one type of text—as important as life story narrative is—but also as a paradigm for future research. This book's demonstration of the linkage between linguistic levels is important both for the future development of linguistics and for the clarification and expansion of its relation to the other social sciences.

# REFERENCES

Aries, Philippe, 1981. *The Hour of Our Death*. Translated by Helen Weaver. Alfred A. Knopf.

Atkinson, J. Maxwell, and John Heritage. 1984. *Structures of Social Action: Studies in Conversation Analysis*. Cambridge University Press.

Auerbach, Erich, 1957. *Mimesis: The Representation of Reality in Western Literature*. Doubleday Anchor Books.

Bakan, David. 1958. *Sigmund Freud and the Jewish Mystical Tradition*. D. Van Nostrand.

Bales, R. F. 1950. *Interaction Process Analysis*. Addison-Wesley.

Barthes, Roland. 1982. *The Empire of Signs*. Hill & Wang.

_____. 1972. *Mythologies*. Hill & Wang.

Becker, Alton, 1979. "Text Building, Epistemology, and Aesthetics in Japanese Shadow Theater." In *The Imagination of Reality*, ed. by Alton Becker and Aran Yengoyan, pp. 211–43. Ablex.

_____. 1975. "A Linguistic Image of Nature: The Burmese Numerative Classifier System." *International Journal of the Sociology of Language* 5: 109–21.

Bellah, Robert N.; Richard Madsen; William M. Sullivan; Ann Swidler; and Steven M. Tipton. 1985. *Habits of the Heart*. Harper & Row.

Benstock, Shari. 1988. "Authorizing the Autobiographical." In *The Private Self: Theory and Practice of Women's Autobiographical Writings*, ed. by Shari Benstock, pp. 10–33. University of North Carolina Press.

Blake, Nicholas. 1935. *A Question of Proof*. Harper & Brothers.

Bloom, Lynn A.; Karen Coburn; and Joan Pearlman. 1975. *The New Assertive Woman*. Delacorte Press.

Bloomfield, Leonard. 1933. *Language*. Henry Holt.

Bourdieu, Pierre. 1977. *Outline of a Theory of Practice*. Cambridge University Press.

Braun, Bennett G. 1988. "The BASK Model of Dissociation: Clinical Application." *Dissociation: Progress in the Dissociative Disorders* 11: 4–23.

Brooks, Peter. 1984. *Reading for the Plot: Design and Intention in Narrative*. Alfred A. Knopf.

Brown, Roger, and A. Gilman. 1960. "The Pronouns of Power and Solidarity." In *Style in Language*, ed. by Thomas A. Sebeok, pp. 253–76. John Wiley & Sons.

Bruss, Elizabeth. 1976. *Autobiographical Acts: The Changing Situation of a Literary Genre*. University of Michigan Press.

Buhler, Charlotte. 1933. *Der Menschlicher Lebenslauf als Psychologisches Problem*. S. Herzel Verlag.

Carroll, John B. 1991. "Benjamin Lee Whorf." In *Oxford Encyclopedia of Linguistics*, pp. 240–41.

Cerling, Charles E. 1980. *Holy Boldness*. Christian Herald Books.

Chafe, Wallace, and Johanna Nichols. 1986. *Evidentiality: The Linguistic Coding of Epistemology*. Vol. 20 of *Advances in Discourse Processes*. Ablex.

Chatman, Seymour. 1978. *Story and Discourse: Narrative Structure in Fiction and Film*. Cornell University Press.

Chodorow, Nancy. 1974. "Family Structure and Feminine Personality." In *Women, Culture, and Society*, ed. by Michelle Z. Rosaldo and Louise Lamphere, pp. 43–66. Stanford University Press.

Chomsky, Noam. 1965. *Aspects of the Theory of Syntax*. MIT Press.

———. 1957. *Syntactic Structures*. Mouton.

Cicero, Marcus Tullius. *Orations*. Translated by Charles Duke Yonge. Colonial Press (1900).

Clancey, William. 1992. "Model Construction Operators." *Artificial Intelligence* 53: 1–115.

Clanchy, M. T. 1979. *From Memory to Written Record*. Edward Arnold.

Clark, Eve. 1978. "From Gesture to Word: On the Natural History of Deixis in Language Acquisition." *Human Growth and Development: Wolfson College Lectures 1976*, ed. by J. Bruner and A. Garton, pp. 85–120. Oxford University Press.

Cole-Whittaker, Terry. 1983. *How to Have More in a Have-Not World*. Rawson Associates.

Coles, Robert. 1980. "Civility and Psychology." *Daedalus* 109: 133–41.

Cross, Whitney R. 1965. *The Burned-Over District: The Social and Intellectual History of Enthusiastic Religion in Western New York, 1800–1850*. Harper & Row.

Daly, Mary. 1978. *Gyn/Ecology: The Metaethics of Radical Feminism*. Beacon Press.

D'Andrade, Roy. 1987. "A Folk Model of the Mind." In *Cultural Models in Language and Thought*, ed. by Dorothy Holland and Naomi Quinn, pp. 112–48. Cambridge University Press.

Dresser, Horatio. 1919. *A History of the New Thought Movement*. George G. Harrap.

Eckert, Penelope. 1990. "Cooperative Competition in Adolescent Girl Talk." *Discourse Processes* 13: 92–122.

———. 1989. *Jocks and Burnouts*. Teachers College Press.

Ellenberger, Henri. 1970. *The Discovery of the Unconscious: The History and Evolution of Dynamic Psychology*. Basic Books.

Erikson, Erik. 1969. *Gandhi's Truth on the Origins of Militant Nonviolence*. W. W. Norton.

———. 1963a. *Childhood and Society*. W. W. Norton.

———. 1963*b*. "The Legend of Hitler's Childhood." In *Childhood and Society*, pp. 326–58. W. W. Norton.

———. 1962. *Young Man Luther: A Study in Psychoanalysis and History*. W. W. Norton.

Foucault, Michel. 1985. *The History of Sexuality, Volume II: The Use of Pleasure*. Pantheon Books.

———. 1980*a*. *The History of Sexuality, Volume I: An Introduction*. Pantheon Books.

———. 1980*b*. *Language, Countermemory, Practice*. Edited by Donald Bouchard. Cornell University Press.

———. 1979. *Discipline and Punish: The Birth of the Prison*. Vintage Books.

———. 1972. *The Archaeology of Knowledge*. Pantheon Books.

Frank, Gelya. 1981. *Venus of Wheels: The Life History of a Congenital Amputee*. UCLA Department of Anthropology.

———. 1979. "Finding the Common Denominator: A Phenomenological Critique of Life History Method." *Ethos* 7: 68–94.

Frankel, Richard. 1984. "From Sentence to Sequence: Exploring the Medical Encounter Using Microinteractional Analysis." *Discourse Processes* 7: 135–70.

Friedman, Susan S. 1988. "Women's Autobiographical Selves: Theory and Practice." In *The Private Self: Theory and Practice of Women's Autobiographical Writing*, ed. by Shari Benstock, pp. 34–62. University of North Carolina Press.

Fuller, Robert C. 1986. *Americans and the Unconscious*. Oxford University Press.

Fussell, Paul. 1975. *The Great War and Modern Memory*. Oxford University Press.

Garfinkel, Harold. 1959. "Aspects of the Problem of Common-Sense Knowledge of Social Structures." *Transactions of the Fourth World Congress of Sociology*, vol. IV, pp. 51–65. International Sociological Association.

Garfinkel, Harold, and E. Bittner. 1967. "Good Organizational Reasons for 'Bad' Clinical Records." In *Studies in Ethnomethodology*, ed. by Harold Garfinkel, pp. 186–207. Prentice-Hall.

Gay, Peter. 1986. *The Bourgeois Experience—Victoria to Freud: The Tender Passion*. Oxford University Press.

———. 1984. *The Bourgeois Experience—Victoria to Freud: The Education of the Senses*. Oxford University Press.

Geertz, Clifford. 1983*a*. "Common Sense as a Cultural System." In *Local Knowledge: Further Essays in Interpretive Anthropology*, pp. 73–93. Basic Books.

———. 1983*b*. "From the Native's Point of View: On the Nature of Anthropological Understanding." In *Local Knowledge: Further Essays in Interpretive Anthropology*, pp. 55–70. Basic Books.

———. 1973. *The Interpretation of Cultures*. Basic Books.

Gilligan, Carol. 1982. *In a Different Voice: Psychological Theory and Women's Development*. Harvard University Press.

Goffman, Erving. 1972. "The Moral Career of the Mental Patient." In *Symbolic Interaction: A Reader in Social Psychology*, ed. by Jerome G. Manis and Bernard N. Meltzer, pp. 234–44. Allyn & Bacon.

Goguen, J. A.; J. L. Weiner; and C. Linde. 1983. "Reasoning and Natural Explanation." *International Journal of Man-Machine Studies* 19: 521–59.

Goldman, Emma. 1931. *Living My Life*. Dover Publications.

Goodwin, Charles. 1986. "Audience Diversity, Participation and Interpretation." *Text* 63: 283–316.

———. 1984. "Notes on Story Structure and the Organization of Participation." In *Structures of Social Action*, ed. by J. Maxwell Atkinson and John Heritage, pp. 225–46. Cambridge University Press.

Goodwin, Charles, and Marjorie H. Goodwin. 1987. "Concurrent Operations on Talk: Notes on the Interactive Organization of Assessments." *IPRA Papers in Pragmatics* 11: 1–54.

Goodwin, Charles, and John Heritage. 1990. "Conversation Analysis." *Annual Review of Anthropology* 19: 283–307.

Goodwin, Marjorie H. 1982. "Processes of Dispute Management Among Urban Black Children." *American Ethnologist* 9: 76–96.

Green, Harvey. 1986. *Fit for America: Health, Fitness, Sport, and American Society*. Pantheon Books.

Grice, H. P. 1978. "Further Notes on Logic and Conversation." In *Syntax and Semantics 9: Pragmatics*, ed. by Peter Cole, pp. 113–28. Academic Press.

———. 1975. "Logic and Conversation." In *Syntax and Semantics 3: Speech Acts*, ed. by Peter Cole and Jerry Morgan, pp. 41–58. Academic Press.

Gusdorf, George. 1980. "Conditions and Limits of Autobiography." In *Autobiography: Essays Theoretical and Critical*, ed. by James Olney, pp. 28–48. Princeton University Press.

Hale, Nathan, Jr. 1971. *Freud and the Americans, Volume 1: The Beginnings of Psychoanalysis in the United States*. Oxford University Press.

Halliday, M. A. K., and R. Hasan. 1976. *Cohesion in English*. Longman.

Hallowell, A. I. 1955. "The Self and Its Behavioral Environment." In *Culture and Experience*, pp. 75–110. University of Pennsylvania Press.

Hill, Napoleon. 1985. *Think and Grow Rich*. Ballantine Books.

Holland, Dorothy, and Naomi Quinn. 1987. *Cultural Models in Language and Thought*. Cambridge University Press.

Holmes, Ernest S. 1919. *Creative Mind and Success*. Robert M. McBride.

Hymes, Dell. 1972. "Models of the Interaction of Language and Social Life." In *Directions in Sociolinguistics*, ed. by John Gumperz and Dell Hymes, pp. 35–71. Holt, Rinehart & Winston.

———. 1964. "The Ethnography of Communication." *American Anthropologist* 66: 21–34.

Jakobson, Roman. 1984. *Russian and Slavic Grammar: Studies, 1931–1981*. Edited by Linda Waugh and Morris Halle. Mouton.

Jefferson, Gail. 1972. "Side-Sequences." In *Studies in Social Interaction*, ed. by David Sudnow, pp. 294–338. Free Press.

Jelinek, Estelle C. 1980. "Women's Autobiography and the Male Tradition." In *Women's Autobiography: Essays in Criticism*, ed. by Estelle C. Jelinek, pp. 1–20. Indiana University Press.

Jordan, Brigitte. 1989. "Cosmopolitical Obstetrics: Some Insights from the Training of Traditional Midwives." *Social Science and Medicine* 289: 925–37.

Joshi, Aravind; Bonnie Webber; and Ivan Sag. 1981. *Elements of Discourse Understanding*. Cambridge University Press.

Kalcik, Susan. 1975. ". . . Like Ann's Gynecologist or the Time I Was Almost Raped." In *Women and Folklore*, ed. by Claire R. Farrer, pp. 3–11. University of Texas Press.

Katz, Jerrold J., and Jerry Fodor. 1963. "The Structure of a Semantic Theory." *Language* 39: 170–210.

Kelley, H. H. 1967. "Attribution Theory in Social Psychology." In *Nebraska Symposium on Motivation*, ed. by D. Levine, pp. 192–240. University of Nebraska Press.

Kermode, Frank. 1966. *The Sense of an Ending: Studies in the Theory of Fiction*. Oxford University Press.

Kirshenblatt-Gimblett, Barbara. 1975. "A Parable in Context: A Social Interactional Analysis of Storytelling Performance." In *Folklore: Performance and Communication*, ed. by Dan Ben-Amos and Kenneth S. Goldstein, pp. 105–30. Mouton.

Kluckhohn, Clyde. 1945. "The Personal Document in Anthropological Science." In *The Use of Personal Documents in History, Anthropology, and Sociology*, ed. by Louis Gottschalk. Social Science Research Council, Bulletin 53.

Kohlberg, Lawrence. 1981. *The Philosophy of Moral Development: Moral Stages and the Idea of Justice*. Harper & Row.

Kondo, D. K. 1990. *Crafting Selves: Power, Gender and Discourses of Identity in a Japanese Workplace*. University of Chicago Press.

Krainer, Elizabeth. 1988a. "Challenges in a Psychotherapy Group." *Proceedings of the Berkeley Linguistics Society* 14: 100–113.

———. 1988b. "Challenges in a Psychotherapy Group: Reflections of Direct and Indirect Discourse Strategies." Doctoral dissertation. Department of Linguistics, Stanford University.

Kroeber, Theodora. 1961. *Ishi in Two Worlds: A Biography of the Last Wild Indian in North America*. University of California Press.

Labov, William. 1972a. *Sociolinguistic Patterns*. University of Pennsylvania Press.

———. 1972b. "The Transformation of Experience in Narrative Syntax." In *Language in the Inner City*, pp. 354–96. University of Pennsylvania Press.

———. 1966. *The Social Stratification of English in New York City*. Center for Applied Linguistics.

Labov, William, and David Fanshel. 1977. *Therapeutic Discourse: Psychotherapy as Conversation*. Academic Press.

Labov, William, and Joshua Waletsky. 1967. "Narrative Analysis: Oral Versions of Personal Experience." In *Essays on the Verbal and Visual Arts*, ed. by June Helms, pp. 12–44. University of Washington Press.

Langness, Lewis, and Gelya Frank. 1981. *Lives: An Anthropological Approach to Biography*. Chandler & Sharp.

Larson, Martin A. 1985. *New Thought or a Modern Religious Approach: The Philosophy of Health, Happiness, and Prosperity*. Philosophical Library.

Lasch, Christopher. 1979. *The Culture of Narcissism*. W. W. Norton.

Le Roy Ladurie, Emmanuel. 1987. *Jasmin's Witch*. George Braziller.

Levinson, Stephen. 1983. *Pragmatics*. Cambridge University Press.

Linde, Charlotte. 1991. "What's Next: The Social and Technological Management of Meetings." *Pragmatics* 1(3): 297–318.

———. 1988*a*. "Politeness and Accidents in Aviation Discourse: The Quantitative Study of Communicative Success." *Language and Society* 17: 375–99.

———. 1988*b*. "Who's in Charge Here? Cooperative Work and Authority Negotiation in Police Helicopter Missions." In *CSCW 88: Proceedings of the Conference on Computer-supported Cooperative Work*, pp. 52–64. Association for Computing Machinery.

———. 1987. "Rank and Status in the Aviation Cockpit: Linguistic Consequences of Crossed Hierarchies." In *Fifteenth Annual Conference on New Ways of Analyzing Variation in Language: NWAV-XV*, ed. by Keith M. Downing, Sharon Inkelas, Faye C. McNair-Knox, and John Rickford, pp. 300–11. Department of Linguistics, Stanford University.

———. 1986. "Private Stories in Public Discourse." *Poetics* 15: 183–202.

———. 1981. "The Organization of Discourse." In *Style and Variables in English*, ed. by Timothy Shoper and Joseph Williams, pp. 84–114. Winthrop Publishers.

———. 1974. "The Linguistic Encoding of Spatial Information." Doctoral dissertation. Department of Linguistics, Columbia University.

Linde, Charlotte, and Joseph Goguen. 1978. "The Structure of Planning Discourse." *Journal of Social and Biological Structures* 1: 219–51.

Linde, Charlotte, and William Labov. 1975. "Spatial Networks as a Site for the Study of Language and Thought." *Language* 51: 924–39.

Luhrmann, T. M. 1989. *Persuasions of the Witches' Craft: Ritual Magic in Contemporary England*. Harvard University Press.

Lyons, John. 1968. *Introduction to Theoretical Linguistics*. Cambridge University Press.

Martin, Jay. 1988. *Who Am I This Time?* W. W. Norton.

Mead, George H. 1934. *Self and Society: From the Standpoint of a Social Behaviorist*. University of Chicago Press.

Meehan, Albert J. 1986. "Record-keeping Practices in the Policing of Juveniles." *Urban Life* 151: 70–102.

Merton, Thomas. 1948. *The Seven Story Mountain*. Harcourt.

Meyer, Donald. 1980. *The Positive Thinkers: Religion as Pop Psychology from Mary Baker Eddy to Oral Roberts*. Pantheon Books.

Michaels, Sarah, and Courtney Cazden. 1986. "Teacher/Child Collaboration as Oral Preparation for Literacy." In *The Acquisition of Literacy: Ethnographic Perspectives*, ed. by Bambi B. Schieffelin and Perry Gilmore, pp. 132–54. Ablex.

Miller, Peggy J., and Linda L. Sperry. 1988. "Early Talk About the Past: The Origins of Conversational Stories of Personal Experience." *Journal of Child Language* 15: 203–315.

Misch, George. 1973. *A History of Autobiography in Antiquity*, vols. 1 & 2. Greenwood Press.

_____. 1950. *A History of Autobiography in Antiquity*. Greenwood Press.

Moerman, Michael. 1987. *Talking Culture: Ethnography and Conversation Analysis*. University of Pennsylvania Press.

Newman, John Henry Cardinal. 1864. *Apologia Pro Vita Sua*. Modern Library (1950).

Ochs, Elinor, 1979. "Transcription as Theory." In *Developmental Pragmatics*, ed. by Elinor Ochs and Bambi B. Schieffelin, pp. 41–72. Academic Press.

Olney, James. 1972. *Metaphors of Self: The Meaning of Autobiography*. Princeton University Press.

Orwell, George. 1956. "Politics and the English Language." In *The Orwell Reader*, pp. 355–66. Harcourt, Brace & World.

Palmer, Richard E. 1969. *Hermeneutics: Interpretation Theory in Schleiermacher, Dilthey, Heidegger, and Gadamer*. Northwestern University Press.

Parker, Theodore. 1879. *Collected Works*. Trabner & Co.

Peacock, James. 1984. "Religion and Life History: An Explanation in Cultural Psychology." In *Text, Play, and Story: The Construction and Reconstruction of Self and Society*, ed. by E. Bruner, pp. 94–116. American Ethnological Society.

_____. 1978. *Muslim Puritans: The Reformist Psychology in Southeast Asian Islam*. University of California Press.

_____. 1969. "Mystics and Merchants in Fourteenth-Century Germany: A Speculative Reconstruction of Their Psychological Bond and Its Implications for Social Change." *Journal for the Scientific Study of Religion* 81: 47–59.

Peacock, James, and Dorothy Holland. 1988. "The Narrated Self: Life Stories and Self Construction." Symposium on Self Narrative, American Anthropological Association Meeting. Phoenix, Arizona.

Polanyi, Livia. 1990. "Toward a Formal Analysis of Discourse Structure and Interpretation." *Text* 10: 81–85.

_____. 1989. *Telling the American Story: A Structural and Cultural Analysis of Conversational Storytelling*. MIT Press.

_____. 1985. "Conversational Storytelling." In *Handbook of Discourse Analysis*, Volume 3: *Discourse and Dialogue*, ed. by Teun A. Van Dijk, pp. 183–201. Academic Press.

_____. 1978. "So What's the Point?" *Semiotica* 25(3–4): 208–24.

Prince, Ellen. 1979. "A Comparison of Wh-clefts and It-clefts in Discourse." *Language* 54: 883–906.

Propp, Vladimir. 1968. *Morphology of the Folktale*, 2d ed. Translated by Lawrence Scott. University of Texas Press.

Ragland-Sullivan, Ellie. 1986. *Jacques Lacan and the Philosophy of Psychoanalysis*. University of Illinois Press.

Rosaldo, Renato. 1976. "The Story of Tukbaw: 'They Listen as He Orates'." In *The Biographical Process: Studies in the History and Psychology of Religion*, ed. by F. Reynolds and D. Capps, pp. 121–51. Mouton.

Rowbotham, Sheila. 1973. *Woman's Consciousness, Man's World*. Penguin.

Rubinstein, J. 1973. *City Police*. Farrar, Straus & Giroux.

Sachs, J. 1983. "Talking About the There and Then: The Emergence of Displaced Reference in Parent-Child Discourse." In *Children's Language*, vol. 4, ed. by K. E. Nelson, pp. 1–28. Gardner Press.

Sacks, Harvey. 1992. *Lectures on Conversation*, ed. by Gail Jefferson. Blackwell.

_____. 1974. "An Analysis of the Course of a Joke's Telling in Conversation." In *Explorations in the Ethnography of Speaking*, ed. by R. Baumann and J. Sherzer, pp. 337–53. Cambridge University Press.

Sacks, Harvey; Emanuel Schegloff; and Gail Jefferson. 1974. "A Simplest Systematics of the Organization of Turn-taking in Conversation." *Language* 50: 696–735.

Schafer, Roy. 1980. "Narration in the Psychoanalytic Dialogue." *Critical Inquiry* 8: 29–53.

_____. 1978. *Language and Insight*. Yale University Press.

Schank, Roger, and Mark Burstein. 1985. "Artificial Intelligence: Modeling Memory for Language Understanding." In *Handbook of Discourse Analysis*, Volume 1: *Disciplines of Discourse*, ed. by Teun Van Dijk, pp. 145–66. Academic Press.

Schegloff, Emanuel A. 1972. "Notes on a Conversational Practice: Formulating Place." In *Studies in Social Interaction*, ed. by David Sudnow, pp. 75–119. Free Press.

Schiffrin, Deborah. 1985. "Everyday Argument: The Organization of Diversity in Talk." In *Handbook of Discourse Analysis*, Volume 3: *Discourse and Dialogue*, ed. by Teun A. Van Dijk, pp. 35–46. Academic Press.

Schreiber, Flora Rheta. 1982. *Sybil*. Warner Books.

Schur, Edwin M. 1976. *The Awareness Trap: Self Absorption Instead of Social Change*. Quadrangle Books.

Scott, James. 1985. *Weapons of the Weak: Everyday Forms of Peasant Resistance*. Yale University Press.

Sennett, Richard. 1977. *The Fall of Public Man*. Alfred A. Knopf.

Shames, Laurence. 1989. *The Hunger for More: Searching for Values in an Age of Greed*. Time Books.

Sheehy, Gail. 1977. *Passages*. Bantam.

Shweder, Richard A., and Joan G. Miller, eds. 1985. *The Social Construction of the Person: How Is It Possible?* Springer Verlag.

Silberstein, Sandra. 1982. "Textbuilding and Personal Style in Oral Courtship Narrative." Doctoral dissertation. Department of Linguistics, University of Michigan.

Skinner, B. F. 1976. *The Particulars of My Life*. Alfred A. Knopf.

———. 1948. *Walden Two*. Macmillan.

Sleeman, Major General Sir W. H. 1893. *Rambles and Recollections of an Indian Official*. Archibald Constable & Co.

Smiles, Samuel. 1859. *Self Help: With Illustrations of Conduct and Perseverance*. John Murray Publishers.

Smith, Dorothy E. 1984. "Textually Mediated Social Organization." *International Social Science Journal* 361: 59–75.

Stern, Daniel N. 1989. "Crib Monologues from a Psychoanalytic Perspective." In *Narratives from the Crib*, ed. by Katherine Nelson, pp. 309–19. Harvard University Press.

———. 1985. *The Interpersonal World of the Infant: A View from Psychoanalysis and Developmental Psychology*. Basic Books.

Sullivan, Harry Stack. 1954. *The Psychiatric Interview*. Edited by Helen S. Perry and Mary L. Cawel. W. W. Norton.

Sulloway, Frank J. 1979. *Freud: Biologist of the Mind*. Basic Books.

Tannen, Deborah. 1984. *Conversational Style: Analyzing Talk Among Friends*. Ablex.

Terkel, Studs. 1972. *Working: People Talk About What They Do All Day and How They Feel About What They Do*. Pantheon Books.

Trine, Ralph Waldo. 1896. *What All the World's A-Seeking: Or the Vital Law of True Life, True Greatness, Power, and Happiness*. Thomas Y. Crowell.

Turner, Jim L. 1980. "Yes I Am Human: Autobiography of a 'Retarded Career'." *Journal of Community Psychology* 8: 3–8.

Turner, Victor. 1974. "Religious Paradigms and Political Action: Thomas Becket at the Council of Northampton." In *Dramas, Fields, and Metaphors: Symbolic Action in Human Society*, pp. 60–97. Cornell University Press.

Van Dijk, Teun A. 1972. *Some Aspects of Text Grammars: A Study in Theoretical Linguistics and Poetics*. Mouton.

Veyne, Paul. 1987. *A History of Private Life Volume 1: From Pagan Rome to Byzantium*. Belknap Press.

Wald, Benji. 1978. "Zur Einheitlichkeit und Einleitung von Diskurseinheiten." In *Sprachstruktur-Socialstruktur, zur Linguistischen Theorienbildung*, ed. by Uta Quasthoff, pp. 128–40. Scriptor.

Weiner, J. L. 1980. "BLAH, a System Which Explains Its Reasoning." *Artificial Intelligence* 15: 19–48.

Weintraub, Karl Joachim. 1978. *The Value of the Individual: Self and Circumstance in Autobiography*. University of Chicago Press.

White, Hayden. 1987. *The Content of the Form: Narrative Discourse and Historical Representation*. Johns Hopkins Press.

———. 1973. *Metahistory: The Historial Imagination in Nineteenth-Century Europe*. Johns Hopkins Press.

Wilcox, Ella Wheeler. 1902. *The Heart of New Thought*. Psychic Research.

Willis, Paul. 1977. *Learning to Labor: How Working Class Kids Get Working Class Jobs*. Columbia University Press.

Wolfson, Nessa. 1982. *The Conversational Historical Present in American English Narrative*. Foris.

Wright, Louis B. 1958. *Middle Class Culture in Elizabethan England*. Cornell University Press.

Wylie, Irvin. 1954. *The Self-Made Man in America: The Myth of Rags to Riches*. Rutgers University Press.

Zaleski, Carol. 1987. *Otherworld Journeys: Accounts of Near-Death Experience in Medieval and Modern Times*. Oxford University Press.

Zimmerman, Donald. 1969. "Record-keeping and the Intake Process in a Public Welfare Agency." In *On Record: Files and Dossiers in American Life*, ed. by Stanton Wheeler, pp. 319–54. Russell Sage Foundation.

# INDEX

Abnormal production of narrative, 59

Abstract, 69–70

Abundance, in common sense system, 203–4, 210–11

Accident
adequate causality and, 131, 141–51, 221
in author's life story, 6–7
common sense and, 197
minor vs. major life events and, 149–51

Addressee
appropriateness expectations and, 7–12
demand for coherence and, 12, 16–18

Adequate causality. *See also* Accident; Discontinuity among life events
character traits and, 129–34
common sense and, 197–98
defined, 221
forms of, 129–40
individual creativity and, 128
presuppositions underlying, 197
proper balance and, 128–29
richness of account and, 135–40
temporal depth and, 135, 136–37

Advice literature. *See* Self-help literature

Affirmations, 214

Age
life story and, 23–25
sense of self and, 100

Agency, lack of, 142, 149, 171–73

Announcement. *See* Abstract

Anthropology, life history in, 47–50

Apolcalyptic thought, 31

*Apologia* (term), 5*n*

Apparent break strategy, 152–54

Appropriateness, 7–12

Archetypes, 189

Art forms, and openness, 27–31

Astrology, 176–78, 187, 211, 222

Atkinson, J. Maxwell, *xii*

Auerbach, Erich, 28

Autobiography, 37–42, 102

Bakan, David, 184

Bales, R. F., 94–95

Becker, Alton, 109, 110

Behaviorism, 169–76, 187, 222

Behavior modification, 175

Beliefs, and coherence systems, 165, 216

Bellah, Robert N., 200, 217

Biography, 42. *See also* Autobiography

Bloom, Lynn A., 204–5

Bloomfield, Leonard, 62

Boswell, James, 38–39

Brooks, Peter, 28–29

Bruss, Elizabeth, 38–39

Bunyan, John, 38

Burmese numeral classifiers, 109

Catholic confessional practice, 178, 180–82, 222

Causality. *See also* Accident; Adequate causality; Discontinuity among life events
in Freudian psychology, 169
inadequate, 140–51, 197–98, 221

235

Causality (*continued*)
  lexical devices and, 127
  management of inadquate causal-
    ity and, 140–51
  narrative presupposition and, 68,
    111
Cerling, Charles E., 205–6
Character. *See also* Richness of ac-
    count
  adequate causality and, 128, 129–
    34, 221
  unsuccessful career choice and,
    132–34
Childhood experiences as causality,
    168
Children, life stories of, 23–25
Chodorow, Nancy, 103–4
Chomsky, Noam, 62, 63
Christian Science, 209, 211
Chronicle
  as discourse unit, 85–89
  distinguished from history, 85–86
  example of, 86–87, 88–89
  structural characteristics of, 87–88
Cicero, *Pro Archia*, 15
Citation conventions, transcription
    conventions for, *xiv*
Clanchy, M. T., 15–16
Coburn, Karen, 204–5
Coherence. *See also* Adequate cau-
    sality; Discontinuity among life
    events
  defined, 12–18
  personal demand for, 17–18, 220
  principles for creation of, 127–62,
    220–21
  social demand for, 16–18, 220
  texts and, 12, 220
  truth and, 14–16
Coherence systems, 163–91. *See also*
    Astrology; Behaviorism; Catho-
    lic confessional practice; Com-
    mon sense; Feminism; Freudian
    psychology
  assumptions of, 216–17

  defined, 163–66
  historical relation between popular
    and expert systems, 184–87
  mixed metaphors and, 190–91
  notion of, 18–19, 221–22
  social practice and, 187–90
  synchronic relation between popu-
    lar and expert systems, 182–84
  types of, 165–66
Coles, Robert, 200
Cole-Whittaker, Terry, 202–4
Common sense
  abundance in, 203–4, 210–11
  adequate causality and, 128, 197–
    98
  assumptions about professional
    choice and, 222
  as coherence system, 18, 192–218
  coherence systems and, 163
  cultural codifications of, 198–99
  defined, 164, 192–94
  history of, 206–14, 222
  history of term, 195–96
  study of, 196–206
Contiguous utterances, transcription
    conventions for, *xiii*
Continuity, as principle for coher-
    ence, 151–52, 221. *See also* Dis-
    continuity of life events
Conversational implicature, 63–64
Conversation analysis
  vs. discourse analysis, 65–66
  text structure and, 13
  transcription conventions for, *xi–
    xiv*
Courtship stories, 113
Cultural system vs. coherence sys-
    tem, 165
Culture
  construction of self and, 101, 102
  notion of life story and, 3–12,
    220

Daly, Mary, 180
D'Andrade, Roy, 169

Data. *See also* Discourse unit
  analysis of discourse data and, 61–67
  choice of profession as topic and, 52–57
  interview as source of, 57–61
Diaries, 42–43, 112
Discontinuities
  in history of common sense, 212–14
  life story and, 3, 25–27
Discontinuity of life events
  common sense and, 197–98
  management of, 140, 151–62, 221
  as meta-continuity, 157–58
  as only apparent break, 152–54
  self-distancing and, 156–57
  as sequence, 155–56
  as temporary, 154–55
  without account, 158–62
Discourse, as term, 223–24
Discourse analysis
  vs. conversational analysis, 65–66
  interpretation and, 94–97
Discourse grammar, 64–65
Discourses, in social sciences, 212, 223
Discourse unit. *See also* Chronicle; Explanation; Narrative
  chronicle as, 85–89
  defined, 62
  explanation as, 90–94
  internal structure and, 67
  narrative as, 67–84
  properties of, 66–67
  property of definable boundaries and, 66–67
  types of, 61–67
"Discursive formations," 212, 223
Distancing of the self, 147–49, 156–57, 168. *See also* Reflexivity
Distinguishability of the self, 101–5

Eckert, Penelope, 24–25, 104–5
Eddy, Mary Baker, 209

Ellenberger, Henri, 184
Elliott, Laura, 40
Erikson, Erik, 100
Ethics, in terms of rights, 204–6, 207
Ethnicity, 166
Evaluation
  chronicle and, 87–88
  kinds of, 81–83
  moral value of self and, 122–26
  in structure of narrative, 71–81, 220
Evaluative point, 21–22
Expert systems, 211, 222
  coherence systems and, 163
  relation between popular coherence systems and, 182–87
Explanation, 90–94
  structure of, 90–92
  use of, 92–94
Explanatory material, transcription conventions for, *xiv*

Facts in life story, expected types of, 8–11. *See also* Truth
Fantasy life story, 11–12
Fedders, Charlotte, 40
Feminism, 178–80, 222
Feminist theory, and construction of self, 102–4
Fictional identities, 189–90
Form, and meaning, 95
Foucault, Michel, 212, 213, 223
"Four Corners of Truth," 203–4
Freud, Sigmund, 45
Freudian psychology, 222
  as coherence system, 18, 166–69
  common sense and, 164
  metaphor of levels in, 169
  relation between popular and expert systems in, 169, 183–87
  richness of account and, 138–39
Freudian slip, 185, 186
Friedman, Susan S., 103
Functional accounts of discourse, 65–66

Garfinkel, Harold, 192
Gateways Institute, 214–15
Geertz, Clifford, 48–50, 99, 165, 193–94
Gender differences in discourse, 80–81, 102–5. *See also* Feminism
Generative grammmar, and discourse, 64
Genre, and openness, 28–31
Gilligan, Carol, 104
Goffman, Erving, 5*n*, 113
Good judgment, 193
Goodwin, Charles, 66, 69–70, 72–73, 79
Goodwin, Marjorie H., 66, 72–73
*Grace Abounding* (Bunyan), 38
Grammatical categories
  existence of pronouns and, 111–12
  obligatory, 107–10
Green, Harvey, 212
Grice, H. P., 63
Gusdorf, George, 102

Hale, Nathan, Jr., 184
Halliday, M. A. K., 65
Hallowell, A. I., 10
Hasan, R., 65
Heraclitus, 101
Heritage, John, *xii*
Hill, Napoleon, 202
History, distinguished from chronicle, 85–86
Holland, Dorothy, 48
Holmes, Ernest S., 210
*Holy Boldness* (Cerling), 205–6
Homer, 28
*How to Have More in a Have-Not World* (Cole-Whittaker), 202–4

Independent income as conversational problem, 8–9
Individual creativity, and adequate causality, 128, 152
Individualism, 197, 199–201, 207, 217

Interpretation, and discourse analysis, 94–97
Interpretive openness, 29–31
Interruption, 26
Intervals in utterances, transcription conventions for, *xiii*
Intimacy, level of, 7–8, 36
Irish luck, 161–62

Jakobson, Roman, 112
Javanese, 99, 110–11
Jelenek, Estelle C., 42, 43
Jordan, Brigitte, 53–54
Journals, 42–43

Kermode, Frank, 31
Kirshenblatt-Gimblett, Barbara, 29–31

Labov, William, 24, 67–69, 129, 193
Lacan, Jacques, 121–22
Ladurie, Le Roy, 211
Lakoff, Robin Tolmach, 15*n*
Landmark events, 23
Language. *See also* Grammatical categories; Linguistic theory
  characteristics of self maintained through, 100–106
  temporal sequence as consequence of, 107–10
Levinson, Stephen, 65
Life history
  in anthropology, 47–50
  in psychology, 43–47
Life story
  age of development of, 23–25
  autobiography and, 37–42
  compared with life history in social sciences, 43–50
  cultural notion of, 3–12
  defined, 20–37
  diaries and, 42–43
  as discontinuous, 3, 25–27, 219–20

interpretive openness and, 29–31
journals and, 42–43
nontechnical definition of, 20–21
private, 11–12, 17–18, 220
relations among stories in, 25
revision of, 31–37
structural openness and, 27–29
technical definition of, 21–25
Linguistic theory. *See also* Discourse
analysis; Grammatical categories
discourse and, 62–66, 223–24
pronouns in, 111–12
text structure and, 13
*London Journal* (Boswell), 38–39
Luhrmann, T. M., 178
Lyons, John, 62

Martin, Jay, 189–90
Maxim of Quantity, 63, 64–67
Mayan midwives, 53–54
Mead, George H., 105–6
Meaning, and form, 95
Mental states, and behaviorism, 171
Meta-account, 34
Meta-continuity strategy, 157–58
Methodology. *See also* Data; Dis-
course unit
analysis of discourse data and, 61–
67
data and, 52–61
interpretation in discourse analysis
and, 94–97
interview as source of data and,
57–61
transcription conventions and, *xi–
xiv*
Meyer, Donald, 209
Miller, Joan G., 10
Miller, Peggy J., 23–24
"Mind cure school," 209–12, 214
Mirroring. *See* Reflexivity
Misch, George, 38
Mixed metaphors, 190–91
Moral values. *See* Values

Multiple accounts. *See also* Richness
of account
adequate causality and, 135–40
as life story strategy, 5–7
Multiple personality disorder, 101
*Mystères de Paris, Les* (Sue), 28–29

Nabokov, Vladimir, 38, 39
Narrative
abnormal production conditions,
59
creation of identity and, 98–126
Labov's definition of, 67–69
as linguistic unit, 62
reflexivity and, 120–26
relation of self to others and, 111–
20
structure of, 69–72, 83–84, 220,
223
temporal continuity of self and,
106–11
types used by mental patients, 5*n*
as unit of discourse, 67–84
Narrative clauses, 70–71
Narrative presupposition
causality and, 68, 111
chronicle and, 87
coherence and, 13–14, 68, 111,
127
defined, 106–7
Labov's definition of narrative
and, 68
richness of account and, 136
temporal continuity of self and,
106–11
Near-death experiences, 212
Negotiation
agreement on group values and,
114–20
evaluation of narrative and, 72–
81
*New Assertive Woman, The* (Bloom,
Coburn, and Pearlman), 204–5
Newman, John Henry (Cardinal),
40–42

Olney, James, 101
Omissions from life story, 196. *See also* Coherence systems
Opportunity
adequate causality and, 131–32
discontinuity without account and, 160–62
ethnicity and, 166
individualism and, 200–201
Oral narrative. *See* Narrative
Order of events. *See* Discontinuities, life story and; Narrative presupposition; Self, temporal continuity of
Orientation clause, 70
Oriyans (Brahman community), 10
Orwell, George, 190
Otherworld journeys, 212
Overlapping utterances, transcription conventions for, *xii*

Peacock, James, 48
Pearlman, Joan, 204–5
Personal influence and career choice, 141–42
Personality, metaphor of levels of, 169
Polanyi, Livia, 12–13, 57, 58, 70, 74–78
Portal approach to life history, 48
Positive thinking, 199–206, 216
Power relations and discourse, 223
Preface. *See* Abstract
Prince, Gerald, 15*n*
Private life story, 11–12, 17–18, 220
*Pro Archia* (Cicero), 15
Process approach to life history, 48
Professional choice
coherence systems in data on, 165–66
common sense assumptions and, 222
data on, 52–61
as expected part in life story, 8–10
unsuccessful, 132–34

Programming metaphor of behavior, 176
Pronouns, 111–12, 188, 223
Protestant theology, American, 208–12
Proverbs, 206
Psychology. *See also* Behaviorism; Freudian psychology
life history in, 43–47
theories of self in, 99–106

Quimby, Phineas Parkhurst, 208–9

Race, 166
Reflexivity of narrative, 120–26
Reflexivity of the self, 105–6. *See also* Distancing
Reinforcement, 170–71
Religion. *See* Catholic confessional practice; Common sense, history of
Reportability, 22–23, 37, 81
Revision, 31–37. *See also* Self-correction
Richness of account, 135–40, 144–47, 197, 221. *See also* Multiple accounts
Rights, ethics in terms of, 204–6, 207
Rosaldo, Renato, 47–48
Rowbotham, Sheila, 103

Sacks, Harvey, 34–35, 36, 37
Sacks-Schegloff-Jefferson transcription system, *xi*
Sad tale (term), 5*n*
Sapir-Whorf hypothesis, 108
Schegloff, Emanuel A., 56–57
Schiffrin, Deborah, 90
Self. *See also* Character
characteristics maintained through language, 100–106
creation of, and narrative, 98–126
fictional identity and, 189–90

moral value of, 122–26
psychological theories of, 99–106
reflexivity and, 105–6, 120–26
relation to others, 101–5, 111–20
temporal continuity of, 100–101,
 106–11
Self-correction, 128–29. *See also* Revision
Self-distancing, 147–49, 156–57. *See also* Reflexivity
Self-help literature, 198–200, 207–9,
 214–15, 216
*Self Help* (Smiles), 208
Self-history, 101
Sequence, strategy of discontinuity
 as, 155–56
Sexuality, common sense notions of,
 212, 213
Shadow plays, Javanese, 110–11
*Shattered Dreams* (Fedders), 40
Shaw, George Bernard, 29
Shweder, Richard A., 10
Silberstein, Sandra, 113
Simultaneous utterances, transcription conventions for, *xii*
Skinner, B. F., 173–75
Sleeman, Sir W. H., 10
Smiles, Samuel, 208
Soap opera, 27–28
Social demands. *See* Addressee
Socioeconomic status
 adequate causality and, 129,
 132
 coherence systems and, 166, 201,
 204
*Speak, Memory* (Nabokov), 38, 39
Speech delivery characteristics, transcription conventions for, *xiii–xiv*
Sperry, Linda L., 23–24
Stern, Daniel N., 99–100, 101
Structuralist methods, 64–65, 66
Structural openness, 27–29
Success literature. *See* Self-help literature

Success story (term), 5n
Sue, Eugène, 28–29
Sullivan, Harry Stack, 44
Sulloway, Frank J., 184

Tannen, Deborah, 57, 58, 74
Task-driven talk, 26–27
Temporal depth, 135, 136–37,
 197
Temporal ordering. *See* Narrative presupposition
Temporary discontinuity strategy,
 154–55
Terkel, Studs, 55
Texts, and coherence, 12, 220
*Think and Grow Rich* (Hill), 202
Thomas à Kempis, 102
Thoughts are things, in common
 sense system, 201–4, 207
Transcription conventions, *xi–xiv*
Transcriptionist doubt, transcription
 conventions for, *xiv*
Trine, Ralph Waldo, 210
Truth
 adequate causality and, 140–41
 coherence and, 14–16, 220
 Labov's definition of narrative
 and, 68
Turner, Jim L., 33–34

Values. *See* Coherence systems;
 Common sense
 common sense and, 195
 evaluation and, 81–83
 group, and narrative, 114–20
 management of inadquate causality and, 142–43
 reflexivity and, 122–26
Van Dijk, Teun A., 64
Veyne, Paul, 9n

Wagner, Richard, 27, 29
Walter Mitty phenomenon, 11–
 12
Watergate tapes, 58

*Wayang* (Javanese shadow plays),
    110–11
Weintraub, Karl Joachim,
    102
White, Hayden, 85–86
Wilcox, Ella Wheeler, 201

Willis, Paul, 54–56
Wolfson, Nessa, 61
Wright, Louis B., 207
Wylie, Irvin, 207–8

Zaleski, Carol, 212